PASSION
and Social
CONSTRAINT

BY ERNEST VAN DEN HAAG

IN ASSOCIATION WITH RALPH ROSS

PASSION

AND SOCIAL

CONSTRAINT

STEIN AND DAY / *Publishers* / New York

Acknowledgments

It gives me pleasure to thank the many scholars and friends who helped me. The generous, steady, and critical friendship of Ralph Ross has been of immeasurable assistance. Robert Merton read the whole manuscript in its original form and gave unstintingly of his time and erudition; so did Earl Latham. Martha Wolfenstein helped clarify the first four chapters, and Robert Bierstedt corrected my somewhat onesided view of authority. Nancy Toft-Harris had the patience to read my handwriting and to bear with me—no small achievement. Carolyn Andersen manifested equal fortitude and patience. (The index is owed to her labors.) With so much help the reader may wonder how any deficiencies remain: they are likely to be owed to a somewhat willful disposition which in doubtful cases preferred my own to the views of my friends.

The design and content of many chapters are based on Part I of *The Fabric of Society* with the kind permission of Harcourt, Brace & World, who published that book written by Ralph Ross and myself. However, every sentence has been rethought, and nearly every one changed—I hope for the better. There is much new material in the old chapters as well, and new chapters have been added. Perhaps, then, this is more a new than a revised book; no matter; I hope it will be found a good one.

—E. v. d. H.

Introduction

LEARNING

Convinced that an intellectual enterprise can be intrinsically gratifying—though schools often succeed in keeping this a secret—I have tried to avoid obscurity, but not difficulty. Excessive smoothness imperils the absorption of ideas no less than excessive complexity. Like a highway, a book should not be super-smooth: a driver, unchallenged by any intricacy, easily falls asleep; so does a reader; and I would rather challenge his ability to think than his ability to keep awake.

Authors are haunted by the temptation to leave no question unanswered and no answer unqualified. Yet if all the qualifications that might quite properly have hedged nearly every one of my statements had been included, I should have obstructed a clear view of the main points. Wherefore, I often preferred, in Bacon's words, "to excite the judgment briefly rather than to inform it tediously." Above all, I tried to shun the ease that comes from vagueness. A spade is called a spade and never an "interpersonal interrelationship."

Readers inured to a terminology lifeless and soporific enough to protect them from experiencing issues as real may be shocked. To learn is to be moved by ideas that are new to the learner and may upset or threaten ideas held before. No mind is blank— hence learning is a rearrangement of mental furniture and is uncomfortable at first. Simple ignorance can preserve comfort;

so can pretentious ignorance. While the former may or may not be worth preserving, the latter is not worth laboring to create. Armed with pretentious ignorance, one can manipulate ideas, but they never quite become part of oneself; they are used to dress up a mind which they do not actually touch or train. By writing in the most direct possible form I want to make it harder merely to replace simple with pretentious ignorance and easier to learn. With Martin Luther (Thesis 95, Oct. 31, 1517), I trust that we "enter heaven rather through many tribulations than through the false confidence of peace."

ANALYSIS

This is essentially an analytical book: contemporary society is described in terms of its regularities observed by social scientists. Ultimately, this should help understanding and controlling one's own conduct and the environment which limits and influences it. The following letter illustrates what is meant by analysis.

Executive Mansion, Washington
February 3, 1862

Major-General McClellan:

My dear Sir:—
You and I have distinct and different plans for a movement of the Army of the Potomac—yours to be down the Chesapeake, up the Rappahanock to Urbana, and across land to the terminus of the railroad on the York River; mine to move directly to a point on the railroad southwest of Manassas.

If you will give me satisfactory answers to the following questions, I shall gladly yield my plan to yours.

FIRST. Does not your plan involve a greatly larger expenditure of time and money than mine?

SECOND. Wherein is a victory more certain by your plan than mine?

THIRD. Wherein is a victory more valuable by your plan than mine?

FOURTH. In fact, would it not be less valuable in this, that it would break no great line of the enemy's communications, while mine would?

FIFTH. In case of disaster, would not a retreat be more difficult by your plan than mine?

Yours truly,
Abraham Lincoln

FACTS

Facts can be selected, organized, and presented only on the basis of hypotheses (tentative conclusions to be proved or disproved). Otherwise we would not know which facts to choose as possibly relevant nor how to distinguish facts from fancies. Not to make the reader aware of the hypotheses used is not to know, or not to let him know, what one is doing. Further it would suggest erroneously that an implicit theory is "factual" and an explicit one is not; or that "the facts" are all that is needed and that they present themselves organized and selected. Yet learning consists not in knowing "facts" but in being able to interpret and select them so as to draw conclusions from them. There is an infinity of facts; we cannot know them all but we can learn methods enabling us to make sense of them. The mere presentation of unanalyzed material (as though it could be unselected!) does not inspire reasoning or interpretation. Better to provoke reasoned dissent than to give readers the impression that science consists of being on both sides of every question without every clarifying or deciding anything.

OBJECTIVITY

It is often said that there are two sides to every question. This is true; but answering consists of choosing one. The adage (derived from an injunction to the Roman judge: *audiatur et altera pars*—let the other side also be heard) is a rule of procedure, suggesting how to investigate and make decisions, not how to avoid them. Just as to fanatics everything is black or white, so others, who project their own indecision and confusion onto the world, see only murky colors; but there is black and white *and* grey; and many other colors, too.

To be objective is to present all reliable facts and competent arguments relevant to a judgment—and to make it. Judgments are needed for action (and inaction). And the writer encourages them more by presenting his own than by abstaining—even though there be dissents. Lincoln used to tell of the woman who was impartial. She saw her husband struggling with a bear and shouted, "Go to it, husband! Go to it, bear!" The scholar, of course, is not wedded to either party. But does this mean that he cannot point out that one is a bear?

VALUE JUDGMENTS

I have made value judgments then. A work about society would otherwise be valueless. Nor are there any works about society without value judgments—judgments not of but about facts, evaluations of right and wrong, good and bad, beautiful and ugly. The real difference is once again between works that make readers aware of the value judgments that necessarily enter at some points and those in which value premises remain hidden and are therefore not distinguished from statements of fact.

To abstain from value judgments would (if it were possible) have another disadvantage. It would divide the minds of men into two wholly separate parts. In one part, orderly crops of factual and logical judgments are scientifically raised; in the other, a jungle of wild opinions, inconsistent evaluations, and unscrutinized experiences thrives untended. This might bring the very calamity feared by those who advocate the presentation of only what is scientifically knowable: some ferocious and undomesticated beast might break out from the uncultivated part of the mind to ruin the orderly crops planted in the other. For to disregard what cannot be proved is to omit from discussion but not from experience. Indeed, the greater part of human experience would be excluded from articulate reflection.

Men must make value judgments to live—even if the results will never be as conclusive as they may be in science, and the premises never as certain. To discuss only the testable would be to lay undue stress on the trivial, and to ignore what is vital— by what values shall we live, what ends shall we strive for? Reason, though not sufficient, is surely a most necessary instrument in this endeavor. I do not pretend that my judgments are necessarily better than those others might make. They spring from my experience, and the reader must test them against his own. If he does, I have been successful.

Contents

Part Two: Society

PART ONE

Personality

CHAPTER I *The Humanization of Infants*

BIOLOGICAL AND SOCIAL INHERITANCE

Biology sets limits, but within them society forms the human personality. How is this done? What psychological losses and gains occur in making us fit society?

Infants are born with reflexes, automatic reponses, such as make the pupil of the eye contract in response to light. There is no denying either that we have inborn drives—impulsions which are felt as discomforts when not discharged. Hunger and libido— sexual hunger— need no external stimulation to recur. They crave the satisfaction of inborn needs. The number, the mutual relation, the relative strength, and the goals of our drives are in doubt. And there is much argument about the extent to which they can be reinforced, frustrated, transformed, and shifted from one goal to another without harm. Libido, for instance, is quite plastic. It can be gratified in countless indirect and far-fetched ways. But hunger cannot.

Besides many quarrels over the classification and definition of our drives and even quibbles over the use of words, there is actual uncertainty about how much of our observed behavior is begot by biological inheritance. In the past, nearly all customs were thought to be inborn. The rise of anthropology in the twentieth century has made us chary of linking any custom directly to an

3

inborn drive. Many customs thought to be inborn are, we know now, instilled in each individual by his group. Anthropologists never tire of telling how different customs are learned in different societies. As for the quibbles, the mistranslation of Freud's German *Trieb* [drive] as "instinct" led psychoanalysts to call "instincts" what Freud actually had called drives. And Freud meant by *Triebe* what American psychologists now call drives: inborn impulsions to action toward a goal (sometimes mere potentialities). Such "drives," unlike "instincts," do not fix the *pattern* of action though they give direction and force to it.

In all societies something has to be done about hunger, sex, and aggressiveness. If nothing were done there would be no society: people would starve and kill each other. But what is done differs from society to society and even from individual to individual. Inborn drives, at most, impel and limit human behavior within quite a wide range. Drives are a far cry then from the inflexible instincts which set the complex ways in which different kinds of birds mate, build nests, hatch eggs, and take care of their chicks. Unlike bees, we have no instincts to lay out the physical or social architecture of our hives, or our techniques of food gathering. For honeybees are *born*

> *Creatures that by a rule in nature teach*
> *The act of order to a peopled kingdom.*
> *They have a king and officers of sorts;*
> *Where some, like magistrates, correct at home,*
> *Others, like merchants, venture trade abroad,*
> *Others, like soldiers, armed in their stings,*
> *Make boot upon the summer's velvet buds;*
> *Which pillage they with merry march bring home*
> *To the tent-royal of their emperor:*
> *Who, busied in his majesty, surveys*
> *The singing masons building roofs of gold,*
> *The civil citizens kneading up the honey,*
> *The poor mechanic porters crowding in*
> *Their heavy burdens at his narrow gate,*
> *The sad-ey'd justice, with his surly hum,*
> *Delivering o'er to executors pale*
> *The lazy yawning drone.*
>
>   (HENRY V)

To us, nature does not prescribe from within the means to be used in satisfying our drives, nor fix priorities, set patterns, or lay out sequences of action. By giving us less, nature gives us more: it allows us to develop countless designs for living, each subject to change.

By endowing the human race with inborn drives but not with patterns for satisfying them, nature has made it necessary for each infant to be molded anew by the group in which he grows up. Fortunately, the capacity of our infants to learn exceeds that of animals as much as the need. As babies, we don't do better than, in fact not even as well as, the babies of other species. But we go on to learn more when they stop. Though not born with the beaver's dam-building instinct, we can learn not only to build a dam but also to draw a blueprint of it from which others can build dams. Animals can barely express their current feelings and almost incidentally impress them on others. They cannot say "I *was* hungry *yesterday*" or "*He* is hungry *now*" or "Life can be deadly." They can neither describe nor convey ideas. In short, they cannot communicate. We can, because we use symbols. Symbols allow us to profit from the experience of others and of the past. (This is one reason why protracted "learning by doing" is not sufficient for children: it does not develop the ability to learn abstractly, that is, to take over the experience of others *without re-enacting it.* Yet this ability is most important in the development of *human* intelligence.)

Socialization—the process by which infants become human by becoming members of society—transmits customs, ideas, and ambitions from the stock cumulatively developed in the past. The process starts at birth and never quite ceases throughout life, though its basic imprint is made in the first few years, when the group's culture—its design for living—is impressed on a comparatively weak and plastic individual who is as yet able neither deliberately to select from that design nor to contribute to it.

The importance of biological endowments—and of individual differences among them—must not be underestimated, however. Even if we all had the opportunities and the upbringing that helped produce a Shakespeare or an Einstein, few of us would equal their achievements. Talent (or genius) is developed, trained, and used socially, but talent itself is inherent. We know not whence it comes. What the Romans said of the poet—*nascitur, non fit,* "he is born, not made"—is true at least as far as talent, the inborn capacity that can be developed, is concerned. And it is true for any talent. Certainly the opportunities provided by society play a role: Napoleon might have languished as an undistinguished artillery officer had not the French Revolution given him specific opportunities. Yet would someone else have used them as he did? Hardly. A favorable environment can utilize and develop talent, though not create it. Perhaps, in a different environment, Napoleon might have made a successful businessman or college president. Would he ever have made a great musician, mathematician, or anthropologist? Probably not. Most talents seem to be fairly specific and, for this reason alone, much depends on how much use society has for them.

   That we develop individually and do not inherit our characteristic ways of doing things—that we inherit only a greater or lesser ability to develop (talent)—makes for great differences among us. Even the tendency to self-preservation is by no means uniformly distributed. Though most of us hang on for dear life as long as we can, some of us deliberately commit suicide. (The incidence of suicide apparently depends on the individual's relationship to his society.) In general, dissimilarities among societies seem to depend more on historical than on biological differences. But dissimilarities among individuals in the same group—the difference, say, between Einstein and a schoolmate of his—cannot be altogether reduced to social influences, however great the importance of different family situations and life experiences. Since social and individual elements mingle in each phase of the development of each member of society, they are hard to distinguish. What society instills early, deliberately or not, becomes a second nature nearly as difficult to dislodge later as biological inheritance.

SOCIALIZATION AND INDIVIDUATION

   We are born with countless needs which only society can satisfy. In William Blake's words:

> *My mother groan'd, my father wept;*
> *Into the dangerous world I leapt,*
> *Helpless, naked, piping loud,*
> *Like a fiend hid in a cloud.*

Although needful of society, we are not born helpful to it. Needing society we are born, nevertheless, asocial, if not antisocial. Therefore, the first aim of socialization is to bend the inborn drives of the infant into socially acceptable directions. Our inborn drives can disrupt society or be satisfied at its expense. The infant must be taught to still his needs in socially acceptable ways—for instance, when, where, and how to sleep, eat, defecate, respond to sexual stimuli, give, and take—so as not to disrupt the organization around him or to harm himself. Society teaches the infant what he cannot do, what he must do, and what he may do. Infants must learn to postpone satisfaction of their needs, to find acceptable goals, to stifle unacceptable desires, and finally, to satisfy the needs of others to some extent. Discipline and tolerance of frustration must be taught gradually if the infant is to mature successfully, that is, to fulfill his basic needs by becoming an acceptable member of society. (Very full gratification very early—during the first year—makes the necessary discipline and frustration easier to accept a little later.)

Though the patterns *transmitted* by society may be identical, the patterns *received* never are. In the first place, the receiving infants are not identical. Each sifts for himself what is offered: each accepts or rejects different things, according to his inheritance and previous experience. Secondly, "society" does not transmit. Individual members do. Each child, therefore, receives his social heritage from different hands which sift, shape, and transmit differently so that each child receives a somewhat different selection from the social stock of ideas, attitudes, and views. Finally, each child grows up in a unique family situation which leaves a specific mark. Even the impact of the same family on each child differs. The first-born sees his monopoly of parental attention destroyed. The second-born has parents who have had experiences which the parents of the first-born did not have; and he has an older brother or sister. Thus the very process of socialization also contains elements of individuation.' To paraphrase

Clyde Kluckhohn and Henry A. Murray (in *Personality in Nature, Society, and Culture*), <u>every man in some respects comes
to be:</u>

1. *like all other men*—he is a member of the species;
2. *like some other men*—he is a member of a society characterized by a distinctive culture: he underwent common
   experiences with his fellow members (such as upbringing,
   language, schooling, work, control by laws) which cause
   him to react as they do in many respects;
3. *like no other man*—he is an individual owing to original
   endowments and to experiences peculiar to him.

FREDERICK II AND DR. SPITZ ON INFANT CARE

The burden of socialization, of civilization, of life itself can
be borne only by infants motivated first and stimulated by maternal love. Mothers have always known this. The first reported
relevant experiment confirmed it. It is described (in *The Portable
Medieval Reader* edited by J. B. Ross and M. M. McLaughlin) by
Salimbene, the thirteenth century chronicler of the "misfortunes
and follies" of Frederick II (A remarkable emperor who was called
stupor mundi [the world-shocker], Frederick had the personality
we find frequently in the Renaissance although he lived in the
Middle Ages [he died in 1250]. He not only had a truly scientific
temper; he also supported literature, wrote a treatise on falconry,
and founded the University of Naples):

> . . . His second folly was that he wanted to find out what
> kind of speech and what manner of speech children would have
> when they grew up, if they spoke to no one beforehand. So he
> bade foster mothers and nurses to suckle the children, to bathe
> and wash them, but in no way to prattle with them or to speak
> to them, for he wanted to learn whether they would speak the
> Hebrew language, which was the oldest, or Greek, or Latin, or
> Arabic, or perhaps the language of their parents, of whom they
> had been born. But he laboured in vain, because the children all
> died. For [*N.B.*] they could not live without the petting and

the joyful faces and loving words of their foster mothers. And so the songs are called "swaddling songs," which a woman sings while she is rocking the cradle, to put a child to sleep, and without them a child sleeps badly and has no rest. . . .

What Salimbene knew—that infants "could not live without the petting and the joyful faces and loving words of their foster mothers"—was forgotten, if not by mothers, by institutional administrators. It had to be rediscovered in our own day. The American Pediatric Association in 1915 was told that 90 per cent of the infants in the institutions of Baltimore died in their first year. The remainder were saved only because they were taken out in time. In the same discussion, it was noted that at Randall's Island Hospital the mortality rate was probably 100 per cent. Since then matters have improved. Bellevue Hospital in New York City now registers less than a 10 per cent mortality rate. But the improvement has revealed another problem. The development of children is impaired by lack of maternal love: they become more often asocial, delinquent, feeble-minded, psychotic, or, at the least, neurotic in institutions than in families. This fact has now prompted replacement of institutionalization by foster-home care whenever possible. Where this is impossible, impairment can be minimized only if the institution approximates a home environment, offering maternal love and stimulation—a hard thing to arrange in an institution but not impossible once the need is understood. Institutionalization without this maternal element for more than eight months during the first year often leads to severe psychiatric disturbances which may become irreversible after three years. Even the most destitute home is better than the most hygienic institution, unless the institution can also provide maternal affection.

Dr. René A. Spitz undertook (in "Hospitalism" *The Psychoanalytic Study of the Child*, Vol. I, 1945, and "Hospitalism: a Follow-up Report," *ibid.*, Vol. II, 1946) to establish the precise effects of environmental stimulation on infant development. His conclusion does not differ from Salimbene's. (The effect of institutionalization on the old is in many ways analogous. Human beings of all ages seem to need love and social stimuli. But the need seems greatest at the start and toward the end of their career on

earth. It seems that we are now doing as badly with the aged as
we did with the young in the past.) According to Dr. Spitz:

The children in *Nursery* were at the end of their first year
well-developed and normal on the whole. The children in
Foundling Home, though starting at almost as high a level as
the best of the others, had spectacularly deteriorated. They
showed all the manifestations of hospitalism, both physical and
mental. In spite of the fact that hygiene and precautions against
contagion were impeccable, the children showed, from the
third month on, extreme susceptibility to infection and illness of
any kind. No figures could be elicited on general mortality;
but during my stay an epidemic of measles swept the institution,
with staggeringly high mortality figures, notwithstanding liberal
administration of convalescent serum and globulins, as well as
excellent hygienic conditions. Of a total of 88 children up to
the age of 2½, 23 died. It is striking to compare the mortality
among 45 children up to 1½ years to that of the 43 children ranging from 1½ to 2½ years: usually, the *incidence* of
measles is low in the younger age group, but among those infected the mortality is higher than that in the older age group;
since in the case of *Foundling Home* every child was infected,
the question of incidence does not enter; however, contrary to
expectation, the mortality was much higher in the older age
group. In the younger group, 6 died, i.e., approximately 13 per
cent. In the older group 17 died, i.e., close to 40 per cent.
The significance of these figures becomes apparent when we
realize that the mortality from measles during the first year of
life in the community in question, outside the institution, was
less than 0.5 per cent.

In view of the damage sustained in all personality sectors of
the children during their stay in this institution it is likely
that their resistance to disease was also progressively sapped. In
the ward of the children ranging from 18 months to 2½ years
only 2 of the 26 surviving children speak a couple of words.
The same two are able to walk. A third child is beginning to
walk. Hardly any of them can eat alone. Cleanliness habits
have not been acquired and all are incontinent.

In sharp contrast to this is the picture offered by the oldest
inmates in *Nursery,* ranging from 8 to 12 months. The problem
here is not whether the children walk or talk by the end of the
first year; the problem with these 10-month-olds is how to tame

the healthy toddlers' curiosity and enterprise. They climb up
the bars of the cots after the manner of South Sea Islanders
climbing palms. Special measures to guard them from harm have
had to be taken after one 10-month-old actually succeeded in
diving right over the more than two-foot railing of the cot.
They vocalize freely and some of them actually speak a word
or two. And all of them understand the significance of simple
social gestures. When released from their cots, all walk with
support and a number walk without it.

Dr. Spitz found nothing in the different parental backgrounds
to explain the sharp difference between the thriving *Nursery*
children and the high susceptibility to illness and retarded development of the *Foundling Home* children. There were no
significant differences in the quality and quantity of food, housing, clothing, sanitation, and medical care. And children with
congenital defects were excluded from both institutions.

There was one major difference however. In *Nursery*—where
the infants thrived—each received a great deal of attention.
Nursery was part of a prison where the mothers were detained.
They had entered prison with their babies, or given birth to
them there. The mothers spent all day taking care of their own
and each other's children. They gave the infants a great deal of
attention—probably more than they might have given them on
the outside. For the babies became the only present objects of
their love, ambition, interests, and competitiveness. There are
few distractions in a prison. Finally, the nursery was so arranged
that each infant could observe and participate in whatever was
going on. And a great deal was going on most of the time—
the environment was highly stimulating because of the constant
presence of so many mothers.

In *Foundling Home* nothing happened to stimulate the infants. The nurses took care of them—but that was all. They
came in on schedule, did what was required, and left. (In *Nursery*, the nurses merely supervised and instructed the mothers.)
Bed sheets were routinely hung over the railing of each crib and
cot, effectively closing off the infants' vision. Thus in each cubicle
there was a baby completely screened off from the world as
though in solitary confinement. Even when the baby could stand

up, the wooden partitions of each cubicle did not permit seeing what went on in the next. (The glass panes were beyond the babies' eye level.)

When Dr. Spitz revisited *Foundling Home* two years after his first visit, 33 children (37%) had died. About 36 had been taken back by their families. The 21 children that could be reobserved were now between 2 and 4 years old. All were retarded more or less severely in speaking, walking, toilet training, etc. Their physical development was similarly retarded—although, as a result of the first visit, the environment had been made far more stimulating and warm. But it seemed that these children could no longer be helped by ordinary means.

Dr. Spitz's evidence suffers from various technical defects (see S. R. Pinneau, "The Infantile Disorders of Hospitalism and Anaclitic Depression," *Psychological Bulletin*, 1955, pp. 429-452), mainly because the same infants were not observed over a sufficient length of time. Further, it is not altogether clear what role the absence of maternal affection played, and what role the absence of general social stimulation, coming, for instance, from other infants, may have played. (In the sciences dealing with human beings, evidence is seldom as conclusive as it can be in sciences concerned with nonhumans.) Nonetheless, everyday clinical experience seems to confirm Dr. Spitz's observations. And the literature is full of other reports, none altogether conclusive but all confirming the hypothesis that maternal love and social stimulation are essential to an infant's growth and wellbeing and that isolation from both is detrimental. (E.g., Margaret A. Ribble's observations on six hundred infants reported in *Personality and the Behavior Disorders*, edited by J. McV. Hunt, 1944, Vol. II.)

Dr. Spitz's observations point to a simple moral: the infant, reaching the outside world after dreadful travail, must be made to feel at home if he is to stay. Even the greatest material comforts cannot replace what he has left behind. The warmth of maternal affection is needed to comfort him, to kindle his interest, and to turn his awakening senses toward grasping what the world has to offer.

If affectionate maternal encouragement does not whet the infant's appetites, sharpen his responses, and respond to his initiatives, neither his intelligence nor his senses develop. He will, if he stays alive at all, bear traces of the indifferent welcome. He will not feel at home in the world. He will remain an alien, uneasy, uncomfortable, and likely as not hostile to the society which met him coldly when above all he wanted warmth. He will crave to take, more than to give, and he will find it as hard to renounce his wants as to gratify the wants of others. Or, having been rebuffed, he will not dare demand anything from the world. He will be overly detached and withdrawn. In short, he will not easily recover from the stunning blow received. If he does not wither away, he will bear the marks of crippling psychological injury.

ANNA AND ISABELLA

Kingsley Davis reports on two children kept in isolation until they were six years old. ("Final Note on a Case of Extreme Isolation" reprinted in *Sociological Analysis*, edited by Wilson and Kolb.)

After much shifting around among institutions during her first six months, Anna was finally taken back by her mother. Because of her illegitimate birth, Anna was kept apart from the family. Her mother worked during the day but did not give friendly attention to the child even in her free time. The infant was seldom moved from one position to another in her filthy bedding. At the age of six, Anna, extremely undernourished, could neither talk nor understand. She could not walk, was apathetic, could not feed herself, and had no toilet training. She was taken to a home for retarded children where she learned to walk, to understand directions, to form a few simple sentences, and to control her bowels. However, when she died in her eleventh year, Anna had reached a mental age of only about two and one-half years. She was classified as feeble-minded. This may have been the effect of her initial isolation and neglect, but since her mother was mentally deficient, there might have been a congenital defect as well.

Isabella, too, because she was illegitimate, was kept in seclusion for the first six years of her life. However, her mother, a deaf-mute, spent much of her time with Isabella—in a darkened room shut off from the rest of the family. Owing to lack of sunshine,

Isabella suffered from rickets when found at the age of six. She could not speak, though she made croaking noises; toward strangers she behaved like a fearful and hostile animal. Nonverbal tests indicated a mental age of less than two years and a social maturity of two and one-half years. Unlike Anna, Isabella underwent intensive individual training after she was discovered. In two years she went through the stages of learning which ordinarily take six. By the time she was eight years old, Isabella had caught up with her coevals; she spoke, understood, ran about, and generally behaved like a cheerful little girl of her age. She entered public school and had no particular difficulties.

Why was the belated socialization of Isabella so much more successful than that of Anna? Professor Davis points out rightly that the circumstances do not allow us to decide whether Isabella's rapid progress after she was discovered was due to the special care taken with her or to an inborn capacity more normal than Anna's.

However, Dr. Spitz's observations suggest a third possibility not mentioned by Professor Davis. Unlike Anna, Isabella was not shifted among various institutions during the first months of her life; and, unlike Anna, during her six years of social isolation she had continuous though mute contact with her mother, who spent much time with her and, it stands to reason, gave her attention and some affection. Isabella's learning opportunity was injured but not her learning capacity. She was able to make up the time lost. It might well be that Anna's development after her rescue was limited, perhaps irremediably, by impairment of her learning capacity through absence of affection suffered in the first six years of her life. This, or congenital defects, or insufficiently intensive care after her rescue may have caused Anna's belated socialization to be so much less successful than Isabella's. There is no deciding. But in the light of much clinical observation, it seems entirely possible that lack of maternal affection in the first few years of life deals a blow which cannot be mended later by ordinary means. Isabella's successful humanization, on the other hand, proves that mere social isolation during the first six years leaves no incurable wound, if there was maternal affection and attention.

CHAPTER 11

The Oedipus Complex

Love is needed first of all to keep us alive and eager. But this is only part of the story. As we grow, many drives assert themselves. Some are apparent from the start; others, like teeth, emerge as we mature. A Viennese neurologist, Sigmund Freud (1856-1939), distinguished in the human personality several "systems" which develop under different influences in different stages of maturation. Freud arrived at this systematization after long exploration of the human personality led him to found a new science: psychoanalysis.

The conclusions of experimental psychology are much better established than those of psychoanalysis. Carefully controlled experiments, which every competent psychologist can repeat, have solidly advanced our knowledge of the mechanics of learning, of perception, and of many other processes. It is otherwise with psychoanalysis. There are periods and nations in history that have left vast hoards of documents. Numerous historians specialize in exploring them minutely. Other periods and peoples—no less important in actual history—have left scarcely any documents. Historiography perforce neglects them. Some historians, confusing historiography with history, wrongly think the well-documented is the only important part of history. So it is with human personality. The aspects accessible to experimental proof of the customary sort were minutely investigated, as indeed they should be.

But, until Freud came on the scene, the less accessible aspects
were neglected or consigned to metaphysical speculation. And
some psychologists still deny, or act as though denying, that parts
of personality that cannot be investigated by experimental methods can be important. There is no merit in this contention although experimental verification would indeed be desirable whenever and wherever possible.

How much of Freud's pioneering work might be experiment-
ally validated no one can yet say. Recent collaborations among
experimental psychologists and psychoanalysts have led to tests
which have confirmed some of Freud's views. (see pp.   ) But
much more needs to be done. Meanwhile there is clinical evidence. Clinical evidence, such as case histories, is not as clear-cut
as experimental evidence, but there is so much of it, and it seems
so convincing that it has led to wide acceptance of many psychoanalytic concepts by psychiatrists and psychologists. For the
time being, moreover, those facts about human behavior which
are fully established by experiment do not yield a theory explaining it. Whatever the defects of his explanation, Freud so far has
made the most generally accepted full-scale attempt to explain
the development and function of human personality in society.
It fits the facts and casts light on countless aspects of human
behavior. Thus to describe socialization, for instance—which is
indispensable to a description of society—is in effect to use
Freud's hypotheses. One might as well be plain about it, however much one might bear in mind that most of these hypotheses still await further clarification, possibly modification, and
certainly confirmation.

ID, EGO AND SUPEREGO

Freud, like Plato before him, broke personality down into
three "systems." Plato distinguished the seat of appetites, of reason and morals, and of honor and courage. Freud locates appetites
in the Id, reason in the Ego, and morals in the Superego. Plato's
division differs from Freud's chiefly because Plato puts reason
and morals together and separates the will from the appetites.
The Christian image of man torn between the divine and the dia-

bolic, with reason telling him how to discriminate, also, in effect, acknowledges these personality components.

Freud's German words, *Es* (it), *Ich* (I) and *Über-Ich* (super-I), in American usage have been replaced by Latin ones. The idea of the Id stems (as Freud acknowledges) from the philosopher Friedrich Nietzsche who meant to refer to that which is not individually acquired. But Freud went further in specifying what we inherit and what role it plays, above all, in systematically investigating the relation of the Id to the rest of the personality.

The "system" constituted by our inborn drives, and the original source of the energy that animates us Freud calls the *Id*. (This is a matter of definition, not of topography.) The Id strives solely for pleasure and avoidance of pain by achieving directly the goals of our inborn drives. But the world interposes many obstacles. Experience must teach each of us how the impulses coming from the Id may be fulfilled. We cannot always act impulsively. It is this experience which leads to the formation of a second psychological system, the *Ego*. The Ego mediates between the Id from which it grew and the reality in which our inborn impulses are to be satisfied. The energy of the Ego comes originally from the Id's impulses. But the Ego becomes a rather independent agent of the Id. The Id impels toward immediate gratification, but the Ego strives toward realistic long-run adjustment and self-preservation. In Freud's metaphor, the Ego guides and bridles the Id as a rider does a horse—except that the horse here is the ultimate source of the rider's energy and also influences the basic direction of the ride. To stay in the saddle, the rider sometimes must go where the horse wants to. Still, it is the rider who shows the way, skirts obstacles, avoids excessive risks, and finds forage.

The Ego develops as a result of the clash of the Id with reality, of the frustration met by the unbridled attempt to gratify impulses. Were all our drives gratified immediately—if reality presented no obstacles at all—we would never have to take cognizance of an independent outer world or understand that it is not necessarily obedient to us. Since some degree of frustration is unavoidable—our primeval impulses do not even seem to take into account the limitations of our own bodies—there arises some recognition of reality. We learn to distinguish between subject (self) and object (world); and the chracteristics of the world, of time, space, and causality slowly dawn on us.

It is as an obstacle that the world first impinges on our consciousness or, rather, calls it into being. It is when the mother withdraws the breast (or the bottle) that the infant dimly feels that there is an outer world on which he depends. He loses the sense of omnipotence which only magic later can restore. When the infant starts to learn how to influence the dimly acknowledged outer world—for instance, by timing his yells—education starts. His first awareness of an outer world forms the nucleus of the Ego.

There, too, is one source of the need to be loved: to be loved is to regain some of the feeling of omnipotence which constitutes the original self-esteem. Without our need to be loved, however abstractly and indirectly expressed (even in the belief that posterity or God will give us the love our contemporaries deny us), civilization is hard to imagine. For, though laws may restrain our aggression, they work only if most of us voluntarily refrain from most of the acts the law prohibits: most of us refrain from killing, stealing, etc. because we want to be accepted—loved—and not just because we are afraid of being caught and punished. We need the emotional support of our fellows and particularly of the parental figures. However, if self-esteem continues to depend entirely on the direct, tangible expression of the love of others and remains unrealistic, the Ego and the Superego (see below) have remained weak. The person colloquially accused of having a "big Ego"—the person who needs flattery, the expression of the love of others and who, if necessary, flatters himself—has a weak, undeveloped Ego which depends on external supplies.

Not all our impulses can be gratified. The Ego often must choose among them. Reality imposes a choice between eating and having one's cake—a dilemma that stays with us through life: to satisfy one's appetite or to keep one's figure? to drink more or be esteemed as a sober man? to work and earn more or to rest? to rape, steal, cheat, and murder or to satisfy one's wishes in a more realistic and morally accepted manner, perhaps discarding some altogether? Some impulses conflict with others or with the wishes of other people; some are simply unfulfillable this side of paradise. Still other impulses would lead to pain or self-destruction, at least in the long run. Our drives do not, without the help of the Ego, adapt to reality or foresee the effects of their gratification. To carry out impulses we must exert ourselves; to have our own demands fulfilled we must often grant demands made upon us. All this management, both of the environment and of the primitive drives, Freud entrusts to the Ego, which seeks a feasible course of action leading to the greatest satisfaction compatible with self-preservation.

The Ego's task is further complicated as the *Superego* comes into being. Essentially the Superego is defined as the seat of moral restraints and of moral passions and compunctions. Like the Id, the Superego may be compared to a horse—of a different color —for the Ego to ride. The Ego must bridle it and then ride the two horses without being torn asunder, for however discordant the elements of our personality, the Ego must try to move so as to gain the backing of all. Frequent inconsistent and self-defeating action means that the personality is torn—the Ego has not been able to integrate it.

As infants we are cared for and taught by parents. From them we learn such notions as "duty," "good," "bad," "right," and "wrong"—in short, morality. To very small children, the approval and disapproval of parents is mysterious. All they understand is that some things they like to do are welcomed while other actions are followed by disapproval or punishment. This quite literally puts the fear of God into us—the conviction that our actions must follow a path laid out by a Being whose word is law, whose will is inscrutable, and on whose benevolence we depend—who is as omnipotent, incomprehensible, and unaccountable as parents are to infants.

Somewhat contrary to Freud's own apparent belief (particularly in *The Future of an Illusion*), logic teaches us that the psychological origin of a belief, or the motive for holding it, or the condition that leads to its acceptance, is irrelevant to its truth or falsehood. Hence, no psychological explanation of how Newton created a theorem or of how religious beliefs arise says anything at all about their truth or falsehood. Thus Freud's explanation of how belief in God is born need not be inconsistent with that belief, any more than an explanation of how babies are born need be inconsistent with the belief that God created men in His image. In fairness to Freud, it must be said that he thought the explanation of its origin and function relevant to the truth of religious belief because he was convinced that there is no evidence for religion other than people's belief. Which, if true, would mean that faith is not part of science, but not, certainly, that faith cannot be part of a religion that does not claim to be founded on science.

The foundations for the Superego are laid through the experience of parental approval, or that of other figures important to the young child. The Superego shares with the Id an unreasoning imperative quality. This quality distinguishes the amoral drives of the Id and the moral imperatives of the Superego from the reasonableness of the Ego. The Ego through which Id and Superego come in touch with the environment must attempt to temper the amoral drives and the moral imperatives realistically, to make them consistent, and to carry them out, as well as to justify them.

The moral notions originating in the Superego are not identical either with the desire of the Id for pleasure or with the Ego's aim of realistic fulfillment and self-preservation. The Superego may tell us to avoid what is pleasant and possible (hence desired by the Id and acceptable to the Ego) or to do what is unpleasant and avoidable (hence rejected by Id and Ego). As the German philosopher Immanuel Kant pointed out, a choice becomes moral if it is made for the sake of morality: to eat candy is not a moral act, nor is it moral not to eat it because you are full or afraid of a stomach-ache. But not to eat the candy (though it won't hurt and you want it), to leave it uneaten because it belongs to someone else and you have no right to it, or because you learn that someone has less than you, or because candy eating is thought to be evil *per se*—that is a moral act. The Ego may afterwards explain and justify the moral act intellectually in utilitarian or other terms. But the feeling that leads to the moral act is unreasoning and originates in the Superego. And psychology—investigation of the origin and character of a feeling—must not be confused with philosophy—justification (or condemnation) of the feeling by rational reasoning from some standard, utilitarian or not.

The Superego is the psychological source of moral prohibitions and goals. These are experienced by the child first as restrictions on its pleasure for the sake of parental approval, benevolence, and protection. The uneasiness experienced in various forms when disobeying Superego commands—the pangs of conscience—has its origin in the infant's fear of parental disapproval or punishment. The fear of external punishment or disapproval can be distinguished from anxiety, due to the Ego's fear of a wholly internalized authority. Only when the process of internalization has occurred (about the fourth year, with the Oedipus complex) does the institution that is, strictly speaking, called the Superego come into being. Kant, too, would call an act moral only when it is motivated not by fear of external punishment, or expectation of reward, but solely by internal feelings of rightness or wrongness.

Some rashly leap to the conclusion: avoid punishment of the child, be permissive and indulgent, and thus avoid unnecessary suffering later. This is a mistake for three basic reasons. (1) Total indulgence is impossible. Children must be subjected to toilet training, inhibition of aggressiveness, and so forth, and they must learn to make efforts. And parents cannot make girls into boys or grant other impossibilities. In short, parents are not omnipotent as children believe them to be. To the children they must necessarily appear frustrating. (2) The Ego must defend itself against Id impulses that threaten its existence. If it is not helped by parental approval, if it does not have a firm guide coaching and pointing the way, the Ego, left to its own devices, has a much harder task which, if accomplished at all, compels it to oppose the Id more fiercely and sweepingly than otherwise necessary. Fearful of being overwhelmed, the Ego might resort to desperate measures and might be injured by the excessive strain. Parents must represent reality, they must ally themselves to the child's Ego, if they wish to help the child. This means firmness, security, and limitation, though not harshness and restrictiveness. In contrast, "permissiveness" often amounts to emotional nonsupport; the child is confronted with too unstructured an existence, which makes the task of restraining his own impulses and finding his own direction overly hard. Tender plants need support. (3) Parents are the most immediate target of the aggressiveness generated by the unavoidable frustration of some Id impulses. The parent who is a kind but firm guide allows the discharge of aggres-

siveness toward an external goal—himself—and subsequent recon-
ciliation. If he has angered the child before, there will be no
guilt feeling in the child who had discharged the anger. The parent who is so indulgent that the child cannot discharge his aggressiveness toward him actually turns the child's aggressiveness inward. His child is likely to suffer from guilt feelings and un-
focused anxiety—generalized qualms of conscience. His task has
been made harder, not easier. The children of parents who indulge them, reason with them, and manipulate them are more
likely to have difficulties than children who are spontaneously
loved, and punished.

We are only intermittently and partially aware of the continuous processes, conflicts, and integrations that go on within us.
Even what goes on in the Ego is not all conscious. Most of the
Ego's defense activities are unconscious; other things are preconscious—stored in memory and easily available. The Id is
altogether unconscious and has no direct contact with reality
while the Superego is partly unconscious and partly preconscious.
Impulses generated in the Id and Superego enter consciousness
only through the Ego. In the process they are often transformed:
what may enter consciousness is not the unacceptable impulse but
the guilt-feeling it generated in the Superego or the anxiety it
caused in the Ego; and sometimes only a symptom caused by the
anxiety—be it a sore throat, an upset stomach, or a depressed
mood. Since the Ego often slams the door to lock out Id impulses
or to push them back, sometimes these impulses, to be admitted,
disguise their original nature and purpose. The Ego thus may
carry out an impulse which actually has an aim that would be rebuffed were it recognized.

The keys to reality—perception through the senses, notions of
space and time, of cause and effect, command of body movements, conscious thought—are located in the Ego. Two legisla-
tives, the Id and Superego, urge their unworldly desires on a
practical executive agency, the Ego.

To avoid being swamped by orders of its two principals, the
Ego erects defenses and ignores signals and importunities when
they might lead to ruin in reality. Such defenses are needed also
because overwhelmingly strong impulses might flood the Ego
so that it would be unable either to restrain or to satisfy them. A

moderately hungry man may work to get food and cook it. But a ravenous man might be so obsessed with desire that he could not hold out and make appropriate efforts to satisfy it. He might eat indigestible food or steal. Experiments show that a moderately hungry animal uses his training and intelligence to get food, but a very hungry animal is unable to use an indirect method that works and insistently tries direct methods, even when they do not work And the ravenous animal is careless of danger. The overwhelmed Ego is put out of commission like an electrical appliance connected with too strong a current. Similarly, the Ego may be paralyzed, or frenzied, by perceiving a strong external threat. The effect is called panic. Finally, the Ego may be paralyzed, or thrown into a sort of oscillation, when it falls under the domination of conflicting Id and Superego commands. Against all these dangers, and many others, complex defense mechanisms are on call.

The observations on which Freud's notions of the forces contending within the human personality are based had struck others before him. Religious literature speaks of the many cunning disguises of the devil and is rich in descriptions of the psychological pitfalls awaiting the man who tries to be virtuous. "Conscience" which "doth make cowards of us all," (Hamlet) "the flesh" which "is weak," whereas "the spirit indeed is willing" (Matthew: 24) —all these notions in untold variations describe the same phenomena Freud describes. The novelty of Freud's discovery lies in the specific tracing of the formation and of the relationship of the forces that constitute personality.

PROOF OF FREUD'S PUDDING?

Freud's view of human personality seems at first so anthropomorphic—he seems to pack the human personality with little men cannily negotiating with each other—and dramatic that it strikes scientists as improbable. Much of it, indeed, is speculative. The Ego, Superego, and Id are, of course, metaphors, compressed similes. And one never observes an Id—only actions attributed to it. But then one never observes gravity either—only actions attributed to it. "Gravity" as well as the "systems" which Freud distinguishes in our personality are concepts, ideas derived from observed data that summarize and relate all the characteristics that distinguish a class of events. Concepts cannot be observed directly. Their usefulness lies in clarifying observations and in explaining them—in relating past experiences in such a way that future ones can sometimes be predicted, or produced, or even avoided. (Strictly, concepts are helpful in the formulation of propositions from which predictions may be inferred. They are not predictions.) The concepts invented by Freud must be judged in this light. So far they have not been superseded, though future observations, no doubt, will lead to modifications. The great majority of people concerned with clinical psychology and psychiatry find Freud's concepts useful in studying the origin of personality and the influences shaping it. There is no doubt, for instance, that what Freud calls Ego and Superego are acquired rather than inborn. (Some psychoanalysts believe now that the rudiments of the Ego exist much earlier than Freud thought though there is no doubt that the Ego *develops* through interaction with reality.) His concepts help not only to trace the origin but also to describe the forces and processes which in time produce alterations of personality: they permit a dynamic as well as a genetic view.

PSYCHOANALYTIC METHOD

Freud's views sprang from perceiving unconscious feelings, impulses, and fantasies through psychoanalysis. "Psychoanalysis" refers (1) to Freud's technique of investigation, (2) to the theories to which he was led by the use of his method, and finally, (3) to a treatment of personality disorders which uses the method and the theory.

The psychoanalytic method interprets manifest behavior in terms of latent, unconscious wishes, fears, ideas, and conflicts. Manifest behavior includes actions, fantasies, day and night dreams, thoughts, feelings, somatic events such as gestures, postures, sensations, blushing, or ulcers; relationships with the social environment such as job behavior, personal relations, or politics; and relations with the physical environment such as the choice of food, or the accidents one suffers. Freud explains that the person who forgets something wanted consciously to do what he forgot. But there was some unconscious opposition to his intent which made him forget. Though the forgetting indicates opposition (and the opposition wins most easily when one is tired) it need not be logically connected with the forgotten object. You might forget to meet Joan not because you are unconsciously reluctant to meet her but because there is an unpleasant association with her name, or with the meeting place, or with someone or something she is linked with in your unconscious. There need be no *logical* connection with her.

To Freud's eye the human personality appears like an iceberg. Only parts are visible above the surface. By learning the way the unconscious expresses itself, we can fathom the latent fears, desires, fantasies, and conflicts that underlie manifest behavior. Actions are often generated by several motives, conscious and unconscious, and by external conditions. When *all* conditions and motives together generate the action and none could have done so by itself—when each is necessary and none alone sufficient—we speak of *joint causation*. When *any* one of several motives or conditions present could generate it—when each is sufficient by itself—the action is said to be *overdetermined*. Actions are often overdetermined. Therefore, pointing to a sufficient conscious motive for an action (or attitude, fantasy, etc.) is not an argument against the existence of an unconscious one—although lack of a conscious motive is an argument for an unconscious one. The unconscious motive—even when there is a reasonable conscious one—may still be needed to account for part of the action or for the feelings associated with it.

The language of the unconscious—the signs by which we identify and trace what goes on unawares now and what must have gone before—differs from person to person because things and situations acquire different meanings for each individual in the course of his experience. But many experiences are common to the human species—after all, all men are born of women and go through the same stages of maturation, and the human species shares many other experiences. Children, psychotics, and primitives often use symbols with full awareness of their meaning, whereas in normal adult Western culture the meaning is uncon-

scious. Even from person to person there are differences in awareness of symbolic meaning and more so from group to group.
Much confirmation for Freud's interpretations of symbols is found
in comparative studies of language, art, mythology, and ritual.

Psychoanalytic technique has found a number of nearly universal symbols with fairly constant meaning from individual to
individual. For instance, flying usually stands for sexual intercourse. But variations of universal symbols—their significance to
particular individuals—are as important as their universality. For
this reason, the language of the unconscious cannot be made intelligible by means of a dictionary. Thus flying may have numerous
additional, perhaps prevalent, meanings to a person who has had
an airplane accident or even some less incisive association with
flying. Therefore, the significance of the expressions of the unconscious can be uncovered only in the context of individual
analysis. Knowledge of universal meanings merely sensitizes the
analyst to possibilities.

In sleep, the Ego's vigilance against disturbing impulses and
fears is somewhat relaxed. Sleep, after all, is rest for the Ego—
withdrawal from contact with reality. But sleep does not affect
the Id and Superego, which have no contact with reality from
which to withdraw. They remain active. If upsetting impulses
and fears, or external danger signals such as noise, break into
consciousness, the sleeper awakens. But dreams often succeed in
keeping the Ego asleep. They produce fantasy fulfillments for
inopportune wishes, fantasy assurances against inopportune fears,
and fantasy explanations for noises. In the dream, impulses and
fears may appear in the unrealistic form in which they exist before the Ego transforms them, and since the Ego is asleep, time,
space, causality, and logic are often disregarded. Further, impulse
and dream fulfillment, fear and dream reassurance, usually are
disguised to prevent alarming the Ego and thus awakening the
sleeper. The camouflage is produced by the dream-work of the
Ego defenses which, though relaxed in sleep, still are awake, unlike
the conscious Ego. The Ego defenses act like a watchman who
lets the contraband pass as long as he has made sure the boss won't
notice. Sometimes the impulse succeeds in circumventing the Ego
and getting hold of the motor apparatus. The result is sleepwalk-
ing. Analogously, we have in a waking state an "acting out" of

impulses the true nature of which remains hidden to the Ego.

Often the unconscious meaning of an action or dream is suggested by time sequence, or juxtaposition. For instance, a boy might suffer a small accident, even though he is not clumsy, each time report cards are issued and he gets the highest marks in his class. Or to his own surprise, he often gets a headache when he has a date, though he does not normally suffer from headaches. The timing might make us look for the possible unconscious relationship and meaning to the boy of the report card and the accident or the date and the headache. The order in which things come to mind also helps establish the relationship that links them unconsciously. The nature of the action is significant as well. Freud mentioned a patient who did not recall that he had been defiant toward his parents—but behaved defiantly toward the analyst. Another patient did not remember that he had given up his childish search for the truth in sexual matters as hopeless. But he produced a mass of confused dreams and associations and complained that he never succeeded at anything and never could carry anything through.

A pat, standardized interpretation glibly translating dreams and symbols can easily mislead. The unconscious does not speak standardized language. Even if the vocabulary be similar, the grammar and syntax needed to make sense must be found in the context of a full analysis. They can never be imposed from the outside without doing violence to the actual contents of the unconscious we are trying to understand.

THE OEDIPUS COMPLEX IN INDIVIDUALS

The Oedipus complex, to which we now turn, is a phase of normal development. Freud thought that this most formative psychological experience of the child, once the Ego has been created, is of basically sexual nature. Perhaps this is the most controversial aspect of his theory. The Oedipus complex is hard to swallow for it denies the proverbial purity of the child—his childlikeness. Reluctantly one might accept this—after all, if one's eyes are open, the sexual life of infants and children is difficult to overlook. Childlikeness actually consists not in not having a sexual life but in regarding it innocently, without shame and guilt. But worse is to come. Freud also appears to deny the purity of the child's relationship to his parents. Incestuous desires are attributed to the child. Our whole image of the parent-child relationship, which keeps entirely free of sexual connotations the sentiments that bind children to parents and parents to children, is questioned. No wonder Freud met anger, the indignant denials and vehement accusations which messengers bearing unwelcome news have met since time immemorial.

Many post-Freudians have cut loose from Freud's conception of the Oedipus complex though still traveling, they insist, on the course he set. Freud reacted by noting that "the more the hard-won truths of psychoanalysis are sacrificed the less resistance is encountered." With Hamlet he insists: "Lay not that flattering unction to your soul,/That not your trespass, but my madness speaks."

Though attempts to interpret the Oedipus complex away or to desexualize it within the psychoanalytic framework are unconvincing, the proofs outside the analyst's study for the existence of the Oedipus complex are by no means incontestable. The most persuasive evidence is clinical. (Unfortunately it cannot be presented here.) Moreover, even that evidence may be interpreted in different ways. Yet to omit the Oedipus complex would be to omit what Freud considered a most important aspect of human development; and however future research will modify the hypothesis, it seems certain that it will not be altogether discarded. Even now the hypothesis itself is so widely accepted and so influential in many forms that one should know and understand it, regardless of whether he believes it true.

Freud thought that the first external object of desire is the mother. When the infant has not yet separated the environment from himself, love for her is part of self-love, narcissism, as Freud with his weakness for Greek mythology called it. During the first year, as the infant perceives her as a separate entity, the mother becomes an external love object. The source of all that is pleasant, the mother is the first person the child wants to appropriate, to make his own, knowing that she is not him—nor his, for she belongs also to the father, not to speak of the other children. (With girls, the father in time takes the mother's place, at least in part, but she remains the object of the boy's desire.) Since the mother frustrates as well as gratifies his desire, the infant's feelings toward her are ambivalent—rage and vindictive aggressiveness are fused with overwhelming desire. When, later, the Superego adds to the ambivalence, it also drives part of it underground— usually the resentment and the socially unacceptable part of the desire. It can reappear only if suitably disguised.

Jealousy of the father (or in girls, of the mother) becomes quite apparent around the fourth year. By this time also the center of sensuality has shifted from the mouth (during the first year) and the anus (in the second and third) to settle in the genitals. Nutritional and excretory functions are finally separated from sexual ones. That the infant's main pleasure during his first year consists in sucking is hardly open to doubt. As maturation permits sphincter control, and toilet training is introduced, the child can use his control for his pleasure, or to win the approval of the mother. Observation leaves little doubt that his bathroom "duty" plays an important role in the second year.

But why does Freud call these stages sexual? Because they partake of some of the traits that later characterize the activities usually called sexual. And, more important, in adult sexual life the originally erogenous zones continue to have erotic significance. The not uncommon activity of kissing recalls the oral stage; so does calling what we like "sweet." The sexual character of the anal stage leaves less directly recognizable traces. Though children originally take delight in their excrement and in dirt generally, they are trained to cleanliness and learn to despise dirt. We all must go beyond pregenital sexual activities and, finally, also beyond oedipal object choices. Both later strike us as immoral. They are tabooed and we usually succeed in entirely forgetting them. If there is a fixation on, or (later) regression to, a pregenital center of sexual excitement so that it habitually replaces the genital center, we speak of perversion. (Note that perversion involves habitual replacement, not occasional addition.) The same term is used when sexual activity has a habitual main terminus other than the genitals of the opposite sex. Perversions are usually symptoms of an underlying psychic disorder. Most perverts display other symptoms as well, but the fact of perversion—deviation from a cultural norm—is not itself a disease.

In our culture, the child's sexual life nearly ceases by about the sixth year. It is followed by a latency period lasting until about the twelfth year. Puberty then initiates a post-oedipal adult sex life. The infantile one is forgotten.

Full gratification of the child's inchoate desire for the mother is at first physically and later socially impossible. The social taboo is impressed on the child long before there is any physical possibility of breaking it. Sexual advances are rejected. The child's Ego is urged to control sexual impulses. The mother might explain to the child that his interest in nudity and in the genitals is "not nice." Even if she tries to deal with the matter without overt disapproval, he will perceive her discomfort. The child's Ego must also try to keep within bounds the hostility against the parent of the same sex who is felt as rival for the possession of the parent of the opposite sex. For the Ego learns that when this hostility is carried into unbounded aggression, it may bring retaliation. And the Ego realizes that the stronger forces are on the other side. Moreover, restraint may also become the price of acceptance by the parent of the opposite sex. And there is love for the rival as well as hate, and ultimately a desire to emulate him.

The Oedipus conflict is overcome as the child partially identifies himself with the parent of his own sex or, more precisely, with his image of the parent, and finds friends of the opposite sex outside his family. The boy identifies himself with his father by internalizing—making his own—feelings and threats attributed to the father. The Ego acts in accordance with the rule, "if you can't beat them, join them." And it is here that the Superego becomes an independent entity.

While this is going on, the child does not yet fully see the outside world as separate from himself. One remnant of the early connection is the assumption that the rest of the world is animated by his own feelings. Hence, the boy, who would like to get rid of the father, attributes to the father the wish to get rid of him. The boy's Ego then, for the sake of security, pushes back the wish to get rid of the father. The boy is rewarded with approval and reduced fear of the father. The paternal threat to wayward impulses is now incorporated and becomes one of the Superego's weapons with which to restrain the Ego from carrying out the Id's desire for the mother, or even allowing the desire to return to consciousness. Specifically, the Superego reminds the Ego from within through anxiety of the punishment which was feared from the father: deprivation of the organ needed to carry out the forbidden sexual intent. (In the pre-oedipal stage the infant, enraged at times by his mother who can never fully satisfy him, may develop hostile reactions to her and immoderate fears of retaliation. These pregenital antecedents of castration fear loom large in certain types of personality disorder.)

The little boy usually knows by this time that not all human beings are formed as he is. This confirms his fears. Indeed, there are many other apparent confirmations. Actual castration threats ("if you don't stop sucking your fingers, or playing with yourself, we'll cut if off") have probably become rare. But the modern parent who tells the child "If you don't stop you will damage yourself" achieves the same effect. The child, moreover, does see how parts of the body can be lost: teeth fall out, hair and nails are cut, and he may even see a mutilated person. To him the fear of losing his valued organ is by no means unreasonable. Castration fear, according to Freud, plays a major role in character formation, particularly in shaping the Superego and overcoming the oedipal conflict. The widespread ceremony of circumcision—and other ritual mutilations—can be explained as symbolic sacrifices *in lieu of* castration. Characteristically, in our age this ritual as well as many others is frequently explained as a sanitary measure. Yet the primitives in question had no notion of its sanitary significance—indeed, no notion of sepsis and of antiseptic measures. The replacement of a psychologically less acceptable explanation by a more acceptable one of a plausible sort is called *rationalization*.

With girls, the Oedipus conflict involves first a change of love object from mother to father and then feelings of rivalry for the mother and a wish to take her place. Further, the little girl dimly feels that the mother deprived her of her original maleness. And she feels that the father might restore it, often in the form of giving her a baby—a fantasy equivalent. However, her hostility against her mother is held in bounds even as is the boy's aggressiveness toward the father: the little girl fears the loss of maternal affection no less than the little boy fears the father's retaliation. Both sexes not only fear the parent they feel as a rival, but also love him. The many folktales involving evil stepmothers clearly indicate the ambivalence of little girls toward their mothers and their fantasy of the ideal (real) mother.

For her fantasy of once having been a boy and for her hope of becoming one again, the little girl finds the same sort of confirmation the little boy finds for his fears. She sees that parts of the body can be lost and sloughed off. She sees also that they can grow again like teeth or hair. Her hope may lead her to be more submissive, accepting, possessive, and receptive than a little boy. But it is not easy to distinguish the impact of early and later cultural conditioning in the psychological differentiation of the sexes.

The Oedipus complex as a whole is highly controversial. The development that Freud believes takes place in girls is easily its most controversial part. (Karen Horney—and other neo-Freudians as well—insists that girls need never resent the lack of a penis.)

The manner in which the Oedipus complex is overcome depends largely on the relationship of the child with his environment, which is patterned in the main on cultural tradition. The type of Superego created—and the influence of the paternal and maternal model—vary accordingly. It seems likely, for instance, that in America the child's Superego incorporates larger portions of the maternal Superego than elsewhere. Note also that there are significant variations in the oedipal pattern when there is more than one child, or fewer or more than two parents. For the sake of brevity, we have schematized the oedipal conflict without even mentioning the many problems that may arise in overcoming it. Our account has been like a timetable, listing points of departure and arrival and some of the scheduled stops. But many unscheduled stops, and even derailment, are possible.

The complexity of psychic development leaves one impressed and, perhaps, a little incredulous. Physical maturation is simpler and fairly automatic if food and shelter are provided. But human personality does not develop automatically; it depends on the human environment. Our prolonged utter dependence on parents probably causes the Oedipus complex to loom so importantly in human development.

It is impossible here to rehearse the evidence for the pattern

Freud traced. It convinced many competent people but left others with reservations. (Anyone who wishes to inquire further should start by reading Freud himself. Although much has since been added to Freud's original results—by himself and by many others —Freud's own *A General Introduction to Psychoanalysis* remains the most lucid and lively introduction. And none of his later expositors has equaled Freud's literary skill. Charles Brenner's *An Elementary Textbook of Psychoanalysis* is an extremely competent and comprehensive presentation of psychoanalysis, including many recent developments.) However, people not professionally concerned with these explorations should not be altogether heedless of the advice Jocasta gave to Oedipus, her troubled husband and unwitting son:

> *Chance rules our lives and the future is all unknown . . .*
> *Best live as best we may . . .*
> *Many a man ere now in dreams has lain*
> *With her who bore him. He will endure best*
> *Who with such omens troubles not his mind.*

SOCIAL EFFECTS OF THE OEDIPUS COMPLEX

Though there is an immense variety of conceptions of the family and of relationships within it, there are incest taboos— prohibitions of sexual intercourse among some family members— in all societies. The taboos concern different family members; and membership in the family is often determined by traditional conceptions as well as by biological relationships. But in all societies, mother-son incest is taboo. This itself, according to Freud, testifies to the universality of the desire. Its universal frustration by taboo is a most important influence on the development of normal human personalities everywhere.

A taboo is an interdiction believed to be self-enforcing and to originate in nature, or the divine or demonic will. Nature or spirits punish the violator and the society that, ignorantly or knowingly, tolerates the unexpiated violation of the taboo. This belief may lead to more or less deliberate social punishment of the violator to avoid punishment of society. Large parts of our legal systems are derived from primitive taboos and the notions of retribution and expiation connected with them; they also remain prominent in most religions. Sophocles' three tragedies about the House of Thebes are concerned with the suffering of a group that unwittingly tolerates an unwitting incest-taboo violator, as well as with his own suffering and self-imposed retaliatory punishment and expiation. The complex of wishes and fears, guilt and expiation, which Freud found to be shared by all human beings in many different ways is named after Sophocles' mythical hero. Much of the sacred and profane literature of the world is concerned directly and indirectly with this topic.

Some cultural anthropologists (students of different and, particularly, of preliterate societies) have objected to Freud's assertion that the Oedipus complex is universal—a condition for each rather than an effect of any culture. In a number of societies, they point out, children either are not brought up by their biological parents or are brought up by them in a manner very different from that which conditioned Freud's patients. Other anthropologists have countered that in most societies children are brought up by their biological parents and that strong incest taboos exist everywhere. Further, the Oedipus complex need not be based on *physical* parenthood as depicted by Sophocles. What matters is the psychological relationship between the child and those from whom it receives parental care. Freud not only grants, but insists, that the pattern of the oedipal conflict and of its influence varies with the type of parent-child relationship, which in turn depends on social custom as well as individual variations. Freud asserts that (though other influences are not excluded) different personality types and cultural patterns are related strongly to different parent-child relationships and that these relationships always include some form of the Oedipus complex: the desire for the parent (or parent figure) of the opposite sex is always present and must always be overcome. The incest taboo is a necessary condition for the existence of human society and of any type of culture. The incestuous desire cannot be gratified else fathers could not safely bring up sons, or mothers daughters, for the children would not succeed but would displace and kill their parents—who would be tempted to murder them beforehand. But each family and each society deals somewhat differently with these psychological forces. And these differences go a long way toward explaining both individual and social differences—though certainly not all the way.

According to Freud, the Oedipus complex helps explain the origin and function of many things—primitive behavior toward totem animals, the killing or eating of which is frequently taboo except on special occasions, and even the rituals of religious communion services, as well as the psychological origin, effects, and limitations of civilization itself. Freud speculated that in prehistoric times human groups were led by domineering fathers who reserved all females for themselves and cowed their sons until finally overthrown and murdered by them. (This form of social organization and change of leadership is observed among a number of animal herds. Human groups are exceptional inasmuch as leaders are not necessarily killed or even dismissed when their physical power wanes.) Civilization, Freud thought, developed from the solidarity, guilt, and fear of the brothers which arose from this primordial revolution. Mankind is united in this hereditary sin. Many ritual actions, guilt feelings, and taboos are explained as symbolizing, expiating, and commemorating the murder of the tyrannical father by rebellious sons. In the Christian religion, redemption—reacceptance by the father—becomes possible by divine grace through the sacrifice of a son—the divine redeemer. The blood of this *Agnus Dei qui tollit peccata mundi* washes away our sins, if we repent and with him submit to the father.

Human and animal sacrifices Freud explains as expiatory acts or, sometimes, ritual repetitions. And he draws attention to many ancient mythologies—Greek, Germanic, Celtic, and Oriental—which report the slaying of a father god by the sons, in direct as well as in symbolic form.

Consider, for instance, the Greek myth of creation as told in Hesiod's *Theogony*. Gaia (earth) lay with Ouranos (sky). Ouranos hid the children "away in a secret place of the earth and would not allow them to rise up into light". Kronos, the youngest, instigated by his mother who armed him with a sickle of adamant, decided to take vengeance: "And now great Ouranos came, bringing on night, and longing for love he laid himself upon Gaia and embraced her all round about." Kronos from his ambush cut off his father's genitals and threw them into the sea;

he foam (seed) they produced Aphrodite, the goddess of
Kronos married his sister, Rhea, and reconfined his siblings
arkness. He swallowed his children at birth, fearing that
they would dethrone him. Rhea was dissatisfied and managed to
hide one of her children, Zeus, giving Kronos a stone wrapped
in swaddling clothes to swallow instead. Zeus, grown up, made
Kronos disgorge his brothers; and, with their aid, he won a long
battle against Kronos and instituted the reign of the Olympian
gods.

These myths have many meanings and occur in numerous
forms among all the peoples of the world. One thing, however,
seems clear in Hesiod's tale: fathers had reason to fear their sons
who would dethrone them and sons their fathers. Unless this fear
is reduced by incest taboos, no society can long continue.

Anthropologists have pointed out that, aside from its convenience for explanatory purposes, there is no evidence for the original patricide. Where, when, and how did it take place? And
since the many far-flung primordial groups did not communicate,
was it repeated in each one? And wherein would the unconscious
collective memory reside that transmits knowledge of an event
long past and nowhere recorded? Evidence for a hypothesis of
this kind is not likely ever to stand up in criminal courts. The primordial patricide is a bold speculation—no more. Freud himself
never considered it more than that.

The explanatory value of the idea is scarcely reduced if it is
reformulated to assert, not that a patricide took place, but that
patricide and the feelings that stem from it are part of the unconscious fantasy life of human beings. The institutions and beliefs
which Freud speculated may be ritual historical reminiscences in
a collective mind are equally well explained as the outcome of
universally shared wishes, prohibitions, and guilt feelings related
to an intent, or to a fantasy, and not necessarily to an actual event.
The evidence Freud offered for the psychological existence of
the individual Oedipus complex then also would be evidence for
whatever social effects it may have without need to postulate a
historical event or a collective unconscious memory of it. And
the evidence for the universality of the fantasy is overwhelming—
while there is none for the fact. (The fantasy, itself, certainly is
evidence only for the wish.) Treating patients, particularly cases

of hysteria, Freud at first thought that he had found the cause of their disorders when they offered histories of early childhood mistreatment, seduction, rape, and so forth. Only later did he find out that the patients' reports were not about actual happenings in their past as they believed (and led him for a time to believe) but fearful and wishful fantasies. These fantasies, however, were found to play no less important a role in the illness than actual external happenings. The case for the social Oedipus complex may be analogous. (Recent clinical evidence indicates that often there is an external stimulus to the fantasies in the unconsciously seductive behavior of parents who act out *their* fantasies under the guise of being "modern" and "hiding nothing from the child" or under guise of caring for his physical health and cleanliness.)

Bronislaw Malinowski (in *Sex and Repression in Savage Society*) and other anthropologists objected to Freud's theory of culture. They pointed to observations which indicate, as they see it, that the Oedipus complex, where it exists, occurs as an effect of culture. Therefore, Freud notwithstanding, they maintain that culture cannot be the effect of the Oedipus complex. But is it not possible that culture and the Oedipus complex developed together, creating and shaping each other? The task is to trace concrete developments rather than to worry about the old conundrum: which came first, the chicken or the egg? One could not exist and, as far as observation goes, nowhere does exist and continue without the other.

Malinowski also thought his observations among the matrilineal Trobrianders, where paternal authority is held by the maternal uncle rather than the father, prove that the boy's hostility is aroused by the paternal authority and not, as Freud thought, by the father's sexual possession of the mother, for resentment is directed against the maternal uncle, not the father. In short, the Oedipus complex is absent in matrilineal societies and therefore not universal. Where it exists, it is an effect of patriarchal family organization in which the father is also a figure of authority. However, Malinowski's evidence and his interpretation of psychoanalytic theory can be questioned. Might the child's hostility not be aroused by the father's sexual relation to the mother as well as by his authority? Originating with jealousy of the actual father, the child's hostility may later be transferred to the uncle who

stands *in loco parentis*. Such "displacements," far from contra-
dicting it, are acknowledged by Freudian theory as characteristic
of human development.

Careful reading of Freud and of the anthropological evidence
thought to disprove his theories suggests, with little room for
doubt, that the disproof rests on a rather naive or willfully cap-
tious reading of both the anthropological evidence and Freud's
views. However, doubt is cast on psychoanalytic theory from
another angle—and this doubt may be reinforced just because
Freud's views are not easily refuted. At least some psychoanalytic
ideas are hard to disprove—or prove—because they are so formulated that no observation can either prove or disprove them.
The hypotheses are not stated clearly, specifically, and precisely
enough to indicate what facts would prove or disprove them, at
least outside a purely clinical setting.

There is no reason to discard ideas just because they stand in
need of more precise formulation to make evidence relevant and
thus enable us to test them. Explanatory conjectures are useful.
They are the parents of more precise hypotheses and observations—though they may be slain by their offspring. Some of
Freud's speculations deal with matters which perhaps can never
be quite objectively and definitely observed. But only a woefully
pedestrian person would confine his curiosity to the definitely
answerable. Thus to fetter the imagination not only shrinks one's
universe but in the end also limits the knowable portion of it.
However, imaginative and informed speculation, though it need
not be eliminated, must be distinguished from proved facts and
from precise provable hypotheses. Though the same cannot be
said of all his followers, Freud himself has never blurred this
distinction.

Need it be said that, though possibly necessary, Freud's theories— even if fully confirmed—are not sufficient to explain social
behavior as a whole? By making possible the exploration of unconscious aspects of individual and group behavior, Freud has
added a new and, on the whole, promising dimension to social
science. But psychoanalysis is an addition, not a replacement;
other methods of explaining human behavior, the observations
and methods of all the social sciences, remain as necessary as ever.

CHAPTER III   *Who Is Normal?*

So far we have traced the formation of human personality, drawn a map of it, and looked at a few tools of map making. Now to the processes that keep us functioning.

When the personality is molded under favorable conditions—when neither drives nor the environment confront the Ego with impossible demands or obstacles—the Ego can realistically perceive and master both. When the undeveloped, weak Ego, not yet fully separated from the Id, nor itself fully integrated, is given some support and a chance to develop, it grows strong enough to gratify drives beyond mere discharge, through the positive actions which mastery of bodily movement and of the environment makes possible. Impulses that cannot be appropriately satisfied through the Ego's manipulation of the environment may be suppressed for the time being. Though acknowledged by the Ego, suppressed impulses are frustrated until they and the environment are so modified that they can be gratified. Further, under favorable conditions the Ego learns to change the aim of drives from the impossible to the possible, from the less to the more socially acceptable, and from the crude and immediate to the

39

subtle, the skillful, indirect, and lasting. These displacements and refinements are called sublimations, particularly when referring to the diversion of libido from directly sexual aims.

Culture springs from sublimation, and so does individual ability to participate in and contribute to it. One's choice of friends and enemies, culinary, aesthetic, and erotic preferences, choice of occupation, and attitude toward life are all influenced by sublimation. Pregenital strivings are sublimated—satisfied in a desexualized and socially acceptable way—more often than the genital ones which can find direct sexual gratification. To sublimate is not the same as not to engage in sexual intercourse. On the contrary, both excessive and deficient sexual intercourse are often effects of inability to sublimate those needs of pregenital origin which interfere with gratification in adult sexual activity. And this less than full gratification leads to compulsive repetition, or, sometimes, repudiation of sexual activity. Sublimation is largely a successful refinement and desexualization of pregenital desires, a displacement which gives satisfaction all around. If the Ego is not powerful enough to achieve sublimation, displacement is unsatisfactory: it does not gratify the displaced drive fully or it impairs the Ego's activities. This may occur when the developments through which sexual activity comes to be centered in the genitals are not quite successfully completed or when impulses which have been repressed do not participate in realistic development and retain a form unacceptable to the Ego.

Various motivations urge the Ego's development towards organized, purposeful, and realistic activity. There is avoidance of anxiety and pain and expectation of pleasure from the successful gratification of impulses. There is also the reassurance provided by by self-control and by Superego approval. Children can be observed re-enacting in play—in safety—experiences that aroused anxiety. They attempt to come to terms with their experiences. Often, for instance in playing doctor, they play an active role when in reality they had an anxiety-provoking passive role. It seems that mastery of anxiety—as distinguished from mere avoidance—is itself a source of positive Ego pleasure. Children like to be tossed in the air and caught by an adult. They take pleasure in exciting and defeating their own fear. (This is only one element of the pleasure experienced. And pleasure will not prevail over fear in the child who has not mastered his fears, or does not trust the adult.) Again, the toddler takes delight in learning to organize his movements, to walk, partly because of external approval and partly because of self (Ego) approval. This is one element in the pleasure many continue to experience in sports: they court difficulties, and sometimes dangers, to prove their skill in overcoming them. This is also an element in the pleasure many people continue to feel in mastering vicariously experienced anxiety—say by listening to horror stories. Just as in the control of external threats and obstacles, there is in the mastery of drives a source of pleasure, offsetting to some extent the pleasure lost in not gratifying them directly. It is the joy of creation—of self (Ego) creation—by achieving control of brute drives and thereby control of the environment, the joy of creating order and purpose from chaos. It is the joy that made the original fall from grace bearable and the prospect of victory over sin attractive. This joy, which God must have felt in creating the world, is felt by every child when he creates his. It remains a strong element particularly in the personalities of artists and thinkers. But everybody who has in some measure attained mastery of the Ego within his personality experiences some of that joy—the joy of self-creation.

One result of mastery of the personality by the Ego must be stressed: perception of situations and persons, and reaction to them, in their own terms. We all must rely on our past experiences in dealing with current ones. Intelligence chiefly consists in understanding the precise relationship of the new to the old experiences. And the emotional aspect of Ego mastery, too, consists in not reacting to current situations by mere repetition of old responses. When Ego mastery is impaired, a husband may transfer to his wife unchanged the responses felt originally toward his mother; or he may "act out" with his business associates some patterns that originated in his early family situation. In both instances he is repeating roles which were once adequate, successful, or necessary but are not now. In every situation we find reminders of earlier experiences. It is neither necessary nor possible to avoid such unconscious association. But a healthy development means that we are not shackled to the past. We don't do violence to the new by perceiving it and reacting mechanically and solely in terms of the old. We are free from the tyranny of past experience and can use it to meet the new spontaneously and realistically as new. Just as an artist creates a new experience out of old materials and new perceptions, so does a healthy person. However, while the artist can create new experiences for others, the nonartist can create new experiences only for himself, though, of course, he can describe them to others.

HEALTH, NORMALITY, AND MORALITY

Specific psychological disorders can be defined, and the mishaps leading to them can be described. However, no one has so far defined psychological health and illness in a way general enough to cover all cases and concrete enough to be useful. The definitions offered are too narrow or too vague or both. Yet one effect of the popularization of psychology is the erroneous belief that behavior can easily be characterized as "sick" and "immature," or "healthy" and "mature." Hence, a pathogenic striving toward "normality": people want to be "normal" instead of wanting to be "right" or "good." The psychologist, vested with the authority of science, has become the arbiter of morals by deciding what is "normal" and "healthy" and therefore good; and what is "neurotic" and therefore bad. (The works of Carl G. Jung, of Erich Fromm [particularly *Man for Himself*], and to a lesser extent of Karen Horney elaborate this confusion from different angles. Among more orthodox analysts, J. C. Flügel does this.) Thus the psychologist has picked up the authority which the minister has lost with many people. But psychology cannot replace morals. Nor is a moral judgment—whether or not disguised as a judgment of "normality"—psychologically relevant, or deducible from psychological observations. Finally, note that no action ever is "neurotic." Actors may be, but whether they are cannot be inferred from an action, only from the motivation for that action in the context of their personalities.

To be normal may mean simply that one conforms to a "norm" —a socially accepted rule. Both healthy and sick persons may conform, and either may refuse to accept the rule. It follows that we can seldom consider conformity or rebelliousness as an indication of health. The motives—conscious or unconscious—for either may be indicative, but no more than that.

We can call Hitler, Stalin, or Genghis Khan evil men, justifying this by appropriate definitions of evil. But in the absence of other evidence about them as personalities, not as politicians, or prophets of a creed, however repugnant, we can call these men neurotic only if we equate evil and neurosis. To do so is not simply to exchange a less for a more pretentious word, but also, and incorrectly, to suggest that there is a scientific (psychological) basis for moral judgment. There isn't. Moral judgment is not a factual (scientific) statement but an evaluation of the facts in the light of a nonscientific standard of good and evil, or right and wrong. Evil men are not necessarily more (or less) neurotic than good men. Men definitely suffering from a neurosis are not necessarily more (or less) evil than others. Whether a man is psychologically healthy must be decided on a basis other than his wickedness, and conversely his freedom from neurosis does not make him a good man in a moral sense. Moral and psychological criteria are distinct and not reducible to each other, and moral defects are not criteria for psychological defects (or conversely). A moral (or immoral) action, indeed any action, may be explained with the help of psychology. But the psychological data do not make an action moral or immoral; they do not suffice for any moral judgment, just as no moral judgment warrants one about psychological health. Morality is an independent, extrinsic valuation of psychological data (among others). It must rest on a basis of its own. If we reduce morals to psychology, we deprive moral judgment of its independence. If we reduce psychology to morals, we taint its scientific (observational) content with the moral judgments of the psychologist. In the end this must discredit both. Running away with your neighbor's wife need not be unhealthy. Does that make it moral? Not murdering your own wife may make you ill (e.g., neurotic) but not immoral. Psychological data are usually irrelevant in judging actions and useful only (sometimes necessary) in judging actors. They are sufficient only if they prove the actor incapable of making or carrying out moral judgments—if they indicate that a moral judgment of the actor would be irrelevant.

A second meaning of "normal" is, in effect, "happy." This

helps not at all. "Happiness" is not easier to define than "normality." Further, pigs might be happy, and hangmen, and perhaps the dead are content. Finally, a person can be happy and neurotic, unhappy and healthy—unless by definition happy and healthy become synonyms, which would make one of the two terms superfluous and the other more vague than it already is.

A third meaning of "normal" is statistical, referring to an average. It is hard to see how data could be collected to figure out an average. What weight are we to give to various aspects of behavior? Does my preference for an unusual breakfast food make me "abnormal"? If not, some nonstatistical norm decides the significance, and thereby the weight, to be given to the various actions that enter the average. Thus we would not rely on statistics, on facts, but on the norm by which data are weighed to construct averages. Technically such a norm, too, can be derived statistically, but it would be quite meaningless.

There is another more telling objection against giving (moral) norm-setting authority to a statistical norm, an average. Suppose you lived among a malaria-infested, or cannibalistic, or alcholic, or Nazi population. Would it be a symptom of disease then, or of immorality, not to have malaria, not to be a cannibal, or alcoholic, or a Nazi? It would be statistically abnormal. And if most of the population suffers from tooth decay or malaria and you don't, are you sick? Whatever the basis for the moral prescription, "You ought to do such and such," it cannot be that people *do* do such and such. Statistics—not to mention less exact frequency statements—at most define what is "normal" in the sense of more or less frequent. But this has scarcely any bearing on "normal" in the sense of "healthy" or "good." Frequency and health, psychological or physical, are certainly not the same. Nor does frequency determine the correctness of beliefs—the earth does not become flat even if everyone believes it is. Finally, moral judgments— whatever their basis otherwise—cannot rest on any statistics. If many people kill Jews, or enslave Negroes, their "normal" action is no more justifiable morally than if only a few do so. The individual moral responsibility of the actors may be weighed according to whether they are leaders, or followers, and according to the degree of freedom they had in choosing to commit or omit the action. Here statistics may play a role: the degree of individual guilt of the actors must be weighed according to the facts —including psychological and statistical ones—which indicate their degree of involvement and responsibility. But the moral evaluation of the act itself is independent of these facts.

Nor does it help to define psychological health as "maturity," "self-realization," "ability to grow," or "the fullest development of all our potentialities." Growth and maturity have a fairly clear meaning in horticulture and biology. But in psychology these words are but metaphors which help users pretend that they have solved a problem which they have merely disguised by rewording. What is it to be "mature"? What is it to grow? And can we not have unhealthy growth? Which potentialities are to be developed? Are we not born with many potentialities which, if developed, would preclude civilization? With potentialities for illness as well as health? For good and bad? When is development fullest? When do we realize ourselves? Such definitions are reassuring only because they are question-begging. Just a little less vague are definitions which characterize normality by "insight" (you don't have it if you disagree with me) or love (same thing) or by "facing your problems rather than escaping from them." Not that such phrases may not correctly describe behavior in individual cases. But they are useless as general definitions; they lack specificity. Does the revolutionary escape from his personal problems into social activity? Or does the conservative escape from social problems into individual introspection? Such formulations are often worse than useless; they are dangerous. Just as to the political fanatic opposition is always "communistic" or, if he is a Communist, "fascist," so to those addicted to psychologizing any dissent from their views is due to "neurosis," "maladjustment," and so forth. Their pretended tolerance allows them not to take seriously any view other than their own, i.e., to be actually most intolerant, by using a pseudo-scientific criterion to rule all dissenters out of order. Yet the source of a view, even if "neurotic," is irrelevant to the view's truth or falsity. Whether you are right or wrong when you say that Carolyn is 20 years old and unmarried does not depend on whether you are "neurotic"; it depends exclusively on her birthdate and marital status. Anyway, a neurosis can never be diagnosed from an opinion. The totality of an individual's behavior must be studied for any diagnosis. And when the proof of the neurosis is the view to be rejected because of it, the label is question-begging as well.

Perhaps a useful general definition of psychological health and disease is impossible. Is it needed? We must be able to distinguish the presence of specific disorders from their absence. Specific syndromes (patterns of symptoms) can be distinguished clinically— if the whole personality is studied to see what function or dysfunction various actions serve and from what motivation they spring. No more is actually needed. Perhaps the demand for more arises from a craving not for a medical tool but for a handy universal measuring stick with which to judge (or beat) oneself and others. Psychology is no more capable of yielding such a standard than any other discipline—except, as we have shown, in terms that are arbitrary, or so lofty as to be inspirational rather than specific. Personalities are unique historical systems. Therefore general rules, though necessary, cannot be sufficient to distinguish "healthy" from "sick." What applies to a lesser degree to works of art applies to personalities: though we may distinguish styles, and good from bad work, it is not possible to formulate a general criterion of universal applicability.

SANE AND INSANE SOCIETIES?

What has just been said about distinguishing sick and healthy personalities can be said also about insane and sane societies. Yet many otherwise competent scientists let themselves go on this topic. For instance, Ernest W. Burgess writes ("Mental Health in Modern Society," in *Mental Health and Mental Disorder*, edited by A. Rose): "Perhaps the most important single factor in mental disorders and disturbances is the failure of society to provide adequately for the social roles essential for the mental health of its members. . . . Society is responsible for the misfits, the unadjusted and the maladjusted persons. . . ." This is an overstatement. There is no known measurement that can tell us what "the most important single factor in mental disorders" is. And that "society is responsible for the misfits, the unadjusted and the maladjusted persons" is as reasonable as to blame the round hole if the square peg does not fit. If Professor Burgess were to show that "human nature" is universally "round" and that we could make the social holes into which it is to fit universally "round," too, he might be right. But as far as history goes, there never has been a social order into which all individuals fitted. Mental disorder is just as unavoidable a feature of social life as mental order. One climate is more favorable to flora and fauna than another, but none avoids disease. Even the mildest climate is unfavorable to some plants, which may thrive in the most inclement one. Forms and incidence of mental disorder change with the social order; possibly one society can do better in this respect than another. But as yet very little is known—though much is said—about this topic.

Neurotic symptoms are frequent even among the most primitive tribes, from the polar to the equatorial regions. Here, for example, is a poem on inhibition written by an Eskimo and transcribed by Knud Rasmussen (*Intellectual Culture of the Copper Eskimos*, 1932. Rasmussen's classic report shows that it was certainly not the modern influence that inspired either neurosis or poetry among these Eskimos):

> *Perhaps—well*
> *It may not matter!*
> *Perhaps—well.*
> *I sing merely of him,*
> *"The Boiling One,"*
> *Who sat, fearful, his mouth fast closed,*
> *Among women.*
>
> *Perhaps—well*
> *It may not matter!*
> *Perhaps—well.*
> *I sing merely of him,*
> *"Caribou Stomach,"*
> *Who sat, fearful, his mouth fast closed*
> *Among women.*
> *His two eyes ill-boding,*
> *Bent like a horn*
> *To be cut into leisters!*

Perhaps—well
It may not matter!
Perhaps—well.
I sing merely of him,
"The Axe,"
Who sat, fearful, his mouth fast closed,
Far, far away from man,
In solitude.

Perhaps—well
It may not matter!
Perhaps—well.
My tongue merely joins words
Into a little song.
A little mouth,
Curling downwards at the corners,
Like a bent twig
For a kayak rib.

And here is an extract of another Eskimo poem, on anxiety:

Glorious was life
In winter.
But did winter bring me joy?
No! Ever was I so anxious
For sole-skins and skins for kamiks,
Would there be enough for us all?
Yes, I was ever anxious,
  Ayi, yai ya.

Glorious was life
In summer.
But did summer bring me joy?
No! Ever was I so anxious
For skins and rugs for the platform,
Yes, I was ever anxious,
  Ayi, yai ya.

Glorious was life
When standing at one's fishing hole
On the ice.
But did standing at the fishing hole bring me joy?

No! Ever was I so anxious
For my tiny little fish-hook
If it should not get a bite,
  Ayi, yai ya.

Glorious was life
When dancing in the dance-house.
But did dancing in the dance-house bring me joy?
No! Ever was I so anxious,
That I could not recall
The song I was to sing.
Yes, I was ever anxious,
  Ayi, yai ya.

No doubt it will ever be a human task to improve the organization of society. Surely much is amiss in ours. But the system that leads to best adjustment is unknown and even undefined. Nor— were it known—need it be the one we might want to choose. What if slavery of selective infanticide as practiced by the Spartans leads to the least "maladjustment"? What if democracy or freedom leads to a great deal of maladjustment? Would we have to reject them? Hardly. Health and "adjustment" are not the only things individuals and societies want.

The specific form that maladjustment most frequently takes and the type of person most susceptible to it depend on social organization. But to say this or even, as Professor Burgess probably meant to say, that a better social organization might avoid some maladjustments is a far cry from saying that "society is responsible for the misfits." Social norms may be more or less hard to conform to. They may fit some and make others misfits. Difficulty or ease of conformity may be one standard for judging the appropriateness of norms. Surely not the only one. But even if we were to follow that standard and knew how to apply it, we would still remain perplexed. A uniform normative order which is rigidly enforced creates misfits. Some people are unable in general to abide by strict rules; others cannot adjust to the particular rules imposed. But a flexible social order which leaves many things to individual choice might create as many misfits. Some people are unable to adjust to even a few indispensable rules. For

instance, you might not be able to abide the rule that your
neighbor may pursue happiness in a way you consider sinful. Yet
you could not interfere. Other people might find no happiness
in pursuing happiness on their own. Indeed, some people are as
unable to stand freedom as others are to stand tyranny. In short,
if "adjustment" were our only goal, we might find that several
incompatible ways of organizing society attain it (or fail) in
equal measure—and we would still not know which to choose.

THE DEFENSES OF THE EGO

The means by which the Ego tries to control danger from
the Id, the Superego, and reality are more or less economic and,
accordingly, more or less healthy. When danger is felt to be very
threatening, whether because the Ego is still weak or because
the danger is ominous, crude and sweeping defense measures
may be resorted to. Just as a community imperiled by the infiltration of a powerful and tyrannical enemy may have to curtail freedom to save itself, so the Ego may inhibit its own growth and
freedom to ward off the hazard. Once a dangerous impulse is
repressed, it is hard to manage rationally. Id impulses expelled
from the Ego by repression remain dissociated and alarmingly
unrealistic. They act, as Freud puts it, like rebellious schoolboys
excluded from class by a teacher who cannot control them. Un-
educated, they continue to hang around, outside the Ego, and try
to break in. The class is tense, torn, and diverted. Not having
been discharged, the repressed impulses retain their energy; the
Ego has built a dam, not a channel, and has to use permanently
some energy to prevent the return of the repressed.

The victory thus achieved is hollow; it may cost only a little
less than defeat. The immobilized energy is unavailable for other
purposes. Even though an older and stronger Ego could well
afford to negotiate, it remains terrified and continues to treat the
repressed impulses as the portentous menace they once were, to
hold at bay dark monsters of the past which might be innocuous
and easily dealt with if scrutinized in the light of the present.

Some popular fairy tales represent the healthy transformation
of such monsters. Thus a prince—someone loved—may awaken

the sleeping beauty, the girl who had withdrawn in fear of her impulses. But it takes a courageous and well motivated man to overcome all the obstacles, his infantile fears as well as hers. Or, the princess is persuaded to love the ugly monster, even more symbolically, to kiss the repulsive frog—the male sex—whereupon he becomes a charming prince. The obstacles to impulse gratification and sublimation are to be expected. It is when they cannot be overcome by the experiences life usually offers, or when these cannot be accepted, that therapy becomes necessary.

THE UNCONSCIOUS

We can now round out the description of the unconscious. It includes impulses, ideas, and fantasies that have never been conscious, and impulses, ideas, and fantasies that once had entered the Ego and consciousness but were expelled by repression. Finally, there are the repressing forces—the mechanisms the Ego uses for defense. Repression and other defense operations still to be discussed, although they originate in the Ego, are, of course, not conscious. If they were conscious, they'd give the show away. Therefore, the defense mechanisms become semidetached from the Ego and, just like the impulses they repress, they miss the education from reality that the Ego experiences.

Things may never rise to the surface (consciousness) or they may disappear from it, but nothing ever seems to leave the personality altogether. In Freud's simile, the psyche is like an ancient city built from materials of many past and forgotten ages. When the archaeologist digs, he finds under each building remnants of still older ones, built in turn on the ruins of previous ones. A person who has successfully used the past to build the future differs from one who is unproductively hampered by it. But they differ in the distribution, not in the sources of their energy. And of course digging is required only when the past has become an obstacle.

The unconscious does not distinguish between impulses, fantasies, ideas—intents—and accomplished facts. To separate the evil thought from the evil deed requires contact with reality, the acknowledgment of the outside world, which occurs only in part of the Ego. Hence a repressed impulse or thought, which not only is not carried out by the Ego but has even been expelled from consciousness, may lead the Superego to react as to an evil deed, with qualms of conscience and threats of punishment. Thus there are guilt feelings and anxiety, an expectation of punishment in the Ego, despite or because of the very repression of the intent. Suppose a beloved person toward whom there was also some repressed resentment is injured or killed. Fate has fulfilled the repressed wish. But the Superego may mete out punishment, abuse, guilt, depression, and self-laceration as if the person had been killed by the repressed fantasy. By insisting on repentance and punishment of sinful thoughts, some religious rules have acknowledged this characteristic of our psyche, and in magical practices the evil intent expressed symbolically is believed to accomplish the evil deed by itself. Primitive law also refused to distinguish between the evil intent—*mens rea*—and the deed. Accidentally inflicted injuries were punished as though themselves proof of intent. And intent was itself considered as though necessarily effective. Certainly nothing evil was thought to happen without it. (Matthew 5:28 may be interpreted as an illustration.)

It has taken societies time just as it does individuals to learn to distinguish consistently between action and mere intent. We no longer punish unintended acts or intentions not acted upon (with a few exceptions: neglect to take proper precautions may be culpable even if the effect was unintended). Sometimes this greater Ego predominance is purchased at a high price: Id intentions are not merely rejected but repressed, and they tend to return in unexpected and undesirable ways.

CHAPTER IV

Sex, Repression, and Beyond

REPRESSION: GENERAL EFFECTS

Repressions usually occur in early infancy when the Ego is still weak. But as they are maintained, perceptions of inner impulses and of the outside world and reaction to them must be selectively distorted throughout life. A somewhat rigid attitude follows. Situations that might upset the applecart and help the repressed impulses to break into consciousness must be avoided in order to maintain what is at best a precarious balance. If the situation cannot be avoided altogether, it might be shorn of its hazards by being sundered from the emotional meaning it would ordinarily have. Thus a person who represses impulses to love persons of the opposite sex, perhaps because he has not quite resolved the oedipal situation, may nevertheless engage in sexual activity. But he may shun the emotional significance of a full relationship which might rearouse the oedipal conflict or the fears connected with it. Or he might have emotional attachments divorced from sexual ones. For him to love a person excludes sexual fulfillment—as it did with the original love object. (Richard Wagner's opera *Tannhauser* dramatizes this unhappy predicament.)

The highly repressed person, instead of reacting to a current situation in current terms, acts in terms of the past to which his repressions link him. There will be a repetitive pattern in his life then. But not because, as he might avow, fate inflicts repetitive experiences on him. It is the other way around. Whatever fate offers is experienced by him in terms of a dominant past. He uses it to re-enact the pattern in which the Ego has imprisoned itself to keep out past dangers. His life may be haunted throughout by the same unsatisfactory personal relations, or the same business failures, unless he lays the ghosts of his own past.

The most general effects of repression directly perceived by the Ego are fatigue, anxiety, and a feeling of futility and boredom, sometimes frantic, sometimes listless. (Occasional listlessness or anxiety is of course not pathological, least of all in adolescence. Generally a problem itself is not a symptom of illness. It is the way we cope or fail to cope with it that makes the difference.) Though the cause remains unconscious, these effects are felt. Of course, they are due to the expenditure of energy on repression on the one hand and on the other hand to the blocking of impulses achieved thereby. A person who through repression has become so unaware of his own desires that he has never allowed himself to come to terms with them can hardly fulfill them in any form. Thus to him life will lose meaning and he will experience it as futile. For whatever gratification he seeks or finds is not what he actually wants, and it leaves him unfulfilled.

However, these are only the most general symptoms of repression. Repression may go further and be completed with other defense mechanisms so that even the symptoms of repression themselves are repressed. A highly repressed person may then insist that he is happy. He may indeed be active and manipulate himself and his environment quite successfully, but without really enjoying it. Repression, instead of impairing his manipulative capacity, strengthened it at the expense of his emotional capacity. He escapes into outside reality instead of fleeing from it, but any ambition, once he achieves it, turns to ashes. With such persons there are often few of the symptoms popularly regarded as neurotic. No one, not even they themselves, may be fully aware of their Midas-like unhappiness—they are too busy and successful, those "who moving others are themselves as stone." Yet the very motive for their continuous search for new successes is that none ever fully gratifies them. They must overwhelm their disappointment in achievement. For they must reassure themselves by constant success and avoid the temptation to indulge their basic impulses. Life is reduced to a series of shallow experiences. This inability to be gratified and the compulsive seeking stemming from this inner impotence must be distinguished from the Faustian quest. It is part of the human fate to suffer and satisfy ever-renewed hunger as long as we live; but compulsive eating is a disease.

Repression, though at times a necessary defense, is always a costly one. Whether the Ego later can replace it with more economic means of control which leave it more freedom and energy depends on many factors. There is no deciding in general. Needs and possibilities, psychological costs, rewards, and risks differ from person to person. No one is entirely free from repression. Indeed, all defense mechanisms are used to some extent by all of us. The difference between neurosis and health is quantitative.

ADDITIONAL DEFENSES

Repression is the most important defense of the Ego against unbearable impulses. There are too many others to list more than a few. "Regression" may occur if gratification on a more advanced level was disappointing, impossible, or aroused too much anxiety. A person who has blocked maturation of other impulses and is basically frustrated may get what gratification he can, for instance, from overeating or drinking, thus regressing to an oral stage. Impulses may be gratified in a more infantile form which is felt to be easier, more rewarding, or beset by fewer dangers. Regression, a return to an earlier pattern, must be distinguished from "fixation" which occurs when this earlier pattern is never left. Overgratification or overfrustration at a given stage of development may bring fixation to that stage, as well as specific "traumatic" events that might injure the psyche so as to inhibit development. The latter, however, are more frequent in popular than in professional literature.

"Identification"—treating something external as though it were internal, as a part of the self—and "projection"—reacting to something internal as though it were outside—also involve a partial return to the stage of development in which the self had not yet been fully separated from the outside world. Basically, identification and projection spring from the infant's initial distinction of the world into things that are good and are swallowed and incorporated, and things that are bad and spat out. The Ego at first, when still hardly differentiated from the Id, regards as "I" or incorporates anything pleasant and as "non I" everything that is not.

Projection may attribute to someone else an unacknowledged feeling of our own. Mary loves me or John hates me, when actually I love Mary and hate John. We can also observe small children reproach any part of the self that has behaved inconveniently —an aching tummy, for instance—as though it were part of the outside world. And many children have invisible companions to whom all naughty actions are attributed. Freud thought even of religions as projections of the content of the human psyche.

The contents of the human psyche themselves are in part introjected from outside at an earlier stage. The Superego, for instance, is largely the result of incorporating the attitudes perceived in the authorities whose love we craved. By identifying with somebody emotionally important to us, we make sure of our possession. We get his power and also make it harmless as a threat to us. Thus children like to play parental roles or to identify with the dog they were afraid of.

Defense mechanisms can be combined with each other, for instance, in the "pecking order" observable in any barnyard. A bird attacked by another that is stronger, and thus not to be resisted, attacks a weaker bird, and so on until the weakest bird is reached. Each bird finds an outlet for his frustration by identifying with the aggressor and shifting the goal of attack. All too often this happens in human affairs, too. But we have other ways of dealing with attacks as well. Sometimes the Superego identifies with the aggressor and turns against the Ego. Sometimes we return aggression to the aggressor even though he be stronger than we are. Sometimes, finally, we succeed in sublimating aggression—instead of attacking anyone, we furiously attack work. Which way will be preferred depends on the strength the Ego commands and on the opportunities and goals offered by the environment.

TWO TYPES OF NEUROSES

The defenses of the Ego all misconstrue reality to some extent
by perceiving it in past, often infantile, terms. But they serve at
least provisionally to prevent worse distortions. When malforma-
tions significantly impair manifest behavior, or the emotional
functioning of the personality, we speak of neurosis: a major conflict involving Id impulses, Ego and Superego restrictions, and
various Ego defense mechanisms. We all experience such conflicts.
Neurosis occurs when the conflicts are not satisfactorily overcome. The Ego prevails in neurosis but precariously, and at so
high a cost that its own freedom and functioning are impaired.
("Traumatic" neuroses, unlike the psychoneuroses just described,
occur when an external event causes more excitation than can be
handled [discharged] without injury. But traumatic neuroses
usually involve psychoneurotic complications.)

Though we cannot fully classify neuroses here, it is useful to
distinguish two types. One—*symptom neurosis*—is characterized
by mobile warfare; a variety of unmistakable symptoms of the
conflicts raging within are displayed. In the second type—*character neurosis*—a truce is achieved. But the truce lines are awkward.
The solution of the conflict, the truce, though it silences discord,
causes the experiences which life offers to become inordinately
shallow, restricted, and unrewarding. The difference is like that
between a broken and unhealed limb and one that has healed, but
badly, so that its function is impaired. It may have to be broken
again to be reset. Often less spectacular than symptom neurosis,
character disorder is also more frequent. Combinations of the two
types of neuroses are common. In most neurotics, some conflicts
remain open, with symptoms readily noted by the patient, such as
anxiety or compulsive hand-washing, while other conflicts may be
closed and hidden by formation of misshapen character traits.
Though in a disorderly, self-defeating, fragmentary, and frustrating way, the open conflict allows for passion if not for fulfillment.
Character disorders can be far more deadening. However, it
would be rash to conclude that the symptom neuroses are inherently unstable. The symptoms may keep the personality in a

sort of equilibrium. It would be equally rash to infer that character neuroses always display a frozen exterior. Some "acting out" of character traits is highly dramatic.

In character disorders, *reaction formation* is frequently paramount: the Ego offsets an unacceptable impulse with an opposite pattern. Where guilt about aggressiveness was felt, an accommodating, submissive trait might emerge. Translation: "I don't really hate anyone, therefore I won't be punished." A love that arouses anxiety may be replaced by truculence and hostility against all those who rearouse the love originally kindled by a forbidden (incestuous) object. Translation: "I don't harbor forbidden feelings, therefore I won't be punished." Arrogant behavior may be a reaction to deep feelings of inferiority. Translation: "No, I can prove that I'm not inadequate." Don Juanism—a show of virility —may be a reaction to an impulse to take a passive, feminine role. When Don Juanism does not offset an impulse by its opposite, but denies a threat (of castration), we speak of *denial*—another defense mechanism. Reaction formation, of course, utilizes the original ambivalence of feelings. And it is prominent also in many symptom neuroses, particularly compulsive ones. Finally, *identification* usually appears in reaction formations: the overbearing person may identify with someone to whom he originally craved to submit.

Instead of reaction formation, or with it, there also may be *phobic* traits: tendencies to fear and avoid situations associated with the dreaded impulse or punishment. Finally, reaction formation seldom occurs without *isolation*: disconnection of parts of the psyche from each other (frequently intellect and affects, or emotions and sensations). In extreme cases there is a split of the Ego. Behavior becomes discontinuous and produces the famous "split personalities." More often we see people alternating between, for instance, excessively strait-laced and excessively libertine behavior, between intemperate "temperance" and alcoholism, and so forth. This would be hypocrisy if there were a crafty, deliberate pretense. But isolation is unconscious—it serves to make hypocrisy unnecessary. Isolation that permits defenses to break down on some occasions and keeps them unimpaired on others can be ritualized. There are times (and places) of indulgence and of atonement, of Carnival and Lent.

Unlike sublimation, the character trait formed as a reaction to the repressed impulse, though it may achieve its conscious goals, does not achieve full gratification since the original impulses remain undischarged. Nonetheless, to the extent a character trait has been formed, the live conflict has subsided. It has been frozen into the personality. And the character trait is not modified without reviving the conflict first.

All human personalities use not only sublimation but also practically all the less economic defenses. It is the extent to which each is used that distinguishes people and ultimately makes the difference between health and illness.

PSYCHOSES

Psychoses, fortunately rarer than neuroses, are also far more severe disorders. In neuroses the Ego wins a Pyrrhic victory. In psychoses, it suffers a serious defeat. Reality exists all too much for the neurotic who tries to deny his inner impulses. Neuroses arise from the Ego's not wholly successful efforts to manage the Id impulses in the service of reality and of the Superego. In psychoses, the Ego has been overwhelmed. Rather than inner impulses, outer reality is denied. The psychotic has never moved beyond, or he has regressed to, a state in which no stable contact with objects realized as such was established. He went further than the neurotic. The world had too little to offer him or appeared too menacing. It shouldn't be concluded that by withdrawing the psychotic becomes happier. He may have jumped from the frying pan because it was unbearable—and fallen into the fire. He may be haunted by his fears more than ever just because he withdrew from reality. But the contact is not easily re-established. It should not be imagined that all psychotics are in institutions. A great many are ambulant—and manage to get along. This is particularly true for borderline cases and for those whose Ego defends itself against psychotic tendencies by a variety of neurotic (often hysterical, or compulsive) defenses; such neurotic defenses against threatening psychotic tendencies are by no means rare—and they can be dismantled safely only when the psychotic threat has been reduced sufficiently, when the Ego is strong enough to mediate between reality and the impulses without the neurotic defense.

Mechanisms—identification and projection, for instance—which also play a role in neurosis and even in healthy development may be driven to extremes in psychosis. Projection degenerates into hallucinations and all awareness of self-identity may be lost in delusive identifications. Further, unlike neurotics, psychotics do not always remain aware of the actual identity of the persons on whom they project; often they cannot distinguish between their hallucinations and reality. Neurotics whose hallucinations are infrequent are usually aware of their delusional nature. (But the labels "psychotic" and "neurotic" are far more discontinuous than the states they refer to.) The coherence which the Ego achieves may be lost, too, in psychosis, and regression may go so far that the psychotic acts like a newborn infant. However, there are untold varieties of psychosis just as of neurosis. Some psychoses break through intermittently. Others affect only a segment of the Ego so that within the hallucinatory system in which the psychotic lives he acts consistently and shrewdly; he is only partially separated from reality. There is reason to suspect that the founders of some parascientific and parareligious cults are psychotics, although they manage to convince nonpsychotic followers. How tenuous is our contact with reality and how easily does it give way, particularly when delusions are shared!

PSYCHOPATHS

Psychopath is used by many as a catchall classification for persons who, though they behave pathologically enough and antisocially, are not easily pigeonholed. Others reserve the term for people who have a very weak Superego or a Superego isolated from the Ego. Perhaps this comes about because of frequent changes of milieu in early childhood, or of excessively inconsistent parental behavior. Unlike neurotics, psychopaths are not bothered by guilt feelings, anxieties, and conflicts. Nor, like psychotics, do they live in a world of their own. The horse (the Id) leads, and uses some horse sense with the help of the rider, the Ego, but it is not bridled and directed by the Ego and not influenced by the

Superego. Psychopaths seem able to do fiendish things without guilt feelings and with little sublimation. Nevertheless it should be stressed that the proportion of psychopaths and neurotics among criminals is not much greater than that in the rest of the population.

In practice many of the processes and symptoms here distinguished blend into each other. The prevalence of distinctive symptoms, not their mere presence or absence, makes classification feasible. Though thread and cloth are identifiable in all, each personality, each fabric, is put together in a way that distinguishes it from all others, and each neurosis has unique historical features. The bare bones offered here are the more likely to become bones of contention because, for lack of space, they were not clothed with the flesh of case histories.

INFANTILE AND LATER EXPERIENCES

Now to a few matters of genesis. Personality—healthy, neurotic, or psychotic—is formed in early childhood. Not that a different later environment could not change behavior. However, early conditioning controls the effect different environments will have. Childhood does not set the personality once and for all, but it does determine the changes it will undergo in different conditions.

How about neuroses appearing under the impact of later events, such as war or the death of a loved person, on a healthy adult? Doubtless neurosis can be precipitated in an adult. Any person might break down under stress at any time. But the degree of stress needed, the kind of stress and its specific effect differ from person to person—precisely because the impact is contingent on the personality formed in childhood.

We might call only that personality neurotic that cannot stand a "normal" amount of stress. But "normal" is very difficult to measure and we might just as well call the person neurotic who has not been able to stand the stress to which he was actually exposed—the person in whom something has come loose or become too constricting, particularly when it does not heal well by itself. Thus neurosis may be precipitated by abnormal reaction to normal stress—in which case it is endogenous, or by normal reaction to abnormal stress—in which case it is exogenous. (In the last case, changes in the environment may become therapeutically important.) Any fabric can be rent. But when, how, and where depends on its strong and weak spots, and on how well it was originally woven. Reweaving must take into account how the strands were knitted together originally and may even require some unraveling. The rending event—the precipitating cause— may happen at any time and to anyone then, but its effect depends on the original strength and resiliency of the personality knitted together in childhood.

"INTERPERSONAL" AND "CULTURAL" FACTORS

Does Freud's account of processes within the personality slight the impact of "interpersonal" relations, of society, and of culture? Or does it explain just how this impact occurs? I think the latter. Socialization is but the adaptation of the infant to a reality patterned by other people around him. The infant is born into a society with a culture—a way of organizing it and assigning roles to its members—that exist before he arrives. The problem then, for every infant, is to find satisfactory ways of dealing with other people—with the society and culture of which he becomes part and which become part of him. The Oedipus complex is surely an "interpersonal" relation, determined by the requirements of all, and the variation represented by each culture and family. Freud does not deny that it is "social"—he denies that society could exist without it. However, he stresses that later interpersonal relations bear the marks of the earlier ones, which have become internalized, i.e., appear as intrapersonal ones. Hence, if the relationship to the environment is to be changed, these internalized relationships which set the reaction patterns of the person to others have to be changed. Their early origin as well as their later reproductions must be traced. Mechanisms such as identification, projection, and repression are ways of dealing with these interpersonal relations as they impinge on and develop the personality of the child. Analysis of intrapsychic processes no more neglects the "interpersonal" or "cultural" relations than a description of the processes of digestion neglects the influence of food and of culturally patterned eating habits; with the difference that we are born with a digestive apparatus but acquire our personality. We are born only with drives and possibilities. They are shaped, developed, sublimated or repressed in response to the internalized impact of society, above all, its early representative, the family.

IS SEX NECESSARY?

It used to be said that psychoanalysis reduces everything to sex. Actually most psychoanalysts would rank the importance of sex somewhat lower than would popular novelists, playwrights, advertisers, and song and movie-script writers. The impression that psychoanalysts stress sex comes about not because they find so much sex but because they find it in unexpected places, particularly in infancy.

Psychoanalysis follows the vicissitudes of drives from their beginning. The malleable energy manifest from birth which ultimately is also released genitally is called libido. It is the force behind most of the infant's strivings and the source of energy for many later activities. But it is the use of this energy that matters. Tracing it back to its original source does not imply that sexual activity (as distinguished from sexual energy) does, or ought to, loom unduly large in the personalities of reasonably well-adjusted people.

In the neurotic personality, however, it does loom large. For neuroses always involve hindrances in the transformation, control, and release of originally sexual energies. If this difficulty could be removed merely by more sexual activity, there would not be much of a problem. On the contrary, it is found that manifest sexual difficulties, such as impotence, homosexuality, nymphomania, or satyriasis originate in problems that are far removed from sex—or at least sex as it is usually understood. (Whereas nymphomania has become a popular term, satyriasis, its male equivalent, has not. The double standard certainly has not disappeared.) They may originate in the past, and present sexual activities are a symptom of the difficulty and not a cure.

In the last century, sexual activity was often publicly regarded as likely to lead to all kinds of diseases if indulged in too much, too early, or in the wrong way. (Private practice was often far healthier than public ideology.) In the current century, the reverse is frequently believed. Failure to engage in sexual activity early and often enough is frequently regarded as cause, or effect, of disease. There is no more evidence for this century's view than there was for the view prevalent in the last. Frequent sexual activity can be as much a symptom of pathology as frequent or total abstinence. And neither is likely to be a cause of disease. Certainly abstinence can be involuntary owing to, say, castration anxiety; and indulgence can be compulsive owing to, say, a denial of castration anxiety. Illness may be connected with the motivation, certainly not with the act. There is no evidence of physical damage through sexual activity—or abstinence; and none of psychological damage: in short, you never have to do it for your health. Indeed, if the motive is to prove your health, the act will be neither healthful nor enjoyable. The belief that sexual activity is a necessary, or even sufficient, proof of health leads to some unnecessary difficulties: people who are not ready for sexual relations may allow themselves to be pushed; other who abstain may be regarded, or regard themselves, with suspicion. There is nothing in psychoanalysis that prescribes sexual activity. Treatment should but remove constriction—e.g., fears or compulsions —which obstruct the individual's ability to decide freely for himself whether, how, and under what conditions he will engage in any activity, including sexual activity.

MORAL RESPONSIBILITY

As the decision becomes a free one, it becomes a moral one, if the alternatives freely chosen are morally significant. Thus, far from relieving patients of moral responsibility, psychoanalysis helps to make them morally responsible. Of course anything may be used as an excuse when you wish to be irresponsible. Confession may be used as permission to commit new sins, but there is nothing in the institution of the confessional to encourage this. Nor in psychoanalysis. To understand is neither to forgive nor to condemn: it is necessary, however, if either is to be done.

Yet, unlike the confessor or judge, the analyst himself does not interpret or impose moral or legal standards. He neither condemns nor condones actions any more than a physician lets his moral ideas about a patient's conduct influence his treatment of a wound. But, although it does not impose moral views of its own, psychoanalysis is intended to restore the patient's psychic and, therewith, his moral faculties. Just as the physician may restore to the patient the use (or possible misuse) of his limbs, and thus his freedom, so psychoanalysis, by making the patient more aware of the motivation for his behavior, helps him to direct it. Only a person able to choose between right and wrong can be moral. Freudian analysis does not impose or advocate the analyst's moral choices. But it does increase the patient's ability to choose—to choose with reflection and without compulsion—in short, to become morally responsible.

"O THE PAIN, THE BLISS OF DYING!"
(ALEXANDER POPE)

One of the faults found most emphatically with Freud's theory is his insistence on the limitation of man's nature and on the tragic nature of human destiny. Dissenters favor a more positive view which finds human nature indefinitely malleable and infinitely perfectible. By reforming society, conditioning, or psychoanalysis, they hope to make this not only the best of all possible worlds but also a good world. For this reason they bitterly reject the hypothesis of a death drive which Freud, late in his life, thought might oppose the libido within the Id (though it is usually fused with the libido). Freud first thought that Id impulses might be destructive, incidental to their gratification or frustration. But after World War I he reached the conclusion that people have impulses aiming at destruction and death, just as others aim at life. Mostly these impulses toward disintegration appeared to him to be fused with the impulses toward integration. We wish to form new units by splitting old ones; and we wish to move in order to come to rest. There seems to be pleasure in tension, in its release, and in the ensuing quiet. Many people feel a will to live, to suffer, to be passionate, to enjoy the tension of existence, alternating and co-existing with a longing for peace and nothingness, the Nirvana of the Buddhists, the return, Freud speculated, to the unfeelingness of the inorganic, whence sometime we must have come.

Some outstanding disciples of Freud, such as Otto Fenichel, doubt the existence of what would in effect amount to opposing drives in the Id. Conflicts, they maintain, occur between the original drives and the Ego, not within the Id. And the existence of destructiveness is explained as a result of unavoidable life experiences. Denial of the death drive may be justified by Occam's razor: *entia non sunt multiplicanda praeter necessitatem* (a rule of scientific economy—"concepts [or entities] should not be multiplied beyond need" generally attributed to William of Occam). Assumption of a death instinct is not at the present time indispensable to explain the phenomena before us.

Many "neo-Freudians" (including Karen Horney, Erich Fromm, Harry Stack Sullivan, and among the older dissenters Carl G. Jung, Alfred Adler, Wilhelm Reich) go further, however, and insist that destructiveness, sadism—one is tempted to say evil in general—always come from life experiences, chiefly frustrations, that are avoidable. They advocate changing cultural conditioning and social institutions. In this extreme form, the dispute is not between two scientific hypotheses but between two philosophical viewpoints. It can be traced back to the conflict between the theology of St. Augustine and the early and later heretics who followed his contemporary, Pelagius. Freud, like St. Augustine, maintains that human nature includes evil and bears the seeds of its own corruption. Both the saint and the psychoanalyst view life as a tragic and heroic struggle against our inborn tendencies to depravity. (Protestant theologians such as Luther and Calvin, and in our time Reinhold Niebuhr and Karl Barth, share this view with Roman Catholics.) The parallel can be spun out. Freud, like St. Augustine, stresses "prevenient grace" (constitution) and this stress distinguishes both from many "Pelagian" heretics.

The neo-Freudians, like the Pelagians and semi-Pelagians, maintain that man is the master of his fate and does not suffer from inherited handicaps (for Freud, constitution, indispensable Oedipus complex, and ineluctable frustration; for St. Augustine, hereditary sin) and thus is far less dependent on grace and far more able to make this earth a paradise than either Freud or St. Augustine would grant. Of course, the neo-Freudians got their notions via Rousseau ("Nature has made man happy and good—society corrupts him and causes his misery"), and in Erich Fromm's case via Marx, rather than directly from Pelagius; but the lineage is clear.

The philosophical and social implications and derivations of the two views are fascinating but irrelevant here. As for evidence, the following can be asserted:

1. There is no positive proof of an inherited death drive.
2. There is no positive proof excluding an inherited death drive, either. The known facts can be explained with or without a death drive.
3. There is much evidence to show that if destructiveness and evil are caused by life experiences (i.e., without a death drive) these are not altogether avoidable even under the most ideal conditions in the most ideal social system—unless "ideal" excludes by definition all characteristics of life this side of the grave, such as death, illness, discipline, work, accident, occasional frustration, injustice, disgust, powerlessness, and defeat.
4. The idea that *all* destructive tendencies are caused by avoidable life experiences is demonstrably false. Yet it can be demonstrated that *some* destructive tendencies are caused by avoidable life experiences.
5. Science can assert that a death instinct is possible, is likely, or is unlikely. To assert that it is impossible or indispensable, one must rely on faith.

It seems worthwhile to define those avoidable life experiences likely to lead to destructiveness and to attempt to minimize them, and, further, to rechannel destructiveness toward the least harmful goals. It seems idle to expect more than moderate and occasional success. Above all, we should remember that the greatest human misery has usually been brought about by leaders insisting on the immediate elimination of all evil.

CHAPTER V *Treatment*

INDICATIONS FOR PSYCHOANALYTIC TREATMENT

Treatment of personality disorders is nearly always arduous, long, and therefore costly. As is common in medical matters, the outcome is uncertain. There is not much at present that can be done about psychopaths. Note, however, that many apparent psychopaths may actually be neurotics. (Dr. Robert Lindner claimed success in treating psychopaths through hypnoanalysis, in *Rebel Without a Cause*.)

With psychotics the main problem is to re-establish contact with reality, to lure them back by helping them to understand that the rewards of reality more than offset the gains of withdrawal, or to see that the original causes of the withdrawal can be controlled. If withdrawal has progressed far, deterioration may be irreversible. But new, hopeful discoveries are made every year. As yet we have only started to attempt seriously to cure psychotics. Shock administered by electricity or chemical means sometimes helps to regain initial contact with reality—though we don't quite know how. Shock cannot be regarded as a cure by itself. It does not solve difficulties, indeed may repress them more deeply. It should be used only when other treatments fail. But at least temporarily shock may remove a symptom such as incoherence or depression, permitting access to the patient, and thus treatment.

There is, of course, no conflict between psychological and physical treatments (though there is between their advocates). In Freud's words: "The future may teach us how to exercise a direct influence, by means of particular chemical substances, upon the amounts of energy and their distribution in the apparatus of the mind." It is unlikely, however, that psychological difficulties can be reduced to physical ones. Brain processes are necessary but not sufficient to explain thoughts. Nor, when a correlation between the physical and the psychic is established, does it follow that the physical is the cause and the psychic the effect.

Many neurotics can be cured or helped by analysis. The neuroses with the most conspicuous symptoms often are easiest to cure. Conversion hysteria, in which an unconscious intent and its equally unconscious punishment are expressed in a physical symptom, such as paralysis without organic basis, is one instance.

Cure always involves replacement of the neurotic defense mechanism, displayed through various symptoms, by less costly means of control. On the one hand, this requires strengthening the Ego; on the other, it requires insight, and reintegration of the impulses toward which the defense is directed and of the defense mechanism itself. Essentially what takes place is a temporary unilateral transfer to the analyst of the relationships the patient originally experienced with persons important in his early life and of the feelings they generated. This *transference* is an essential element in any analysis. It is not necessary that it be expressed positively (love). Negatively expressed transference (hostility) does as well, and both (they usually coexist) must be analyzed in time. The patient must learn to understand that the feelings are transferred and from where they come. Without transference there is no emotional re-experience—and no analysis. Contrary to popular belief, there is no need that the patient "believe" in analysis. (Child analysis would otherwise be impossible.) He need only be willing to follow the rules of procedure.

As the childhood developments that built up the neurotic structure or conflict are re-experienced—in an emotional sense relived in analysis—they are understood and controlled. For in analysis the patient is in a more favorable situation than he was in his childhood. The Ego, being stronger and helped by the analyst who serves as coach, can gain control of matters which previously it had to expel from consciousness. This fosters a better outcome—a productive redistribution of energies and more freedom for the Ego. By his interpretations and other forms of therapeutic behavior, including silence, the analyst helps open the door to the repressed material. The patient, pushed by his suffering and pulled by the transference and by his confidence in the analyst—both of which are built up slowly—becomes able to face the repressed material and to control or use it more fruitfully. Above all, analysis helps the patient to realize what his wishes are. He remembers their origin and understands the function of his own attitudes. The control he gains makes it unnecessary to reproduce ("act out"). He can remember and finds a satisfactory way of sublimating or expressing his impulses. He becomes able to perceive new situations and respond to them spontaneously. (In child analysis, the analyst's task is even more directly to strengthen the Ego and to some extent guide it.)

Though part of the Ego wishes to be freed—otherwise, of course, treatment is hopeless—another part, bound up in the neurotic defense, resists insight and emotional re-experience by operating rather than dismantling defense mechanisms, for the Ego continues to dread the original situation against which it erected them. The defenses can be dismantled only slowly. Any knowledge of unconscious processes which the patient gains is soon jostled aside—repressed again—unless the defense mechanisms are also dismantled. These defense mechanisms are used to resist not only insight but the whole analytic process and, of course, the analyst. Short cuts which outflank these resistances to release repressions are more impressive than helpful. For this reason, hypnosis and various chemical agents—abandoned by Freud many years ago—are rarely decisive in the treatment of neuroses. The defense mechanisms are rearranged, particular symptoms disappear, but the illness which causes them remains, and other symptoms soon appear. Nonetheless, hypnosis and chemical agents are periodically rediscovered by popular schools.

Treatment should help the patient to cope better with his problems—in the long run to be the person he wants to be and realistically can be. Particularly in character disorders, secondary gains—the gratifications, slight and temporary as they might be, reaped by acting out the character traits which arose as reactions to unbearable situations—make lasting changes hard to achieve. A bird in hand seems worth two in the bush: it is hard to forego immediate gratifications now for the promise of long-run gains. This, incidentally, is also one difficulty in the treatment of addictions, alcoholism, perversions, and various impulse disorders. Symptom neuroses are easier in this respect: the secondary gratifications are often offset by the immediate inconveniences. However, it is character disorders and borderline cases that fill the offices of analysts in our times. The more easily handled symptom neuroses so frequent in Freud's time have become proportionately rare. Perhaps our changing customs reduced the severity of externally imposed inhibitions which caused some problems that were curable by fairly swift and direct insights. It is not implied that something better has replaced this puritanism. And there is surely no decrease of neuroses. On the other hand, the refinement of theory has enabled us to perceive previously ignored character disorders as diseases. Perhaps they have become more frequent, too. At any rate, we now attempt to cure them.

Competently done psychoanalysis, like all therapy, is part science, part art. It is not magic: the possibilities are limited. Indeed, treatment is often of small use, and in some cases contraindicated. Psychoanalysis not administered by a properly trained person who, as part of his training was himself analyzed by a trained analyst, is quackery. Lamentably, psychoanalysis is offered by laymen, physicians, and even psychiatrists who have not received the special training needed, or been analyzed. Competent as they may be for other kinds of treatment, psychoanalytic competence does not come therewith; it comes with psychoanalytic training to which, according to Freud, medical and other curricula are not usually relevant.

If there ever was illness, certainly self-analysis is not likely to succeed. It offers no way of re-experiencing originally felt relationships through transfer to a neutral person. The neutrality of the analyst and his interpretation help the patient gain insight into the true nature of his feelings. Without such a person, the patient is too easily beguiled by his own resistances. Freud did analyze himself. Perhaps the first hen did create itself. But all others came from eggs laid by hens. Chicken farmers who insist on creating their chickens from nothing are not likely to succeed.

That the first physician did not go to medical school is certainly
not an excuse for others to practice without schooling.

Unless analysts have been analyzed themselves, they will not
control the human inclination to project one's own problems on
others. They will then respond to their own problems projected
onto their patients. And they will form attachments. This phenomenon is called countertransference. The analyst must understand
it, otherwise it interferes with the analysis of the patient. For the
analyst would succumb to the temptation to react to love and
hate with love and hate, to advise, to argue his views, in short,
to answer his own needs rather than analyze those of the patient.
Advice is not given in analysis, but the need for it is analyzed, as
is the patient's wish to argue and to provoke love or hate. Patients
always believe that the analyst hates or loves them. This is part
of the transference. By responding to the patient's emotion instead
of merely analyzing it, the analyst forfeits his role as a sheer
interpretative screen on which the patient projects his feelings.
He no longer is, in Freud's words, "like a mirror reflecting nothing but what is shown to him." No wonder the patient cannot be
convinced that what he has before him are his own mirrored
(projected) emotions. To the extent to which the patient-analyst
relation becomes actual and personal in the present, it ceases to be
analytical and transferred.

The patient will at times cast the analyst in the role of a forgiv-
ing or condemning parent. He thus transfers to the analyst emotions originally felt toward his own parent. In this way, the patient
re-experiences emotions he had dreaded. With the help of the
analyst, he gains insight into their effect on his behavior. But
once more the insight is possible only if the analyst's equanimity
and objective, neutral behavior make it clear that the emotions
could not be a response to present actual stimulus. If the analyst
acts in a fatherly way, if he does reassure or condemn, then the
patient responds to the analyst and not to his parent. No longer
is the image of the analyst as a parental figure entirely a product
of the patient's emotions. This may be fun. But it is not analysis.
If the patient's feelings are justified by the analyst's being—instead
of being felt to be—at times nice, at times disapproving, the analyst
is of no help to the patient. At best, the analyst—instead of helping his patient to solve his problems—would himself become the

solution. He would add a relationship to those the patient has been engaged in, instead of helping his patient realize why he experiences those relationships as he does. When the treatment is over, the patient is where he started: the magic works only as long as the relationship with the analyst lasts. Cases differ. And exceptions are sometimes needed. In psychoses, support and reassurance that usually must be denied in neuroses (to analyze the need for them) are often useful. The patient, all too aware of his impulses, must be encouraged to find his way in reality. In certain types of phobia and in some other circumstances the analyst may take a comparatively active role. But usually when the analyst goes beyond being an interpretative screen, analysis, cure in the long run, is delayed or precluded in favor of a short-run goal—which only sometimes may be a necessity.

The analyst's task is hard. It requires, in addition to talent and training, more self-control than most people possess. To avoid distracting patients by his facial expressions, Freud placed them so that they could not see him. And to encourage the verbalization and minimize the activity of his patients, Freud did not let them smoke during the analytic session. He himself smoked, however. He felt the analyst's work to be hard enough as it is. American analysts usually feel this to be "undemocratic." They will either not smoke themselves or let the patient smoke, too. But, though it may be necessary for the patient to be uncomfortable, it doesn't help to make the analyst uncomfortable.

The patient's task is onerous, too. Apparently all that is demanded of him is to keep appointments, pay, and—this is the basic rule—say everything that comes to mind during the session, no matter how silly, improper, and irrelevant it may seem. Easy as it sounds, this is a vexatious thing to do. We all have learned to control our speech, and even our conscious thought, to meet criteria of relevance and propriety and the expectations we surmise others place on us. The Ego's sense of coherence also serves to censor unconscious thought; even free association always bears traces of the Ego's work of control. But since the unconscious has a way of making its presence known, even when we want to silence it, a skilled analyst often can gather from the pattern of the patient's conscious utterances his unconscious thoughts. Conscious or unconscious attempts to hide something can be quite as revealing as attempts to reveal. But, of course, much that goes on will puzzle analyst and patient alike. In time the patient becomes aware of his unconscious wishes, ideas, and fears. In the continuous process of treatment, which requires a minimal frequency of several hours a week, successive layers of personality are brought to the fore. The analyst's view of the patient's unconscious processes is continuously confirmed or disconfirmed by the patient's reactions to it. Without these reactions, the analyst's interpretations would be highly speculative as well as useless. We cannot reconstruct the possibilities with an absent person as we could were he with us. Hence analysis of historical figures *in absentia* serves mainly illustrative purposes. Note here that Freud explicitly stated, "it is incorrect to set the patient tasks, such as collecting his memories, thinking over a certain period of his life and so on. . . . Concentrating the will and attention avail nothing. . . ." Freud also rejected "resorting to analytical writing as an aid to patients." The one thing he felt the patient must learn is to try to say what comes to his mind without first evaluating it.

PSYCHOSOMATIC SYMPTOMS

There are bodily conditions clearly of mental origin; conversely, conditions of bodily origin affect the mind. Whatever its origin, the condition may be influenced by psychological *and* physical factors. Cure of a condition of the body by psychoanalysis does not prove the illness was mental, nor does cure by chemical means imply the condition had a physical origin. One may stop sleeplessness by a pill (at least temporarily) or by psychoanalysis. A headache, an ulcer, a skin disease, obesity, hyper- and hypotension—nearly any disease responds to both kinds of treatment. Which is to be preferred is a practical question. When the physical impairment, whatever its origin, is far gone it may be irreversible by psychic means. For example, a broken arm, however much due to accident-prone behavior, first of all must be set.

In many diseases, regardless of mental contribution, a physical remedy is most economical. To label a disease "psychosomatic" means, if it means anything, that in the long run at least, the greatest benefit is reaped by treating its psychological sources. Yet only investigation can establish whether an individual suffers from a "psychosomatic" condition in this sense. Headaches caused by purely psychological stimuli can be cured psychologically. Surgery, of course, is useless in such a case. But brain tumors which also cause headaches do require surgery. Psychological treatment does not remove a tumor—even if the tumor is co-produced by psychological stimuli. It is no argument for one treatment or the other to rehearse the case of the man who was psychoanalyzed, because of his headaches, until he died of a brain tumor, or of the man who died from the effects of an unnecessary operation undergone for a basically psychological condition. The first type of case is newer than the second. But the carelessness and the dogmatism that make both possible are very old indeed.

SOME TESTS OF PERSONALITY-FORMATION THEORY

Confirmation of the curative usefulness of psychoanalysis as a whole is a matter of case histories which hardly lend themselves to meaningful statistical summary. But evidence confirming parts of psychoanalytic theory has been gathered by various methods —though the degree of confirmation is necessarily lower than, for instance, in chemistry.

It is now generally accepted that the character of the adult depends greatly on his experiences as an infant. The importance of infantile experience has been shown even in animals. J. McV. Hunt in "The Effects of Infant Feeding Frustration Upon Adult Hoarding in the Albino Rat" (*Journal of Abnormal Social Psychology*, Vol. 36, pp. 338-60) reports that twenty-four-hour-old albino rats, after having been starved for a period and then fed normally for five months, hoarded two and one-half times as much food as their littermate controls who never experienced short rations in infancy. Further experiments established that the earlier in life rats experience the deprivation which fosters the traits called greed, aggressiveness, and avarice, the more firmly planted and pronounced those traits become. In short, the character of the rats, where it is not determined by inheritance, is

formed by early infantile experience. This does not prove that
it must be so with human beings, but it makes it appear more
likely than the opposite outcome of the experiments on rats would
have made it.

Attention must be drawn, however, to some relevant differences between human infants and those of other species:

1. Human character depends less on instincts than does that
   of rats. Therefore, experience is more important in forming it. If infantile experience is important, as seems likely,
   it follows that it is more so with humans than with rats.
2. Human infants are not only more plastic than those of other
   species but their formative period and dependence on parents last longer proportionally. This, too, suggests that infant rearing patterns have more influence on adult character
   in humans.
3. Human infants learn more, they learn longer, and they learn
   from more sources than the young of other species. Quite
   possibly human beings as they grow up are more able than
   rats to shake off infantile experiences and to balance them
   with others. In short, it is possible that infantile experiences
   leave both more important and more modifiable traces in
   the human species than in others. (But Dr. Spitz's report
   indicates that there are limits to modifiability.)

Though we must hope for more precise observations and formulations in the future, promising investigations have already
been made to confirm statistically the impact of the conditions
to which psychoanalytic theory gives major weight. For instance,
Frieda Goldman-Eisler in "Breastfeeding and Character Formation," reprinted in Clyde Kluckhohn and Henry A. Murray,
Personality in Nature, Society, and Culture, tested some basic
hypotheses derived from the work of the German analyst Karl
Abraham. She describes the "orally gratified" type of character
as distinguished by "unperturbable optimism, by generosity,
bright and sociable conduct, accessibility to new ideas, and ambition accompanied by sanguine expectation" in contrast to the
"orally ungratified" type of character distinguished by "pro-
foundly pessimistic outlook on life, attitudes of withdrawal, a
passive receptive attitude, a feeling of insecurity, a need for the

assurance of getting one's livelihood guaranteed, an ambition which combines an intense desire to climb with a feeling of unattainability, a grudging feeling of injustice, sensitiveness to competition, a dislike of sharing." She tried to find out whether these character traits can be actually shown to be linked to the oral gratification or frustration of infants.

Goldman-Eisler tested forty-seven men and sixty-eight women between the ages of eighteen and thirty-five, (except for three people who were over thirty-five). Fifteen were in psychoanalytic treatment. Though the group was not studiedly representative, its composition probably was not relevantly biased. All, however, belonged to the middle class. This group was asked to answer a number of questions and to react to a number of short statements. Their answers suggested various character traits which were found to form clusters and to permit classification of the members of the group as having either an optimistic or a pessimistic character. Some members were extreme optimists or pessimists but all could be classified as belonging to one group or the other.

Mothers then told the author whether the subjects had been breast-fed or bottle-fed and, if breast-fed, at what age they had been weaned. It was found that the pessimists had been bottle-fed or weaned early while the optimists had been breast-fed; the later they had been weaned, the more optimistic traits they revealed.

On this evidence alone, it would be wrong to leap to the conclusion that infants ought to be breast-fed and weaned late. Some, indeed many, of the men we call great—poets, inventors, scientists, statesmen—belong among the pessimists, and many optimists would be called fools quite rightly. (Their sense of reality is often defective.) Whether the greatness of the great pessimists was because of, in spite of, or regardless of their temperament, we don't know. Too little is known as yet to make universal rules. And there are further reasons for caution. The mothers who bottle-fed their children or weaned them early may differ in other respects from those who produced the optimists. Perhaps the temper of pessimists was related to the general character of the mothers more than to the bottle feeding or early weaning, which might have been only one expression of that general character. Goldman-Eisler's findings—and many similar observations—hint at important relationships among character traits and between character and early experience. In time these relationships may be fully explored. But as yet they pose as many problems as they solve. The safest conclusion so far—like so many safe conclusions, not very helpful—is that excessive gratification as well as excessive frustration (and, of course, alternation between them) should be avoided—which is to say, that infants do best when their parents are reasonable and psychologically healthy. For healthy parents will neither overindulge nor overfrustrate them.

A special difficulty arises from our inability to define character types precisely. The present vagueness probably can be reduced, but it is unlikely that in classifying human characters we can ever be exhaustive as well as precise. In drawing up laws, for instance, extreme care is taken to make the language precise. Yet lawyers make a living in part by disputing whether the law forbids or allows a particular action. Individual cases differ so much, in such unforeseeable ways, that no law, no general rule, no definition can neatly trap all into separate compartments. It is harder still to define and separate types of human personality. Total character is more individual and elusive than any single trait. But despite ineluctable vagueness, the law is not useless in separating permissible from illegal actions. Likewise, the separation of characters into types, however vague, helps relate them to genetic factors even though for the time being we can measure neither the characters nor the genetic factors that shape them.

NATIONAL CHARACTER

Cultural anthropologists (Ruth Benedict, Margaret Mead, and Geoffrey Gorer are among the best known) have been quick to seize on the suspected connection between child care and adult character in order to relate cultural differences to ways of child rearing. Thus, the pattern of infant care now is seen not only as an effect but also as a cause of culture. Child rearing practices are seen as transmitting or reproducing the individual character structures that prevail in each culture. French people not only teach their children French; they implant a French character in their children long before the children reach school age and even before they speak. There is a French pattern of treating, feeding, disciplining, cleaning, and cuddling children. It is this pattern that continuously reproduces "national character," although not consciously by any means.

National character is implanted simply because parents follow the patterns of child rearing that come naturally to them: the French patterns in France, American patterns in America. There are many differences within France: the urban middle class brings children up in a way that differs from the aristocratic, peasant, or working-class ways; and parents in Marseilles do not act like parents in Brest. These regional and class differences help reproduce the psychological characteristics of the respective subcultures. However, all these patterns have in common the fact that they are French.

Patterns of child rearing may change. Perhaps the present security-craving type of American—so different from the prevailing nineteenth century type—grew from changed infant rearing customs. (They changed from spontaneous breast- to the scheduled bottle-feeding—which is now again being abandoned.) One wonders. But we cannot be certain about the actual extent of change in national character nor can we be certain about the influence of wars and depressions, migration, urbanization, and what-not. Margaret Mead, who at one time seemed to support a rather extreme position, has recently warned:

> . . . It is not any single item of child-rearing practice or of culturally patterned child behavior . . . which is significant in isolation. It is the way in which all these thousands of items, most of which are shared with other cultures, some of which are shared with all other cultures, are patterned or fitted together to make a whole.

It is very likely, indeed, that the production of the prevailing adult personality types in any culture or subculture—that is, of the personalities typical of a group because they are most frequent or influential in it—is connected with comparatively uniform child rearing practices. The Zuni society would scarcely remain so markedly different from the Dobu society, described in Ruth Benedict's *Patterns of Culture,* unless each, through its child rearing practices, reproduced personality types adaptable to the roles worked out for them. Child rearing practices are a part of the culture; and their social function is to help reproduce the culture by reproducing the needed personality types.

Two striking instances of this were observed by Geza Roheim ("The Individual, the Group, and Mankind," *The Psychoanalytic Quarterly,* Vol. 25, No. 1, 1956):

> The primitive Australians live in an arid desert where famine is an ever-present threat; yet these people give no thought to the future. We can trace their optimistic outlook on life to the type of childhood they enjoy. Their mothers give them the breast whenever they want it. They wean themselves when they no longer want their mothers' milk. There is a minimum of oral frustration. They have practically no training in cleanliness. Adult natives defecate and urinate in their huts and throw a little sand over the feces. Babies are often smeared with their own excrement and no one bothers to take notice of it. . . .
>
> The Melanesian natives of Normanby Island live in a tropical environment. They are agriculturalists, raising yams, taro and sweet potatoes in their gardens. There is an abundance of edible fruit, animals and birds in the jungle. The ocean abounds in fish, lobsters, turtles and clams. While the island is sparsely populated, the inhabitants nevertheless live in great fear of starvation. In their anxiety, they pile up huge mountains of supplies in their houses. How do we explain the contrast between these people who in the midst of plenty fear starvation, and the Australian natives who in the face of famine are unconcerned?
>
> When the women of Normanby Island nurse their children, they sing. At the end of each verse of the lullaby, the nipple is withdrawn from the infant's mouth. With the beginning of the next stanza, suckling is resumed. We must assume that this experience is a traumatic one. This assumption is verified by the fact that these people live in great fear of witches, whom they call "our mothers."

We can say with some confidence that there are specifiable relations between child rearing practices, personality types, and culture. But we cannot describe particular institutions and social actions as effects of child rearing practices. There is no warrant, for instance, for saying that the American, French, German, or Russian national characters demand either democracy or dictatorship. To speak of a "democratic character" misleadingly suggests a simple relationship between character types and political institutions. Actuallly, domineering personalities may make good democrats, politically speaking. And people who have all the democratic virtues in psychological terms, however defined, may believe in political dictatorship. Christian churches have been able to convert Italians, Germans, Irishmen, Britons, Arabs, Hungarians, Congolese, Americans, Eskimos, and South Sea Islanders. National character affects the way the religion is practiced, but it does not prevent a particular religion from gaining a hold. So it is with political institutions.

Thus dictatorship as well as democracy can thrive with the German national character, and so with the Polish, French, or Japanese national character. Politics and indeed social structure can be related, but cannot be reduced, to individual or social psychology. National character is far more likely to help explain the style of a dictatorship or a democracy in a given nation than to explain the existence of democracy or dictatorship. Thus the *differences* among German, Russian, and Italian dictatorships, and between French and English democracy may be related to national character—although nonpsychological factors play a role here too. Similarly with individuals: the kind of Communist, Socialist, Liberal or Conservative, Catholic or Protestant Mr. Smith becomes is related to his personality. But whether and which of these groups he joins depends mainly on factors other than his personality.

Analogies are seductive. The Ego which represses impulses, engages in reaction formation, and so forth may be said to act like a dictator—unlike the "democratic" Ego that integrates all components of the personality and allows them to be expressed. The domination of the "democratic" Ego is more secure and happy. The "dictatorial" one leads a precarious and cheerless life. This may be all right as an analogy. It becomes a sheer fallacy, however, if we forget that analogies can illustrate conclusions but never establish them.

The fallacy is compounded if it is implied that we know

enough to try to influence a national character linked—by doubtful evidence—to undesirable political institutions. This is to be done by prescribing changes in infant rearing practices. We may produce changes but we do not know enough to know whether they will be desirable. The fruits of science when plucked unripe, or when we are not ready to digest them, can be quite poisonous. Enthusiasts should read Goethe's *The Sorcerer's Apprentice*.

CHAPTER VI   *The Family as an Industry*

THE PURSUIT OF LOVE

To grow well children require, above all, what William Blake called "the lineaments of gratified desire"—parents who are able to love them out of the fullness, not from the poverty, of their hearts. Most mothers are willing, as far as they are aware, to give their infants love. However, love cannot really be "given" deliberately; one loves or one doesn't. Duty can be willed, skill can be taught, but love must be spontaneously felt. Adults feeling an absence of spontaneous love, can sever relationships. Infants cannot. Their inarticulateness and their dependence make it easy to ignore the response of infants. Nevertheless, the response occurs through the development of the child and finally through his adult character. Unhappily, no studied pursuit can create the spontaneous feeling the mother must have if her child is to thrive. Methodical pursuit is apt to drown in anxiety what spontaneity there is and to hobble it by rules. Yet, though it cannot create spontaneous feelings, society can cultivate them. But quite the contrary has happened. On the whole, the institutions, arrangements, and evaluations of our society tend to replace spontaneous maternal feeling with sanitary and psychological rules.

Families consisting only of parents and children under one often-changed roof cannot transmit lore as they did when rooted

83

in a village with several generations and collateral kin. They no longer train mothers by direct informal experience. Psychologically as well as economically, families have become less self-sufficient than they were. They buy their child rearing patterns on the market with the baby food and most other things. Canned products are practical; they are also bland, standardized, and sterile.

Many other developments contributed to loss of faith in custom and in spontaneous feeling. There is the awe inspired by the accomplishments of science in other fields. There was, for a while, the conviction of scientists that the universe could be reduced to mechanical rules mechanically taught. More important, perhaps, many parents were bringing up children in a culture very different from the one in which they themselves had been raised. Even native Americans suddenly found themselves in urban surroundings, as often as not in a class different from that of their own childhood. Or husband and wife came from different backgrounds. They hoped with the help of science to do better by their children than their parents had done by them. After all, hadn't the new scientific ways generally proven superior to traditional ones? Why shouldn't the new rules and schedules be more successful than the old ways, just as new formulas were more efficient than the old baby food?

Material arrangements and social evaluations have standardized and industrialized motherhood. For instance, women are practically compelled to deliver their children in—and to—a hospital. Even when normal delivery is expected it takes inordinate stubbornness to persuade an obstetrician to deliver an infant at home if a hospital is within reach. And hospitals seldom allow mothers to take charge of their newborn infants. Professional care is preferred. The babies, labeled and numbered, are kept in nurseries, as though to affirm from birth that they belong with their age-mates, an American culture trait that will dog them throughout their lives. The mother has little contact with her child until she returns home; in the recent past, overbearing hospitals even dissuaded women from breast feeding. No wonder that, home at last, the mother feels confronted with a mysterious little stranger she hardly dares touch without professional advice. This is the most efficient and safe way to deliver children, and it has greatly reduced mortality. It is also the most convenient routine. But is it apt to foster the spontaneous flow of familiar affection between mother and child, and the sense of conviction so necessary to rear an infant and guide a child? No doubt the routine is not an insurmountable obstacle to spontaneity. But it leads away from it.

SEXUAL AND SOCIAL CAREER

Young women now have not only the experience of formal schooling but also that of employment. What could be more natural than to transfer the techniques of industrial organization —regular schedules, expert advice, generalized rules—to the home? To acquire a status comparable to that of other occupations, motherhood is reduced to a job, a job for which one is formally trained. College courses and hosts of magazines and books establish family life as an industry served by numerous suppliers with ever-new models. Unavoidably, the focus shifts from spontaneous affection to training, gadgets, efficiency, and progress.

Above all, the participation of women in work outside the home changed their conception of their own role and their attitude toward children. To become a wife and mother once had been *the* expectation of young women, the fulfillment and consummation of their lives. Now this is no longer all; for many it is no longer enough. Motherhood has become one among many possible careers. Other careers may be experienced first or combined with motherhood. But motherhood is still the career requiring fewest formal qualifications and most easily within the reach of every female. Motherhood thus confers the least distinguished status of the careers available to women. Not that women refuse to become mothers; but they become less maternal. Owing to the shrunken size of the family, motherhood demands more labor and devotion now than in the past. Among middle-class women who in other countries could count on hired help, it, too, was missed in the United States: the difference between middle-class incomes and lower-class incomes is not great enough to permit the importation of country girls to help in urban households. Yet a woman now no more wants to be *only* a mother and wife than a man wants to be only a father and husband. And too many women become mothers "to save their marriage" (taking quite a risk at the expense of the child) or to prove "their adequacy as women" without feeling an inner wish drawing them to the maternal role, which consequently is neglected.

In all cultures, there is a radical status and role change when a girl becomes a wife and mother. Though by our public standards motherhood is regarded highly, privately the loss exceeds the gain. Therefore, the new role is accepted hesitantly and with a great deal of ambivalence. Not that girls don't like to *get* married; they are ambivalent only about *being* married, and even more, about being mothers—just as many people like eating but do not like the effect—gaining weight. Similarly, money-getting is more prestige-bearing than having money: success in our culture is symbolized more by the process of acquisition than by the result.

An employee who has led a well-regulated, sociable, and diverting occupational and private life as a mother finds herself bound to the house and to never-ending menial chores—chores which do not use her educational skills and qualifications or advance her on any sort of recognized career. She may well resent the infant who so tyrannically imprisons her. That resentment and the guilt feeling it causes contribute to the anxiety expressed in the constant search for scientific, efficient, *certified* ways of rearing infants. To be a mother, for many a woman, means to miss out on the activities vested with glamour and prestige. A woman who actually prefers maternal chores to all she must give up to do them full justice is likely to be exceptional.

Children must suffer from this. If for their sake the mother does renounce what she would rather do, it is likely that some resentment will sneak into her relationship with them—the guilt feeling that follows the resentment will be expressed in over-anxiousness or pseudowarmth. And, if she indulges herself, it is unlikely that they will get all the stable affection they need. Or she might use her children to "succeed" through them as she might have through the career she missed. Instead of being loved, the child is rewarded with love for achievements which are to prove the worth of the parent; he is used the way a race horse might be and becomes, at best, anxious and competitive, for failure means parental scorn.

Women have striven hard to equal men; female achievement has been prized more as it resembles male achievement more closely. And once their physiological functions are regarded mainly as hindrances to more highly valued accomplishments, women lose much of their taste for maternity. Yet there can scarcely be anything more directly creative (and potentially rewarding) than to bear and rear a child. To match the natural creativeness of women, men must go out into the world and create artifacts, brain children, such as books or works of art.

Not that every woman should strive for fulfillment only in motherhood. Neither instinct nor physiology predestines human individuals so specifically and uniformly. Indeed it is culture which very largely specifies what are regarded as male and female tasks. But most societies have taken their cues from physiology: though much has been made of them, the cultures in which feminine achievement does not usually center around childbearing and homemaking are exceptional. The fact that in some tribes the connection between intercourse and childbearing is not acknowledged or known is hardly a reason to consider such a connection "only cultural." Nor does the fact that some tribes do assign to females roles assigned in most cultures to males make the basic role distinction "only cultural." The ignorance or the knowledge involved, not the objects thereof, are cultural.

The troublesome thing is that present social evaluations leave many women dissatisfied with careers, with motherhood, and with the possible compromises. The brunt of parental ambivalences is borne by the children. The problem is tricky. For one thing, in our circumstances the traditional ways cannot be adopted. They won't do now that most women survive long after their children have grown. As grandmothers, they no longer have an important role. Hence, a woman who devotes her life only to motherhood faces a void as she reaches what today is middle age.

Statistics indicate that women of all ages, in increasing numbers, shun domesticity. One-third of the United States labor force now consists of women. Eighty per cent of all single females between the ages of twenty and thirty hold jobs versus 90 per cent of all single males. The most stunning change concerns married women. At the turn of the century, 4 per cent worked; in 1940, 15 per cent; but in 1956 nearly one-third of all married women were at work—double the number of single girls. The more prosperous we have become, the more married women have gone to work, driven obviously by boredom, education, and ambition more than by poverty.

Most married women at work are childless. But the number of married women with children holding jobs is soaring. Seven per cent of all mothers with young children held jobs in 1940—and 18.2 per cent in 1955. The proportion of middle-aged women at work also is mounting fast. Forty-five per cent of the women between forty-five and fifty-four years are now at work and the percentage of women in the thirty-five to forty-four age group who are working has nearly doubled in the last thirty-five years. Time was when a woman went to work only because the husband's income did not suffice to support the family. But that time clearly has passed. The trend is unmistakable. The magnitude of the change may be exaggerated, nonetheless, since women working as farm wives in the past were not included in the "labor force," though they did not work less than women who, as industrial or office workers, are now included in the labor force. However, psychologically, farm work was combined with family life and homemaking, whereas today's work is spatially, and psychologically, separated from family life.

THE ABDICATION OF PARENTAL AUTHORITY

The burden of socialization is heavy, as is the burden of civilization. But it is the price of survival of the species; it must be paid by every individual. The human infant learns over a long time to carry his burden. A young fox has little to learn. He need not control his aggressive tendencies or his wish to get what he needs when he wants it; nor does he observe incest taboos. And nature endowed him with the instincts he needs to survive; the vixen need protect him only during maturation. No education is required. Not so with us. We must learn to make a living and, above all, to control our antisocial tendencies enough to gain the cooperation of society, which is indispensable to us both psychologically and materially.

Education, even when based on love, cannot be unmitigated joy; one of its tasks is to teach that pleasure must often be foregone, that the unpleasant, the tiresome, the hard must not be shunned. Experience alone can teach children to undergo and finally to internalize the discipline which members of society need. In learning to master, as well as to indulge, our drives, we learn specifically to bridle and direct our aggressiveness; in the process it is shifted and concentrated, at times, against those who teach us, who frustrate as well as indulge us. Parents who want to be popular rather than right find this hard to bear. Yet the parent who does not guide and discipline his child introduces into the world an individual unprepared for its ways. He creates a problem for society and for his child who, some time, will have to face people unwilling to indulge him. Spoiled children end up by loving their parents least—they dimly realize that slothful and weak parents have failed them. The child who received no help in mastering his drives might well find it more difficult to forgive his parents than the child who was treated with excessive severity.

Socialization in our own society has been subjected to scientific study. In the long run this might bear useful fruit. Unfortunately, the fruits have been eagerly plucked while still immature. Educators, as experts in scientific socialization, have assumed responsibilities abdicated by parents intimidated by "science." But educators cannot do what only the family is equipped to do: channel and regulate the emotional wellsprings of children. Besides, in attempting to act *in loco parentis*, schools have neglected their proper tasks: the transmission of knowledge and the reinforcement of discipline that goes with it. This may be one reason why there is more teaching and (proportionally) less learning than ever before.

Even in the functions they still essay to carry out, parents struggle to follow the rules of science. This has disadvantages. Scientific methods of child rearing are not as yet well established or even agreed on. Moreover, the only *general* prescription science can provide is to have healthy and loving parents, parents who do not flock anxiously to lectures to find out how to bring

up their children. The harassed parent who looks up in books
what to do with his child is usually too insecure to make a good
job of it regardless of what he reads. And his insecurity is what
harms the child. But rules for behaving—toward children or
anyone—have never yet cured insecurity. Scientists only indulge
it by advice. The more such parents learn, the less they know.
They are like people who constantly look up in home medicine
books, health columns, and so forth, how to be healthy. This is a
symptom of, not a prescription against, disease. Psychoanalysis
is based on the idea that the mere giving of a rule (or explanation of a difficulty) is useless. People cannot follow it, or utilize
the explanation emotionally, even if they accept it intellectually.
Simple ignorance seldom causes psychological problems. Ignorance is more likely to be an effect than a cause of psychological
problems. It is no small paradox to find that people are given more
rules and explanations than ever—"psychoanalytic" ones this time,
even though psychoanalysis has shown the futility of this very
practice.

The effort to be scientific has led also to unwillingness to assert
parental authority. Countless developments have abetted this. In
a society that changes as swiftly as ours, the experience of the
older generations tends to become irrelevant to the younger.
While in less rapidly changing societies authority tends to increase
with years, in ours it often diminishes. Far from being regarded
as vessels of experience, the aged are patronized as old-fashioned;
their experience becomes rapidly obsolete, and makes their adaptation to the rapid changes in our society more difficult. Their
power over the young nearly ceases when their physical ability
to impose it does, and their authority may cease before. The fact
that many immigrant parents did less well, and have a lower
social status, than their children causes a further decrease of
parental authority. The values and practices of these parents,
appearing ill adapted to their new environment, were eagerly replaced. Finally, in a society where income can be easily derived
without property, the economic power of the older generation—
the power to bequeath—has comparatively little importance. All
these factors have contributed variously to parental timidity and
lack of authority which, in turn, leave the child alone to cope
with his antisocial potentialities. The child's problems become

greater while the aged, left functionless, feel rejected, useless, and bereft of dignity—a sad ending to life and a prospect which further encourages the frenzy of the young.

Finally, socialization is increasingly understood to mean not learning to master one's unruly drive but adjusting to a group. Instead of acquiring their own individual standards of conduct through their parents, children are taught to take acceptance by the coeval "peer" group as their standard. Authority so largely shifted to coeval groups produces people who, rather than relying on an internal authority—which has never been implanted—remain forever morally dependent on their neighbors (or the newspaper columnists who replace them). Indeed, children are often deterred from doing disapproved things by being told that people will not love them if they do. Parents thus intill an unquenchable thirst to please whatever group is joined, instead of implanting a moral standard and raising their children to be able to satisfy it. The individuating aspects of socialization are minimized. And society becomes what there is now: the past no longer serves as a model. The result, all too frequently, is a being unfit for society, just because he is not fit for anything else—because he has no identity of his own and is only a compound of roles played for applause—a secondhand character.

PART TWO

Society

CHAPTER VII

Groups

Every man is born into a group of men and will belong throughout his life to many groups. Exceptions such as psychotics, hermits, and some men of genius do not disprove this rule. Isolation (involuntary) is part of the pathology of psychosis and of the arduous and uncommon renunciation (deliberate) of the hermit. Finally, in Jacob Burckhardt's words, it is "the misfortune of genius to make him lonely in whom it dwells all too mightily." A genius, instead of sharing prevailing attitudes and ideas, creates new ones. His originality and depth are understood when that which he pioneered is generally accepted and has lost its singularity. Only some types of genius achieve recognition early enough to lead a group, usually when their innovations bring already accepted trends to full fruition.

The career of the word egregious (from the Latin *ex-grege*, "out of the herd") suggests a change of social attitude unfavorable to genius. "Egregious" was a laudatory adjective. Today we use "egregious" to mean "outstandingly bad" or "wrong." To be outstanding is almost to be bad, and to hold an unshared view is almost to be wrong.

Even the genius, the hermit, or the psychotic starts out as a member of a group. He is born into a family. This *primary group* is itself part of a number of national, local, and religious communities into which the new family member will grow. Later he also may be drafted into a military group, or be compelled to be part of a group of hospital patients or penitentiary inmates. Into many groups he grows without deliberation; others he joins by choice; still others through coercion by men or circumstances.

The word "group" may be used in a purely classificatory sense —regardless of how people feel and act. For instance, we can divide people into groups according to whether they have green or brown eyes. But classificatory orderings matter only when they can be related to the behavior of the group members toward each other, and toward the social and natural environment, or to the behavior of others toward the group members. Every group which behaves as a group or is *felt* to be one establishes, at least on some occasions, more, different, and perhaps closer relations of members with each other than with outsiders.

Group members must have common attitudes. They acquire a structured relationship to each other by their distinctive attitudes to objects, persons, symbols, or actions. A physical or statistical aggregation of people is a group only when the members are related by more than propinquity or common traits, when they share some relationship which they (and outsiders) feel as a distinctive tie. Propinquity may, of course, lead to such a relationship without itself being one. Thus the inhabitants of a village and, perhaps of a suburb, or a tenement, may be a group (but probably not the tenants of an apartment house in a well-to-do neighborhood). Often people become a group because of a common action they undertake; as often they undertake the common action because of their group membership. The importance of the grouping depends entirely on the importance of the behavior related to the group membership.

One may choose to become a member of a group formed mainly for the pleasures of group life, for instance, by joining a fraternity chapter. As the name suggests, fraternities are elective sibling groups affiliated with the campus "family" reared by "alma mater" and with the "parent" body of the chapters. As do many other groups, fraternities draw strength from the family, the original human association. They share some of its symbols and try to elicit sentiments associated with the family. But fraternities must provide artificially the ties which grow naturally in actual families. Their initiation rites are imposed so that, through suffering a common experience, group solidarity and distinctiveness will be strengthened.

One may pay a high price for what one holds dear; and one may also hold dear that for which one has paid a high price. Initiation rites are likely to be more exigent and harrowing the more the need for solidarity is felt and the less previously shared experience can be counted on to create ties. Stringent initiations may also be required when those who undergo them have a great deal in common with others who are not members. The rite helps to weaken the bonds between the new group members and their old nonmember friends (*adhesion*) as well as to strengthen ties between new and old group members (*cohesion*).

Pain, possibly, is a more impressive experience than pleasure and is more easily inflicted. Though they end in feasts, initiations often feature pain. Perhaps pain is inflicted also to purge the resentment of current members against the newcomers who will compete with them, and share in everything painfully created by them and by past generations.

The initiation ceremonies of primitive tribes may be interpreted analogously. But in primitive puberty rites, additional motives are present. They mark stages of biological maturation and usher age and sex groups into their social roles. With us, religious confirmations, the graduation ceremonies of schools, and "coming out" parties have similar significance, though more limited scope.

Groups may be effects of the common experiences members undergo, and at other times the cause. Perhaps we have received the same education—a cause of some of our group attitudes and characteristics. In turn, our common education may be an effect of group membership. Our families may be members of the same religious, national, or economic groups; or perhaps we live in the same town or work together and are functionally dependent on each other. Some groups are formed because of a common endeavor which, however, may be also the effect of group formation. Other groups have no specific purpose. Group membership may be the result of people's dependence on each other for the satisfaction of their needs, or it may create the needs it satisfies, just as it may result from common characteristics or create them. Using the same aftershave lotion may not be enough to form a club, though advertisers seem convinced that it is, but how much more is needed we don't know. Nearly any common experience may furnish the material for a common bond.

We become group-conscious almost as soon as we start discriminating ourselves from the rest of the universe, as soon as we become self-conscious. Our actions and feelings clearly, if not explicitly, distinguish between our group and others. But the form this distinction takes depends on the culture into which we are born—the patterns of behavior which are transmitted to us. Culture also greatly influences the common characteristics, out of many possible ones, which lead to formation of felt groups. Skin color may be important in one culture and political views, occupation, sex, or religion more important in another. Each group usually influences the behavior of members only in selected respects and on selected occasions. This is so because people hold membership in many groups. Only observation can tell which group membership will prevail in controlling individual behavior on a given occasion.

Groups may be ordered according to size and intimacy of members. The smallest and most intimate group is a pair, husband and wife, or two friends, or mother and child. Not far behind come families or classes in a boarding school—associations with personal, intimate, fairly enduring, and comprehensive contacts. These groups are called primary, to be distinguished from secondary groups such as nations or labor unions, which are of greater size. Relations in secondary groups are less personal, usually concerned more purposefully with fewer aspects of behavior, and frequently controlled by formal rules. The primary group often is formed spontaneously. It is formally organized only when changed into a secondary one, which requires designation of officeholders, entrance requirements, and so forth. Within the secondary group there are numerous primary ones. Within the church there are congregations, within the fraternity there are chapters, and within each of these still smaller, more informal, and more intimate groupings. It is, of course, the primary group which is primary in the direct patterning of the developing and still plastic individual personality.

Among the secondary groups, there are permanent and temporary ones. Groups such as nations or churches are permanent:

they continue indefinitely because their characteristic patterns of behavior are transmitted to new members; these patterns change slowly and continuously enough for the group to retain its identity. Permanent groups are united by continuous habits—e.g., speaking a common language, residing on a given territory, being subjected to the same laws—or by recurrent functions, by a common outlook or belief, or by something that is believed about them and that causes them to suffer similar treatment. In contrast, members of temporary groups have only an *ad hoc* relationship which binds them together while they share an experience actively or passively. The relationship, the group as such, disappears with the occasion that led to it. Primary groups by definition end with the life of the participants, if not before.

When the membership changes frequently, when the association is involuntary, or casual and sudden, and when it consists of people who have little in common, group solidarity (cohesion) is transient. Members may act as a group only in the temporary conditions which lead to the group membership—while soldiers, or in the crowd, or in the penitentiary. Yet, while the activating condition exists, the solidarity of temporary groups can be as strong as that of permanent groups.

Crowds (momentary groups) differ according to the kind and binding power of their focus. Audiences sharing a spectacle (planned or accidental) or people sharing a bus ride form crowds. In a bus, the common ride is a means rather than an end and it is not much of a bond. In the theater, the common enjoyment of the spectacle is the final purpose of grouping. Members of crowds who came together to dance in a public hall or to go on a lynching bee also are each attuned to similar sentiments. They often behave as they would not individually. They shed personal characteristics and responsibilities, suspend their individual judgment, and follow their unbridled instincts. They are "beside themselves": that part of their personality which they have in common with others and which is attuned to the crowd focus overwhelms individuating traits—the Ego—and silences calmer counsel. They become anonymous not only to others but, one is tempted to say, even to themselves. Crowd members do not reason, but follow. Inflammatory speeches or martial music or drinking may heighten and focus the anti-individual, anti-intellectual character of crowds, but they are not indispensable to crowd behavior. Any speaker knows that what appears as a great joke to a crowd, owing to the near suspension of judgment, need not be one.

Publics should be distinguished from crowds and, in a sense, from groups. Unlike a crowd, the public is physically dispersed, but is linked together by a common culture or, within it, by a common activity such as reading a newspaper or looking at a television show. Being part of a public may contribute to a group membership, but is not enough by itself to form a group except in the loosest sense. Yet influence of the public on the conduct of individuals and groups is immense and, owing to the spread of mass media of communication, the influence of "public opinion" is rising.

Note finally that the various relationships which we separate analytically—primary and secondary group, crowd and public, and many others—may coexist in the same aggregate of persons and blend into each other.

INTENSITY AND EXCLUSIVENESS

When ties are intensive, the group is often exclusive, making it difficult for newcomers to join. When groups accept newcomers readily, the bonds which are so easily lengthened often become less stringent.

Alexis de Tocqueville found the loosely tied, rather changeable, readily joined and abandoned group most characteristic of America, where "the bond of human affection is extended, but is relaxed." Since differences among groups (and individuals) are felt to be smaller, or less important, than similarities, Americans might be expected to be indifferent to them. But the conviction that differences are small (which, as convictions often do in social matters, helps make itself come true) prompts Americans to resent immensely exclusion from any group as a denial of their equal "right" to belong or of their equal value as persons. Indeed, eagerness to belong remains great in spite of or because of the relatively easy acceptance. The fluidity of groups increases our anxiety to remain "in the swim"; and the generally easy acceptance makes exclusions particularly offensive. In *Democracy in America* de Tocqueville suggests one reason:

The hatred that men bear to privilege increases in proportion as privileges become fewer and less considerable, so that democratic passions would seem to burn most fiercely just when they have least fuel. . . . When all conditions are unequal, no inequality is so great as to offend the eye, whereas the slightest dissimilarity is odious in the midst of general uniformity; the more complete this uniformity is, the more insupportable the sight of such a difference becomes. Hence it is natural that the love of equality should constantly increase together with the equality itself, and that it should grow by what it feeds on.

Because it is so exceptional, the exclusion of groups such as Negroes in a manner so contrary to the general fluidity of American society lies heavily on the American conscience. If egalitarianism is a virtue, our vice stands out because of our general virtuousness.

SOCIOLOGY DEFINED

Sociology studies the formation and transformation of groups, and the relationships of groups and group members as such with each other. In brief, sociology studies sociation—*as*-sociation and *dis*-sociation. "Society" is not a thing but a series of human actions relating people to each other in various ways. These actions are studied by sociologists. In personal behavior, sociologists study what correlation there may be with group membership in general and with the specific location of the person within a group. But sociologists focus on group behavior—in Wordsworth's words, on the "inscrutable workmanship that reconciles/ discordant elements, makes them cling together/ in one society."

For instance, when studying how people vote or marry, or who commits crimes, succeeds in college, or becomes an alcoholic, sociologists relate voting, marital choice, criminality, alcoholism or collegiate success to group memberships. To what extent is alcoholism or success in college related to residence in urban or rural communities? literacy? income? religion? sex? age? type of family? Or, to what extent is criminality or the rate of suicide, fertility, or radio listening related to changes of the group membership, for instance, to migration from rural to urban areas? Sociologists also inquire into the causes and effects of urbanization or of modifications in the techniques of production. Why are inventions made when and where they are made? (They seem to occur in clusters.) What leads to the application of inventions (innovation)? Surely the ancient Greeks were not less intelligent than we are. Yet their technology was primitive compared to ours. Sociologists want to know what leads one group to behave in one way and another to behave in an entirely different way.

All social sciences are related because they all study aspects of the same thing: human behavior. They tackle different aspects with different intellectual instruments, but there is some overlapping. Cultural anthropology, social psychology, political science, to name a few, overlap in part with sociology. But their focus, if not their range, is different. Political science, for instance, focuses on a particular social function: government. Cultural anthropology studies extinct or preliterate cultures. (If concerned with literate contemporary ones, it can be distinguished from sociology mainly by hairsplitting.) Social psychology pursues effects of group memberships further into the individual psyche than does sociology. The overlap is nonetheless undeniable. Even individual psychology is not far away from sociology for it can hardly be confined to intrapsychic matters.

Each group is a strand in the social fabric and each personality is a nexus of group influences. (Under strain, both societies and individuals may unravel or lose their shape.) We can therefore conceive of much psychology as microsociology and of much sociology as macropsychology. But we should not drive such analogies too far. There are irreducibly social elements in sociology and irreducibly nonsocial ones in psychology, even though there are many adjoining and some common areas.

Scientists, too, form groups and they sometimes willfully delight in distinctive terminologies. There is competition and even "imperialism" among learned specialists. Occasionally one longs to reduce the subject matter of other specialists to his own, as though the various approaches to society were not complementary but alternative. Yet there is so much to be learned about ourselves that all groups of social scientists have plenty of opportunity to contribute. And the craving for distinctiveness is not always sterile. Though it may prompt needless terminological differentiations, it also fosters the invention of concepts and hypotheses explaining human behavior.

Groups cultivate distinctive behavior patterns which are more or less adapted to their functions. Permanent group behavior patterns, often accumulated over generations, are called "institutions." Institutions are expected to generate appropriate sentiments. These sentiments are often expressed and the whole institution operated through a cluster of symbolic and utilitarian paraphernalia and specifications. For instance, political institutions such as the state elicit from the members (citizens) sentiments of loyalty, patriotism, respect, and subordination. The state is symbolized by the flag, the national anthem, and numerous shrines and monuments. It is celebrated, and the sentiments reasserted, by rituals on holidays such as Washington's Birthday or Veterans Day. The state is operated and sometimes enforces its requirements, which are specified by laws, with the help of public officials, buildings, courts, schools, and armies.

Most institutions are similarly organized. The family, for instance, elicits sentiments of affection and a disposition to mutual support. It is symbolized by such things as wedding rings and heirlooms, and is celebrated ritually on holidays, on occasions of birth, death, or marriage, and on anniversaries. It is operated with the help of equipment such as furniture and living quarters, according to specifications laid down in laws and usages and accepted in ecclesiastical or civil ceremonies. Churches and schools are similarly operated. Institutions such as banks or labor unions are thought of mainly as means. The conscious sentiments of the groups involved and the symbols are likely therefore to be more directly related to utilitarian functions.

Poolrooms, colleges, prisons, hospitals, Christmas, and baseball also are institutions, each occupying a different place in the network of social relations. Some institutions bind people together continuously in a specific way, others recurrently, some extensively, others only in a particular activity. But each institution fits its members into specific related roles which it defines. The family defines parental, filial, and conjugal roles. The state defines the roles of government and citizens, and baseball those of the player, the fan, and the coach. We may thus conceive of institutions as clusters of related roles outlining behavior patterns to be interpreted by the actors, according to the status each occupies.

Groups are distinguished from each other by their institutions; and societies differ in the total systems formed by their institutions. The system is part of the culture of each society. Culture includes institutions, as well as man-made products and all learned behavior patterns: sentiments, ideas, beliefs, and techniques such as language, art, religion, science, and technology. Culture is not merely an aggregate of all these elements, however. They must be sufficiently meshed together to permit the society to continue. No institution carries out its function by itself. It must be supported by other institutions. If the impact of some institutions is detrimental to others, we are faced with a "social problem" solved only by changing one or more of the institutions.

KINDS OF FAMILIES

Though the culture of each society differs from that of others, some institutions are needed in all societies to perform, in however varied ways, functions essential to any social life. Thus all societies that have offspring have the institution of the family. (Groups such as the Shakers, and monastic orders, can renounce offspring; but there are no societies that do.) Social regulation and limitation of our biological propensity to sexual intercourse and reproduction are a function of the family everywhere. The identity of this one function permits us to identify the family in all societies.

The family is seldom restricted to its basic reproductive function, but it has a different selection of additional functions in each society. It may loom large or small as an economic unit or in politics. All or some family members may live and work together using and inheriting each other's implements. The family may decide who is to be whose bride or groom, or leave it to the individuals concerned. Sometimes only individuals of one sex —usually the male—may choose mates for themselves. Political and judicial power may be inherited through family membership, as it often was in the Middle Ages, or inheritance may be limited mainly to wealth, as it is now.

The usages distributing power, respect, and income among family members also differ enormously. Age may be decisive, or sex, or neither. Qualifications for membership (definitions of kinship) in families differ from society to society to begin with, and so do eligibility requirements. Each culture prescribes different relations of family members to each other, and to outsiders. Some societies have wide kinship systems, others restricted ones; some emphasize avuncular, others matrilineal, others patrilineal, still others adoptive family relations. Finally some emphasize offspring, others stress ancestry, still others mainly the conjugal mates.

The differences in accepted emotional relationships are also staggering. For Eskimos and some other groups it is a matter of common courtesy to lend their wives to guests; but they will take great offense and kill each other for unauthorized wife borrowing. (This is not as odd as it may appear: we too give gifts but punish anyone who takes anything without permission.) The polar night is long and entertainment scarce. However, the Kiwei Papuans in British New Guinea also have sexual hospitality, though their natural environment is very different from that of the Eskimos.

Some societies consider love the cause of marriage; others the effect; and still others consider love irrelevant. It goes without saying that ideas and ideals of love differ enormously in different cultures, though some sort of attraction is always involved. Differences are so great that one might well say that love, as it has been defined for us in a long historical development since the Middle Ages, plays a significant role only in a few places and periods. Just as the family differs in each society, so do other institutions.

Types of marriage also vary. Some societies institutionalize polygyny; a few, polyandry. (Both types of marriage, of course, involve polygamy—plural wedlock.) Byzantine Christendom had strict monogamy. Even widowed persons could not remarry. There was some apprehension lest a widower be embarrassed by several wives upon resurrection. Nonmarital relations, however,

seem to have been rather free. Our own society has a somewhat
looser monogamy. One can be married only to one person at
a time. But the ease in changing partners brings us fairly near
to polygamy now. Through divorce one is able successively
to marry several persons without waiting for the death of any
one. Marriage, moreover, is becoming mainly a union of two
individuals to satisfy their psychobiological needs, whilst in
the past it was largely a union of two families meant to continue
them. For instance, in Deuteronomy 25:5-9 it is declared the
duty of a brother to marry his widowed sister-in-law. If he
refuses: "Then shall his brother's wife come unto him . . . and
spit in his face . . . and say, So shall it be done unto that man
that will not build up his brother's house." The idea of the
family as a device to continue the male's life (his name) through
his descendants, and the many functions of the family beyond
the union of two individuals, explain most of the characteristics
it is now losing.

Once it is no longer hemmed in and supported by other
functions and by religious beliefs which in the past made it a
permanent bond, wedlock becomes synchronous with the satisfaction of the needs felt by the pair linked by it; wherefore it
is often temporary. Our high divorce rate—about 25% of all
marriages in the U.S. end in divorces—does not show that
husbands and wives get along less well now than before (there
is no evidence one way or the other); however, it shows that
when they do not get along they can (and do) divorce more
easily than they used to. Possibly the emotional demands made
on marriage have increased as the material demands have decreased. And divorce is easy enough to be preferred, in some
instances, to serious attempts to overcome marital difficulties.
There is some reason, finally, to suspect that many people expect
from marriage a fulfillment that no human institution can yield;
perhaps they marry and divorce a few times before that realiza-
tion dawns on them.

Every reader of the Bible is familiar with polygyny, which
is still permitted in most of Asia and the East. Polyandry is
less familiar, but according to Christopher Rand's description (in
The New Yorker, Sept. 18, 1954):

Polyandry is universal in Tibet, though it comes in various forms, the most common being fraternal polyandry, in which a set of brothers marry a joint wife to keep their heritage intact. In another form, a woman who owns property takes husbands, who may or may not be related, as she likes; in such households the woman rules the roost. Yet another form, prevailing in the Lhasa region and extending down to Kalimpong, is father-and-son polyandry. This comes about when a mother dies and the father takes to sharing his daughter-in-law with his son, or sons. Or he may find a new wife and welcome his son, or sons, to share her with him. Nor is this done only by single fathers. Joint fathers (that is, the several husbands of one woman, who are all regarded as the fathers of all her children) may do it, too, in which case it is fathers-and-sons, rather than father-and-son polyandry; several joint fathers may share one wife with their several joint sons—though not, to be sure, if she is a joint son's own mother. Still other combinations are possible. Polyandrous families, for instance, need not be restricted to one wife but may have two or more [in other words, they may also practice polygyny. E.v.d.H.].

The main reason for Tibetan polyandry is economic. . . . Tibetans have too few resources to keep dividing them up. When brothers stay home and share a wife, the family is stable from generation to generation. If no sons are born in a certain generation, a daughter can perpetuate the household by taking husbands. Once . . . an old Tibetan was told that in Europe it has long been the custom for younger sons to take private wives, leave the family, and strike out for themselves. The old man thought this expensive and difficult. "Now I understand why you Europeans come here," he said. "That is why you have colonies. If you were polyandrous, you wouldn't need them." . . . Conservative Tibetans think polyandry the best system morally, of course. They point out that it works against selfishness, since it stresses the family above the individual.

According to Mr. Rand, "the main reason for Tibetan polyandry is economic." This view is shared by sociologists Ogburn and Nimkoff (*Sociology*, 1946, p. 458): ". . . The chief factors responsible for polyandry would seem to be the extreme poverty of the people and the small economic utility of women in the culture." Although economic explanations always seem plausible to us, they are not always correct. This one isn't. Analogous economic conditions elsewhere have not led to polyandry. And we do find similar forms of family organization under very different economic circumstances. A combination of elements, including economic ones, produces a particular form of family organization. But we do not know which combination produces which forms of family organization, though we do find many reasons for the existence of a particular form each time we analyze its function in the total context. No single factor—such as variation in economic circumstances—accounts for, or even is of primary importance in the variety of forms of family organization which any geographical or historical survey shows.

CHAPTER VIII *The Basic Tension of*
Group Membership

Groups as disparate as the Campfire Girls, the Communist party, communities of Melanesian headhunters, and the Junior League of New York have in common not only that the members of each feel bound together and separated from nonmembers, but also that each group holds the conviction that it is superior—at least to those other groups that are near enough to compete with it. Our nation—right or wrong—is superior to other nations; our town to similar towns; our team to other teams in its league. The conviction of superiority seems to inhere spontaneously in group formation, but it may also be cultivated to strengthen group loyalties. College fraternities, the Marine Corps, certain Texas groups make deliberate efforts to cultivate a collective superiority feeling. We may asseverate it when it is a matter of opinion. When it is an objective matter, we may strive to achieve or prove superiority.

That so much need is felt to prove superiority suggests that the conviction must be strengthened not only in others, but also in those who proclaim it. Suspicion of ambivalence is buttressed when we note that groups within a society accept inferiority as well as superiority, and that some groups, such as the untouchables in India, may form a prevailing self-image of inferiority

109

to all others. (In European society, workers had a self-image of inferiority corresponding to their low social status until some intellectuals, who felt ambivalent about their own superiority, furnished them a new self-image: they became the wave of the future—the socialist ruling class.) Despite indications of ambivalence, groups usually form their self-images—at least the part that is externalized—in terms of superiority to competing groups. One may speculate that the infant's feeling of omnipotence, mentioned before, is successively shifted to parents, group, and group ideal—God. Through being with these superior entities, one avoids renouncing omnipotence altogether and feeling powerless. We draw our self-esteem from this source.

When the feeling of superiority cannot be sustained in the face of proof to the contrary, solidarity declines. The "morale" of a losing baseball team or a defeated army is lowered. If members lose their feeling of superiority altogether, group identification may be lost. People must be convinced that the group will ultimately prove superior—despite temporary setbacks—if they are to continue to form a group. History is inspiring to nations for this reason. It proves everybody's superiority and indicates that all declines are temporary.

Human society consists of groups as much as of individuals. And competing claims to group superiority are one important motivation of strife. The harmlessness, injuriousness, or even fruitfulness of competition depends on the form it takes; on what is considered a token of superiority, and on the means accepted to achieve it. One can try to prove oneself superior by knocking down a competing claimant, by being quicker on the draw, by making or spending more money, by being more popular, by writing a more popular book—even by writing a better one. One may root for one's baseball team, assert the superiority of the white race, insist on the superiority of French civilization, or of American plumbing. Each of these postures expresses the profound need we feel to be superior by belonging to a group which is.

The wish for superiority is expressed individually as well as by reference to one's group; it is part of the motivation of much of our activity. In the words of Nassau Senior (*An Outline of the Science of Political Economy*, 1836):

... The desire for distinction ... if we consider its universality and its constancy, that it affects all men and at all times, that it comes with us from the cradle, and never leaves us till we go into the grave, may be pronounced to be the most powerful of human passions.

The most obvious source of distinction is the possession of superior wealth. It is the one which excites most the admiration of the bulk of mankind, and the only one which they feel capable of attaining. To seem more rich, or, to use a common expression, to keep up a better appearance, is, with almost all men who are placed beyond the fear of actual want, the ruling principle of conduct. For this object they undergo toil which no pain or pleasure addressed to the senses would lead them to encounter; into which no slave could be lashed or bribed.

Senior's statement that the wish for superiority is "the most powerful of human passions" should not be taken too literally. We have no way of measuring passions, or of identifying them in all their disguises. It should also be stressed that the intensity of competition, as well as its intermediate objectives (such as wealth), varies from culture to culture. Still, Senior is right in asserting that our desire for superiority (competitive prestige, power, prior acceptance, to be the best-loved—the forms, levels and expressions vary) is infinite.

GAMBLING AS AN ATTEMPT TO PROVE INDIVIDUAL SUPERIORITY

How strong, indirect, and destructive the need to prove superior can be is illustrated by gambling. The gambler tries to prove, in the first place to himself, that fortune will favor him. He lays claim to being destiny's darling, to being recognized and proved superior or best-loved in its eyes. If we were to go back into his history, we might find that he belatedly asserts a claim for the unconditional favor of his mother, ever repeating it because it can never be quite fulfilled now. To be fortune's favored is the adult equivalent—not very adult at that. And fortune is always a woman. Incidentally, the nearly universal saying asserting that one cannot be lucky both in gambling and in love seems to confirm this: however unconditional, mother's favor exacts the price of faithfulness. The gambler might have been an overfrustrated

child with unsatisfied demands, or an overspoiled child with demands so increased by the spoiling that life can never satisfy him;
or, most often, a child who was alternately spoiled and frustrated
too much, and thus remains in search of assurance. The very
capriciousness of such alternation—whether apparent or real—
might lead the child to expect to be the prey of an equally capri-
cious fate for the rest of his life. And such expectation would
discourage systematic endeavors and encourage reliance on luck.
"The child," as Wordsworth says, "is father of the man."

Gambling is not confined to gamblers. The man who, drunk
or sober, crosses the street hazardously also invokes, almost hopes
to provoke, protection or destruction by the fates. He challenges
them to prove him fate's favored child. Man's career on earth
unavoidably involves fortuitous elements: "The race is not to
the swift . . . but time and chance happeneth to them all."
Gamblers, some criminals who gamble with their life chances,
and less conspicuously many others are impelled to maximize this
chance element. They entreat fate unceasingly for indulgence, not
content until in terrified, incredulous fascination they receive the
final rebuke they so long invited.

Some nongamblers, on the contrary, try to minimize the fortuitous element in most if not all of their actions. They may deny
it altogether, or try to control it through magic, or explain it
away as providence, but nonetheless try to propitiate it through
religious rituals. The early Puritans trusted God to mark His
grace by the degree of success with which He crowned their
labors. They despised gambling as a rival way of groping for
certainty. Gamblers were suspected of asking (and paying) for
diabolic favors. In contrast, those who labored successfully were
deemed superior because favored by God who, unlike fate or
blind chance, had a benevolent design.

It is no accident that we use the word "fortune" to mean possessions as well as the chance ("good fortune") that brought
them. Thus the influence of fate and chance, of conditions which,
though not necessarily mysterious, are beyond one's control in
shaping life situations is recognized in our language. And the man
who seems overly fortunate or fortunate without intelligible
cause is always suspect. One sees no reason for God to favor him
and resentfully suspects that he obtained the devil's favor by

selling his soul. Else I would have to recognize that he is superior, or preferred by the authorities I recognize. That won't do, for it would mean admitting that I am not. The ancients scarcely disguised their vindictiveness by attributing it to the gods, whose envy the overly fortunate man was always in danger of provoking. In every age, however, communities are prone to throw the overly fortunate, favored, proud, or strange into some well, prison, or concentration camp—or, at least, to tax him heavily.

SOCIALIZATION OF SUPERIORITY FEELINGS

Through joining a group and asserting or attempting to achieve its superiority over others, we indirectly try to certify that we ourselves are superior and are favored with (or by) superior powers. Asserted through membership in a superior group, one's own claim of superiority is less brazenly egocentric. (Some even claim superiority because they are "common men.") It seems less arrogant to claim superiority without singling oneself out directly, and perhaps less dangerous. The resentment of other group members is not aroused and the punishment of the jealous father gods would have to strike all the group members. Finally, one is more easily supported in such a claim: the members of the superior group are readily persuaded to admit each other's superiority over nonmembers. Thus, every people is chosen—whether because Jewish or blond.

Any distinctive characteristic of the group to which we belong, its habits or environment, may be used to prove the group's superiority and thus ours. Blond hair, the true religion, male- or femaleness, good plumbing, martial glory, or a peaceful bent may serve to bolster the claim. Tribes have declared themselves elected by God. Even without such ethnic distinctiveness, members of religious groups may feel that they are superior by virtue of having the true religion. Members of political groups are not far behind. Nations may feel superior because of special divine protection, historical mission, or political or economic circumstances. Whatever actual or imaginary differences appear to justify a feeling of superiority are stressed by the person who needs it. Thus Abigail Adams, wife of John Adams, our first ambassador to England, wrote home: "Do you know that the European birds have not half the melody of ours? Nor is their fruit half so sweet, nor their flowers half so fragrant, nor their manners half so pure, nor their people half so virtuous; but keep this to yourself. . . ."

The alien birds never sing as sweetly as the birds of one's native land. The wife of our second President did not realize this. She thought American birds, flowers, fruits, manners, and the virtues of American people were *objectively* superior. Thomas Jefferson gave more sophisticated reasons for our superiority: it was social, political, economic. In our own days this is still the main point made, though few would go so far as Ralph Waldo Emerson, who, witnessing the Palm Sunday ceremonies in the Sistine Chapel, exclaimed: "to the eye of an Indian . . . it would be ridiculous . . . there is no true majesty in all this millinery and imbecility . . ." Emerson compounded misconceptions of both the papal ritual and the Indian character in his remark. "To the eye of an Indian" the Roman ritual might have been "ridiculous" not because the Indians shared Emerson's aversion to all ritual, or his New England idea of naturalness, but only because the Roman ritual was not like his own Indian (totemistic) "millinery and imbecility"—which is scarcely less elaborate, Emerson notwithstanding, than the Vatican ritual.

Few, today, would rationalize their discomfort as transparently as Nathaniel Hawthorne, who, contemplating Italian painting, wrote, "a genuine love of painting and sculpture and perhaps of music seems to have distinguished men capable of every social crime and to have formed a fine and hard enamel over their characters." In other words, we don't paint so well because we are *nice* people. No doubt the Puritan background and our pragmatic bent, as well as the historical fact of the American revolution against European society, contributed to these judgments. There is little doubt either that some differentiation would have been found to justify the feeling of superiority in any case.

A feeling of superiority is part of any group solidarity. It is not confined to national groups. Thus we find the great twelfth century scholar Peter Abélard reporting that he had to flee secretly by night when he mentioned to the monks in the Abbey of St. Denis that the abbey was not founded by St. Dionysius Areopagita. For the monks felt that he would "take away the honor which was their greatest glory." This is what groups always feel when someone doubts that on which they base their claim of superiority.

"It is not enough," Mr. Justice Holmes declared, "for the knight of romance that you agree that his lady is a very nice girl —if you do not admit that she is the best that God ever made or will make, you must fight. There is in all men a demand for the superlative, so much so that the poor devil who has no other way of reaching it attains it by getting drunk." Since each knight cherished his own lady, they could not agree and therefore had to fight.

What ties a group together is often that all the members agree on the absolute superiority of something that they alone possess. This monopoly makes them superior. It does not matter whether it is American virtue, plumbing, or *"Deutsche Frauen, Deutscher Wein,"* the "German women, German wine" asserted to be superior in the German national anthem, *"Deutschland über Alles"* (Germany above all). The assertion of group superiority may well be the price for which we give up enough of our claim to individual superiority to make association in groups possible. We part with some of our personal conviction of superiority by sharing it with others. And the recurrent wish to prove this superiority reveals that we have also shifted to the group part of our fear of seeing the claim shattered.

The grounds used to justify superiority beggar description. A group may feel superior for disavowing the standards by which others measure their superiority. Internationalists, for instance, reject a national basis for superiority. This rejection becomes the ground for feeling superior to nationalists. Though the rationalization may be different, the superiority feeling need not be less virulent. Pacifists usually feel superior to those willing to resort to arms to assert their superiority. Not unexpectedly, the belligerence of pacifists is stimulated by controversies about peace, just as that of martial people responds to controversies over martial glory. (In fairness, it must be said that peace is a subject likely to lead to belligerence not only among pacifists.) In turn, those who cherish tolerance and lack of prejudice often can be stirred to unreasoning intolerance by the prejudices they detect in others.

One belief may be truer than, or preferable to, another. But a feeling of superiority can be attached to any one belief or group membership. It is a feeling which reason does not cause but merely tries to justify. The vehicle changes but not the cargo. The temptation to turn any actual or imaginary differential characteristic into a mark of general superiority or inferiority seems hard to resist. Sometimes people succeed in resisting only by denying that there are any differences at all; they homogenize humanity in their minds to the point of excluding all discrimination. Yet what is needed is discriminating judgment, to replace the indiscriminate prejudice which asserts fancied differences, or denies real ones.

Nations and groups tend to believe that a *status quo* which favors them is due to natural or divine law and is therefore good. Actually natural law at most *explains* the survival or dominance of a species or group. It does not *justify* it, or suggest that those who survive or predominate are more deserving than those who don't. What is is not, therefore, right—though it is "rational," i.e., performs some function. Nor can we justify any particular distribution of power or predominance as a result of the divine will, since clearly other distributions also are consistent with the divine will. Hence there is no reason to believe that God opposes change as such.

Practically every nation has found theoreticians who more or less naively or elaborately justified its feeling of superiority. The French political theorist Jean Bodin (1530-1596) arranged mankind under a theory of climates. There are outer sectors of partial goodness and a center of political virtue in France, with a concentration of this virtue in French constitutional lawyers, and an ultimate concentration of political wisdom in the principles laid down by Bodin. The novelist Aubrey Menen (in *Dead Man in the Silver Market*) describes ironically one historian's justification for the superiority feelings of a national group:

> Men of all races have always sought for a convincing explanation of their own astonishing excellence and they have frequently found what they were looking for.
> Thus, the Scottish historian Buckle . . . , in an exhaustive survey of the climates of the world, was able to range them in their order of merit. Hot, wet climates produced monstrous civilisations; hot, dry ones produced no civilisation at all . . . Extremely cold climates produced cultures of a low, huddling, grubbing, and contracted nature. The best climate of all was temperate,

varied, moderately rainy and briskly cold in winter. It was to be found . . . in that part of the British Isles which lay to the north of the River Tweed. Buckle's theories were well received in northwest Europe but did not gain much currency among the Spaniards, the Italians, or the Indians. . . .

A later theory was that natural selection determined that certain races should go to the top of the evolutionary tree and that others, owing to their lack of those qualities which led to survival, fell behind and ultimately became absorbed by the lucky winner. This theory held the field for a considerable time in England, particularly during those decades when the English were the greatest power in the world. Nowadays, when it would appear that Nature has selected them to be a secondary one, the theory gains no acceptance at all.

A third theory is that mankind are all brothers, but that some of the brothers are, for the time being, endowed with greater qualities than less fortunate brothers, and this superiority runs through a whole race. . . . It is the duty of the more fortunate races to take the less fortunate ones by the hand (or, if they are stubborn, by the neck) and lead them to higher things. . . .

. . . [This theory was] applied by the Germans, not to coloured people as it was so clearly intended to be, but to white people who were not Germans. When this happened the theory was seen to be absurd and even pernicious. However, it convinced a great number of Germans that they could not lose a war because there was, logically, nobody good enough to beat them. So far, two attempts to introduce a higher standard of civilisation to the white races have met with stubborn resistance on the part of the native. . . .

The most modern theory of all . . . confines itself to history. It says that history, when properly understood, convinces all unprejudiced men that they ought to be Russians. But all men are not Russians. This would be an insuperable barrier if it were not for the Russians themselves, who have no desire to confine their immense advantages to their own nation, but eagerly press them on whoever asks for them. Thus everybody can be happy, if they are only sensible. This thesis has gained such wide acceptance in Russia that the rest of the world can only account for its success by holding that the Russians are not allowed to think for themselves. No doubt they are not, but even if they were, there is no reason to believe that they would come to any other conclusion.

THE IMAGES GROUPS FORM OF EACH OTHER

Each group takes its own superiority seriously as it trench-
antly ridicules the presumption of the others. Yet since the feeling of superiority is one of the basic characteristics of human
association and conflict, we can't let it go at ridicule. Nor is it
enough to preach amity. If tension and conflict are ever to be reduced, their nature, origin, and function must be understood.
Only by facing the fact that even a modicum of group loyalty
usually implies some rejection of what is foreign can we hope to
bridge group hostilities and direct them into the least harmful
channels.

Each society has patterns of behavior separating it from other
societies. In turn, groups within societies differentiate their pattern by adding to, modifying, and selectively stressing some of
the patterns shared by the society as a whole. As group members,
we often resent members of other groups and societies because we
do not recognize that they, too, are subjected to rules, restrictions,
and deprivations—in short, to their own group patterns. Children and very ignorant people think that a foreign language is
what it seems: gibberish. They notice the absence of familiar
sounds, and of their own vocabulary and grammar, and conclude
there are none at all. The Greeks called non-Greeks barbarians
(from *bar-bar*) in onomatopoeic reproduction of the gibberish
non-Greeks were thought to speak. And, of course, since the
strangers lacked Greek culture, they were thought uncultured.
So we often perceive in the behavior of the alien only that he
lacks the rules and patterns of our group. We do not understand
emotionally, even though we might be taught intellectually, that
outsiders follow different rules, but rules nevertheless. We feel
that they are, in Rudyard Kipling's words, a "lesser breed without the law"—not a different breed, with a different law.

We imagine those who are not members of our group to be
ruleless, and free as we are not. We seldom realize that all societies, and all groups, must restrict feedom in some ways. We prefer to believe that our institutions are particularly restrictive, regardless of whether this is actually the case; the basic fantasy of

most people is influenced little by the actually remediable ills of society. (Organized social movements, fired perhaps by fantasies but striving toward concrete goals, are likely to respond a little more realistically to existing institutions.) The "civilized" usually imagine the "primitive" as free, childlike jungle dwellers and "bongo-bongo" they want to go "back to the Congo." Yet anthropological research should make us realize that the "savage," too, is rule-ridden. Since rules are imposed only to restrain people from what they are tempted to do, and therefore are broken occasionally in fact, and frequently in fantasy, the savage, too, is often fear- and guilt-ridden.

Even within our society, groups project wishful and fearful fantasies on each other. The upper-class person may look at the lower-class with a mixture of envy and contempt: "They (slum dwellers, Negroes, *et al.*), being less than I, have freedoms I do not have." The career of the word "villain" illustrates how ancient are distorted intrasocietal group images. This French word for peasant is now generally used as a synonym for "scoundrel," thus perpetuating the French nobility's image of the peasant. The lower class in turn likes to hear of the decadent pleasures of the rich; the urbanite of the simple, direct, and lusty country life; while the farmer is thrilled by tales of the wicked pleasures of the city. Adults envy the freedom of children, and children believe that grownups have it. Yet even heaven and hell are difficult to imagine without irksome laws and restraints.

F. Scott Fitzgerald is said once to have told Ernest Hemingway: "The very rich are different." Hemingway's reply, "Yes, they have more money," is usually applauded because of its egalitarian and debunking air. But didn't each man express a truth though with different emphasis? Money makes a difference beyond having or earning it. The economic group membership influences general attitudes and behavior. Yet outsiders may overstress, above all misapprehend, group differences because they project their fantasies. (Both Fitzgerald and Hemingway were well within the American tradition, one in identifying group differences with differences in wealth, the other in denying them altogether.)

Groaning under the burden our rules impose on us, we have contempt, but also envy, for the lawlessness, the freedom, or

license, which we fancy the alien group enjoys. We resent it
then when the group presumably enjoying such license also wants
the advantages for which we have had to pay with so many
restraints.

Owing to the comparatively great mobility of American society and its small cultural distances, as well as to the equal consumption by all groups of the same popular entertainment, in
America groups possibly do not project such fantasies on each
other quite as comprehensively and continuously as in other
countries. Perhaps this is why fantasies here are so often projected
forward upon people we do not know—in science fiction; or
backward—in historical fiction; or finally, sideways—into the
esoteric adventures described in "comics" and thrillers. Special
fantasies nevertheless are attached to remote groups such as Wall
Street, Hollywood, Negroes, and lately Madison Avenue.

The projection of one's fantasies on the alien group which
serves as a human Rorschach blot is not the only source of resentment of the alien (xenophobia or ethnocentrism) stemming
from envy and fear. (The Rorschach test is a method of measuring personality characteristics through classifying what a person
"sees" in a series of standardized ink blots. What he "sees" in
the ink blots are, of course, the images he projects onto them—
the images that are in his mind.) Even if we do recognize the
behavior of the alien group as patterned, even if we perceive
correctly some of the actual patterns—if Irishmen realize that
Jews are not just free from the rules of the Church, but have
their own; if white men realize that the black man's burden differs from the white man's in color rather than weight—there is
still much that may cause us to resent strangers. (Moreover,
knowledge of others can never be complete enough to preclude
the projection of our fantasies on them.) They are different. And
when we realize that one can be different, feel, act, and value,
deprive, and indulge oneself differently, we become less certain
of our own ways. The very acquaintance with ways foreign to
us confronts us with a choice, demands from us a preference, an
acceptance or rejection. We must leave, or recommit ourselves
to our own pattern, which hitherto we might have accepted unquestioningly. We must change or reaffirm our distinctions of

good and evil. Those who do not succeed in doing either meander through life without compass or aim.

To escape from this increased freedom, and from the renewed need to distinguish between good and evil, to regain paradise— the innocence we are losing when getting acquainted with the ways of the world abroad—we might truculently assert our superiority over those whom we resent because they make us insecure or envious. We may remove the doubt they instill in us by refusing to consider their ways as alternatives to ours—by rejecting them out of hand, declaring them altogether inferior, wrong, immoral, or uncivilized, without daring first to understand them. As Erich Fromm has stressed, in *Escape from Freedom*, what makes totalitarianism attractive to some is that it seems to impose certainty, security, and order, in place of independence, choice, and freedom. The comprehensiveness and absoluteness of the certainty sought seem to be a measure of the anxiety caused by the freedom from which one escapes. In the words of the classic American sociologist William G. Sumner: ". . . Each in-group forms its own ways, and looks with contempt and abhorrence upon the ways of any out-group." Thus we may defend ourselves against alternative ways felt as a threat to our own laboriously internalized restraints and purposes.

In excluding the alien as an equal we may continue to exclude what tempts us. The alien is identified with the part of our personality we repressed and alienated, originally for the sake of our group membership. The less we consciously control and the more we unconsciously repress our desires, the more alienated we are from them, the greater a threat the alien will be to us and the stronger our psychological reaction. As Henry Sidgwick points out in his *Ethics*: "The denial by another of what I hold true, impairs my confidence in it." We may deal with the denial, implicit in alien beliefs, by asseverating that the alien is a "lesser breed," or by rejecting his pattern through hostility. This spares us the strain of examining alien beliefs, comparing them to our own, and perhaps impairing our self-confidence. The very word "hostility" indicates our ambivalence (simultaneous, though inconsistent, feeling) toward what is foreign. It comes from the Latis *hostis* which stood for guest, host, and enemy. And the

English word "strange" means uncanny, as well as foreign. Finally, the same purpose is served if we deny any basic difference between alien ways and our own. We can be indifferent to the world, and relieved of any awareness of choice, if we see foreign parts through enough emotional distance to find in the hazy shapes the familiar outlines we seek.

<h2 style="text-align:center">HOW USEFUL ARE CONTACTS?</h2>

Contact with groups other than one's own is thus a two-edged sword. Contact may lead to a better understanding of oneself and of the world if one's basic pattern is satisfactory and built on more than ignorance of alternatives, or if one is quite able to change, which is rare. Otherwise contact with alien patterns might increase not understanding, but confusion, insecurity, and resentment. William Dean Howells in *The Rise of Silas Lapham* put these words in Mr. Corey's mouth: "I am always saying that a Bostonian should never leave Boston. Then he knows—and then only—that there can be no standards but ours. But we are constantly going away and coming back with our convictions shaken to their foundations. . . ." As irony often does, this sally reveals an unexpected facet of reality.

Indeed, the neighbor's grass is greener mostly because of the distance which adds color. Yet travel seldom disabuses us. Social distance and illusion are increased as often as diminished, when physical distance is decreased. The traveler picks the raisins from the cake of custom and reports on returning that in Paris everyone is carefree, engaged mainly in making love. He found what he sought because he expected it. Parisians, of course, "know" that sex is the main preoccupation of Americans. For this is what the Americans they know seem particularly fascinated by. Both groups disregard the selective and distorting effect of being abroad.

Perception and retention of what we see is filtered. Our mind, with its previously established contents, acts like a sieve. What goes through is highly selected; and the selection depends as much on the quality of the filtering sieve of expectations as it does on the material filtered. Experience can indeed broaden the mind. But when the walls experience would have to break down are too strong, we resort to narrowing and distorting what we experience so as to fit it in. Thus travel can be a fertile source of cross-cultural misunderstanding and misconception, confirming rather than dispelling prejudices, just as it may help understanding. Which it is will depend not on "good will"—conscious friendly intent—but on the general capacity of the traveler to respond to new experiences rather than to answer back (or for that matter merely to echo). This capacity can be cultivated, but only on fertile ground, only in a generally balanced and open personality.

A great deal can be said then in favor of parochialism and even immobility in a geographical as well as a social sense. Little is gained by making our eyes see more than our minds can accept without distortion or rending. Not everyone is always the best judge of what he ought to know and learn. Yet there is no one in the end who has a valid and universally recognized claim to decide bindingly. The most one can argue for then is to arrange matters in such a way that neither knowledge nor ignorance become universal and compelling fashions. The more the uses of *both* are recognized, the greater the chance that individuals and groups will have as much of each as they can digest without upsetting their stomachs.

The belief that prejudice, hostility, and conflict are basically caused by ignorance, and remedied by better acquaintance, is itself an optimistic prejudice. While it remains to be seen to what extent society can divert hostility and agressiveness into harmless channels, experience shows that they are as much generated as they are avoided or settled by acquaintance among groups. Certainly ignorance is more often the effect than the cause of hostility, and it is hardly ever a decisive cause. Judas did not betray Jesus because they were unacquainted; nor were the wars between Protestants and Roman Catholics due to lack of acquaintance. It is hard to believe that American Communists are unacquainted with democracy and hate it because of ignorance; nor did Germans slaughter Jews or try to conquer their neighbors because they did not know them. Was the War Between the States due to lack of mutual acquaintance?

Disagreements, whether the source is a quarrel over material in-

terest or ideologies, can sometimes be settled by mutual understanding and limitation. But just as often, understanding merely
clarifies the reason for the conflict. As for prejudices, it is only
by recognizing their emotional sources, which are hardly affected
by information of any kind, that we can hope to control group
relations a little better. And such recognition will not always
counsel us to foster direct contact unconditionally.

THE GROUP FEELING TOWARD NONMEMBERS

Groups regard some outsiders with indifference, but they are
hostile to those who have split off. A heretic who left is hated
more than a heathen who was never in the group. A heathen may
not know what he misses, but a heretic rejects knowingly, and
thus attacks directly the convictions of the orthodox. We feel
uneasy, knowing he has much in common with us, and yet became an outsider. Though one of us, he rejected and disavowed
us. He left, leaving a doubt in us which we must ward off with
vehemence.

Apostates who have repudiated one group for an opposed one
are seldom fully accepted by it. However honorable their motives might have been, they are regarded askance. The group
the "traitor" joins dimly feels that he has betrayed not only his
former group but group solidarity as such. Thus he has indirectly
rejected the new group, too, and he is felt as a psychological
threat. His own attitudes are likely to reflect this: there will be
hostility against the former group and a craving to prove loyalty
to his new group. This feeling is strongest in nations and groups
organized to be exclusive rather than universal.

The "traitor" is most easily accepted as "convert" by groups
with inclusive ideologies and universal (catholic) ambitions, such
as most Christian churches. Because of their universal ambitions,
on the other hand, these groups have been most intolerant of
those who leave, or refuse to be converted. The same sentiments
characterize a political group with universal or total ambitions.
The members of these groups are linked by strong bonds. Intensive adherence to a common faith is cultivated. Only those
believers in a dogma which expresses the revealed faith, the

depositum fidei, or at least accepting some holy writ, are counted as actual members. Organizational measures are taken, more or less successfully, to keep and transmit the faith pure, and thereby to cultivate the unity and identity of the group. Such groups often think that there can be no salvation for those who leave the faith, or knowingly refuse to accept it. This belief helps them to remain universal yet intensive enough not to lose or water down their identity.

Universal organizations which do not act in this fashion are likely either to keep their strength and lose their universality, or to lose their identity and strength. Religious denominations abound to illustrate these possibilities. Some are universal, yet remain intensive and closely knit through dogma; some are universal, but held together only loosely, with little emotional identification. Some groups (usually called sects) remain intensive and identified by being exclusive, that is, non-universal. Some, finally, gave up the original intensity, became loosely organized, and yet have not achieved universality.

It is always the similar group which seems most to endanger our own claim to superiority. Group members therefore seldom are enthusiastic about other groups with which they may be identified against their will. What outrages us is that they are like us but not quite identical. This seems to imply a criticism. We feel confronted either with a caricature of ourselves—and we are not quite sure of being sufficiently distinguished from it —or with a better edition of ourselves—and we compare ourselves unfavorably with it and suspect that others might do so, too. Either image is uncomfortable; it seems to suggest that we could be different from what we are, and not as incomparable as we think. As Tacitus reports of the Emperor Tiberius: *"ex optimis periculum sibi a pessimis dedecus publicum metuebat"* (he was afraid of the best, ashamed of the worst). Wherefore he liked mediocrities. They are usually liked best.

Not everyone does feel this way, and no one feels this way all the time. But most people do feel this way some of the time. The strength, the direction, and the expression of such feelings depend on actual similarities of people and groups, on whether they are perceived as such, and on the more or less competitive pattern of the culture and of the individuals concerned. Some

compete with everyone directly, others mainly with their own
ideals or ambitions.

THE BASIC TENSION OF GROUP MEMBERSHIP

Though it is nearly impossible to be without, it is often uncomfortable to be with a group. The burden of loneliness is
assuaged—perhaps merely overwhelmed—by the presence of
others. Yet the demands they make, and the restraints with which
their presence must be purchased are an almost equal burden. One
lives in the tension between society and solitude.

The deprivations imposed by each group differ, as do the
psychological and material satisfactions offered. But some are
universal: group members always must inhibit aggressiveness
against other members and tolerate some aggression from them.
They must give up some personal preferences, habits, ideas, and
gratifications and indulge their fellows'. For the sake of support
of the remainder they must surrender not a little of their original
nature. At times, all human beings might ask with Lord Byron:
"Is it not better thus our lives to wear / Than join the crushing
crowd, doom'd to inflict or bear?" But it is a rhetorical question.
We have no choice. Still we are responsible for not surrendering
too much, for remaining ourselves.

As a group member man, frustrated as well as satisfied, remains torn between loyalty to the group and resentment of it.
The existence of rival groups becomes a temptation then. Rejecting the temptation, one rejects the tempter and sometimes ap-
proves the punishment he suffers as a painless way of punishing
one's own disloyal thought.

By splitting the ambivalence of members, by directing hostility
outward and love inward, group social bonds are strengthened.
Civil war leads to particularly intensive intraparty identification
and correspondingly violent interparty de-identification. In 1938,
the French writer Simone Weil, serving as a volunteer on the
republican side in the Spanish Civil War, wrote to George
Bernanos describing with anguished candor how men behave
toward those who are not, or worse, are no longer, members of
their group. "I felt that whenever a certain group of human be-

ings is relegated, by some temporal or spiritual authority, beyond the pale of those whose life has a price, then one finds it perfectly natural to kill such people. When one knows one can kill without risk or punishment or blame, one kills; or at least one smiles encouragingly at those who kill. If at first one happens to feel some revulsion, one hides it, stifles it, fearing to seem lacking in virility. There seems to be in this some impulse or intoxication which it is impossible to resist without a strength of mind which I am obliged to consider exceptional, since I have not found it in anyone."

Just as "some temporal or spiritual authority" relegates people "beyond the pale," so in the first place people are included within the pale (legated, bound, if you wish) by such an authority. "The pale" itself is a creation of culture. But how precarious are these bonds, how limited and how all too easily broken! How much easier to break than to fashion them! The veneer of civilization that binds us together is very thin at best. If to spread it wider is to spread it even thinner, de-identifications might become more frequent. Religions of love—such as Christianity or the religiously inspired nonviolent movements in India—basically attempt to convert hostility into love by formation of broad, inclusive, even universal communities. They are optimistic in believing that this will reduce hostility not only *within* each community but *among* communities in the world. For experience, so far, suggests that communities are formed when love is directed inward to the members, differentiated from outsiders, toward whom aggression is directed in some culturally determined form. If love is to flow inwards and to flow pure, there must be an outside which drains off hate. A world community is unlikely until we find enemies in outer space.

GROUPS AND PERSONAL RELATIONS

Group loyalty usually diminishes one's interest in other groups; often it also reduces one's interest in persons. The more intensive the active identification of members with their group, the less they are usually concerned with individuals as such. As more affection is invested in the collective or group existence, less remains for private persons and relations, sometimes even for the private self. But it does not always seem so. A person endowed with great capacity to love may be able to be quite active in a group and yet more devoted to a few individuals than one endowed with a lesser capacity who does not use much of it for groups. Often, however, the persons most dedicated to group activities are those least capable of intensive and happy personal relationships. Perhaps this is why they are so dedicated. "If anything ail a man . . . if he have a pain in his bowels even . . . he forthwith sets about reforming—the world," says Henry David Thoreau.

In some cases, once affection is devoted to a group, more becomes available for individuals rather than being withdrawn from them. And a man who has not previously been a member of a group that suits him may, on joining one, reveal affection not only for the group he just joined but also for others. Perhaps before joining he converted most of his psychic energy into hostility toward a world in which he did not feel accepted—a frequent form of anticipatory rejection and retribution. Upon finding himself in communion with a group, he may be able to transform more of his energies into love. (The convertibility of intense emotions is proverbial.) Thus despite the new expenditure of love on the group, more love becomes available for the world at large.

Hostile and destructive tendencies can be changed into affectionate ones through acceptance into a group. This is how religious communities or temperance societies such as Alcoholics Anonymous, have been able, through acceptance, to save some alcoholics from self-destruction. They become more tempting for the current sinner when ex-sinners convincingly make him feel acceptable. A similar service can be done for some types of delinquents by acceptance into a community. (But delinquency seems as frequently the cause as the effect of social isolation.) The process may occur also in reverse order. A person who cannot participate in group life because he is overly frustrated in his personal relationships may become capable of group identification upon establishing satisfactory personal relationships.

The presence of a modicum of one relationship seems to release the ability to establish the other, while a great deal of one tends to reduce the other. It may also be that the absence of both group and individual relationships is due to a common cause; once it is removed, both reappear without one giving the impetus to the other. Usually, however, distribution of affection over a group or to private and intimate relationships seems more alternative than cumulative: the bond that unites group members loosens and weakens other positive ties in proportion to its strength and stringency. One would almost think that the total amount of love we have is limited. If a great deal is expended on our group, there is not much left for nonmembers or individual relationships. Surely this is too simple a view. Yet it is a view which fits much group behavior through history though we know too little to do more than suggest tentative hypotheses.

CHAPTER IX

Rivalry, Competition, and Conflict

Though the objectives of the groups to which he is loyal be compatible, various allegiances may struggle within a person for the lion's share of his attention and time, and for primacy in controlling his behavior and outlook. Man, as a multiple group member, on occasion finds himself pulled and pushed by rival and incompatible demands—for instance, from his family, his business associates, or his lodge. Each may wish to pre-empt a particular evening. But groups are not in *conflict* or *competition* when they contend sporadically for devotion within a multiple member's mind, or for his time. A relationship among groups can amount to conflict or competition only when membership in one group is conceived to exclude simultaneous membership in the other. Each person has only one nationality and religion, and can be a fan of only one baseball team in a given league. Persons who regard an accepted basis for rivalry among groups as wrong, for instance, internationalists or interreligionists, only appear to be exceptions. They usually found a group of their own which competes with all national or religious groups, and also with rival international or interreligious groups. The same groups are not regarded as mutually exclusive and competitive by everyone, but some groups are always so regarded.

Group membership can be cumulative or alternative then, depending on subjective conceptions of the goals pursued and of the means required, as well as on objective characteristics of the goals, and, finally, on how intensively they are pursued. A man's family membership, or his personal relations may, but need not, involve a conflict with his membership in a larger group such as the nation. But occasionally there is a clash as described in Verdi's tragic opera *Aïda*, or in Bizet's *Carmen*. (The scene in *Carmen* in which the conflict becomes acute is extensively interpreted in Thomas Mann's *Magic Mountain*.) Only when groups are conceived of as alternative more than occasionally can we speak of competition. Jesus, forming his group of followers, said: "He who loveth mother and father more than me is not worthy of me. . . ."And in his insistence on priority he has been imitated by many group leaders. Such insistence may cause conflicts among groups with overt goals which need not be mutually exclusive, and which otherwise "compete" only occasionally.

There are various types of competition and these shade over into various types of conflict: *competition* and *conflict* each refer to whole classes of relationships. The word "competition," like its analogues in foreign languages, derives from the Latin for racing. It is not used here in the technical economic sense (which assumes absence of differentiation), but in the psychological sense of felt rivalry (which assumes at least putative differentiation).

INDIRECT COMPETITION

When individuals or groups compete in a race, attainment of the goal by any one competitor need not hinder or delay attainment by the others. Actually we race against time, not against each other; no runner can shorten his time by lengthening that of another. This is *indirect competition:* competition is indirect when people striving for the same goal, and achieving it *independently*, nevertheless rank and measure their standing relative to each other by using the goal as a common standard. We find indirect competition also when a teacher grades according to a fixed standard; one's achievement of a top grade does not reduce anyone else's but we rank each other according to grades, and may engage in a psychological rivalry (competitiveness) for them. Similarly, businessmen, or farmers, may compete in relation to an objective—income maximization—without reducing each other's chances or interfering with each other. The time re- quired to reach the goal in the race, the percentage or quality of correct answers, the income achieved by each businessman— all serve as standards for ranking. Though in his achievement each competitor is independent of the others, he vies with them for the highest ranking.

The actions of our rivals have no bearing on our achievement. Yet we feel as though we are running a race against them, and not against the objective. Possibly this is so because the psycho- logical importance of our achievement lies largely in demonstrat- ing our superiority, in running faster or doing better than others, rather than in simply running fast or doing well.

We engage almost constantly in indirect competition. It is a powerful motive for achievement. Its useful effects were recog- nized by Hesiod who in his *Works and Days* (a gloomy and poetic Greek almanac written probably about 700 B.C.) wrote: "A man grows eager to work when he considers his neighbor, a rich man who hastens to plough and plant and put his house in good order; and neighbor vies with neighbor as he hurries after wealth. . . ." The disadvantageous possibilities also were recog- nized early. The objective goal may be lost sight of in the struggle for superiority, which may then be carried on by means which damage some or all competitors (or even noncompetitors) and de- lay, rather than hasten, attainment of the goal. Neighboring com- munities, instead of vying for the greatest harvest by growing "eager to work," may try to destroy or plunder each other's crops. Further, the enjoyment of accomplishment itself may give way entirely to enjoyment of the competitive struggle or of superiority. An overly contentious and invidious spirit may be fostered. Excessive cultivation of competitive attitudes may bear fruit also in a resentful and invidious egalitarianism. Unrest, and even revolutions, may come about not so much because people fare badly, but because they feel they are doing less well than they should, than others with whom they compare themselves. Spontaneous creation and enjoyment, too, become hard when appreciation of the creative act, and of what it creates, inde- pendent of the effect it has on one's ranking, becomes rare.

DIRECT COMPETITION

These disadvantageous potentialities are brought nearer in *direct competition*. Direct competition is illustrated by games like baseball or football. Each team tries not only to maximize its own score, but also to hold to a minimum the score of the opposing team. Each team attempts to reduce the achievement of the other by directly interfering with it. There is only a relative standard of achievement, and no objective, independent one, such as time in a race, or total crop harvested. The extent of the defeat of one team is the measure of the achievement, the victory, of the other team. This is true also of boxing, or chess matches. Achievement consists mainly in defeating the opponent—more than in attaining a goal in itself worthwhile.

However, a theoretical standard of excellence independent of the antagonists' performance can be constructed. The points may be scored more or less elegantly. Mastery of a subject may be displayed indirectly by the manner in which victory is won. The performance of a player, the number of hits or points, may also be scored independently of the outcome of particular games or fights. Yet direct competitors fight in the first place against each other rather than against time or any third thing. They do not so much master the object, and rank themselves accordingly, as they master each other.

To the extent to which businessmen compete not only for more sales but also for a greater share of total sales, they come near direct competition. One's *share* can be increased only by decreasing someone else's. Yet, if the total expands indefinitely, all may still gain in absolute terms. The loser may lose only by not gaining as much as the winner whose share increased. There is no need to hold him back directly. It is enough to advance faster. Direct competition may be approached in attitude and purposive focus, but not in fact. However, to increase their share, businessmen may also try to hold back others. In this case direct competition occurs, even though the sales total could be expanded. Sometimes businessmen have the choice of gaining by expansion of the market or gaining within a limited market. They choose whichever they think is easier—direct or indirect competition. In America, businessmen have usually preferred to stress expansion of the market. In Europe, the pre-capitalist tradition of regarding the market as limited, and stressing direct competition, has been stronger. At present, this tradition is strongest—both in Europe and in America—among the sellers of labor represented by unions. Of course, when total sales actually cannot be expanded, one's gain necessarily involves the other's absolute loss. If anyone tries to increase his sales, he must engage in direct competition. He must not only exceed but push back others. He can gain only at their expense.

The struggle for shares of a fixed total, when one can increase one's share only by reducing that of others, may still be defined as direct competition if two characteristics are present: first, the total can be, and is, shared rather than monopolized by any contender; second, the rivals hold the not unrealistic expectation that the shares may be redistributed through continued or renewed contention, and regard this as legitimate. For instance, struggles about the division of the proceeds of their economic efforts among workers, owners, and managers, or even about the rules of their cooperation, are competitive as long as none of the parties deprives the others of *all* the proceeds, or of any voice in the pursuit of the common task, and as long as any given outcome of the struggle remains open to revision by renewed struggle.

What newspapers call conflicts between labor and employers and between various sectors of the economy (farmers versus consumers, tenants versus landlords) are here defined as *direct competition* even though the feelings involved and sometimes the actions are rather violent. For, as long as these doings take place within a capitalistic system, they involve a continued contention about shares of income, rather than total deprivation of any party and an end to the struggle. However, since these struggles do not result in a ranking of the participants—except inasmuch as struggle as a process always involves it—they lie in part outside our classification altogether.

Probably the most frequent form of competition is that illustrated by a football game. The competitors can increase their standing both by advancing themselves and by holding back others. In many cases there also is a third possibility of increasing one's gain by actually wresting from others what they have, rather than just holding them back. Situations where one can gain *only* by holding back others or only by taking from them, and situations where one can gain only by advancing oneself, where one's objective gain is entirely independent of that of others, are probably less frequent.

The stability of institutions and the attainment of social goals, such as higher production, depend greatly on the way groups compete. Frequently all three possibilities—advancing oneself, hindering others, or taking from them—are open. If we are conscious of competition, we tend to conceive of it as besting others, no matter whether by outdoing them or by holding or by pushing them back. The motivation of rivalry—the wish to achieve superiority—remains largely the same whatever form the competition takes. But the effect is very different.

It may be advantageous that our motivations and feelings do not differ very much whichever the form of competition, even though the effects of the behavior involved vary greatly. The strong motivations of rivalry may be used for extremely useful emulation; then, in Hesiod's words, "a good neighbor is a precious possession." Clearly, indirect competition is usually in the social interest, while direct competition is in the social interest only as a lesser evil compared to conflict. However, the near identity of motivation also makes it possible for indirect competition to become direct. People readily concentrate on hindering rivals, on destroying or taking from them whatever might endanger their own superiority. It is clear that the basic motivations from which the various forms of competition spring require careful cultivation to foster the right kind of growth, and to weed out the injurious kind. Otherwise society cannot hope to harvest much. The psychological usefulness of competitive games lies both in cultivating and in absorbing some of our competitive spirit, channeling the need for superiority feeling into harmless outlets, and, above all, in training us to pursue our aims according to rules that limit the harm we do to each other.

CONFLICT

Direct competition becomes *conflict* when the victory of either party would be total: when the opposing party would be deprived of any share of what is at stake and when the victory would end the struggle. In short, *conflict* occurs when no arrangement to continue the struggle (competition) can be made or when the victorious party is able and willing to utilize its victory to forestall any legitimate future competition. Conflict is likely when no compromise on the object of desire is possible, or believed possible. The object of contention cannot or will not be shared; nor is there agreement on continued or renewed contest in the future. Through conflict, then, at least one of the parties attempts to avoid future competition. Conflict thus leads to unity by annihilation or subordination of one party. Competition in contrast achieves unity by limitation of both parties and continuation of the limited contention. Of course, a struggle may be transformed from conflict into competition by means of compromise, just as competition may become conflict when the rules are violated.

Unlike competition, conflict seldom directly furthers the creation of anything valued. Conflict diverts energies from creation to possession. Beyond that, conflict often leads to destruction. Competition, too, occasionally leads to destruction and nonproductive use of energies. But conflict, as a process, cannot have any other direct effect. Of course, the result—possession of the object by one of the parties—may lead to more or less productive use; and conflicts may have indirect beneficial repercussions. Finally, the avoidance of conflict—continuation of unresolved problems, or disadvantageous compromise—could be worse than the conflict.

It is a major problem of any society to further (indirect) competition of the type illustrated by a race; to find outlets, such as harmless games, for the (direct) competition illustrated by a football match; and to minimize conflicts, partly by replacing them with competition, possibly indirect, but if necessary direct. The more successfully society minimizes conflict, even though replacing it with competition, the greater is its stability. For competition, by definition, takes place with a set of rules limiting the destructive activities of contestants. Competition is based on the acceptance of the institutions of society. Conflicts, in contrast, cannot always be controlled by a system of social rules. Moreover, such rules at most limit the damage.

Yet no society avoids all conflicts. There seem to be two ways of reducing conflict. People may be conditioned to limited aspirations which do not clash with each other. (Competition may be reduced, too, in this manner, and the society is likely to stagnate.) The second possibility is to replace conflict with competition. Conflict gives way to competition most readily when the quantity of the object of desire can be increased, when none of its units is regarded as unique, and when it can be easily transferred among persons and groups. Typically, but not exclusively, these are the characteristics of the objects of the activity we call "economic." The invention of commerce, the discovery that one might get what he coveted without robbing by giving the owner something in exchange, was probably a great impetus to social cohesion. Through competition commerce made it possible to unite groups that would otherwise be rent by conflict. To exchange means to compromise, to give as well as to get, to resign one's childish desire and belief in one's unconditional right of taking. This renunciation, essential to association, is by no means easy. Apart from introspection, crime, and the not uncommon feeling that fighting and robbing are nobler than exchanging and compromising, attest how much this renunciation goes against the grain. It is perhaps for this reason that economists have always encountered psychological resistance to the idea that "profit" is available to both seller and buyer in the same transaction. Many people suspect that business involves mutual exploitation, robbing, taking advantage of somebody. Whole social movements are based on this misapprehension.

Conflict is harder to avoid when the quantity of the desired object is regarded as fixed, as it always is when the object is regarded as unique, and when it cannot be divided or shared. Finally, when transfer from one person to the other is difficult, or when possession makes likely important and irreversible changes contrary to the interests of nonpossessors, conflict is likely.

Money is perhaps the best means to make competition ubiqui-
tous and reduce conflict. Through money it is possible to share
and to compete indefinitely for almost any object. People are
able to purchase rather than to fight for what gratifies them. The
greater the possibility of exchange, the greater the possibility of
competition and the less the need of conflict over anything.
However, much depends on how things are regarded. The ability
to earn money and the range of things that can be purchased for
it—whether this range includes prestige and power, for instance
—depend chiefly on custom, our second nature so often confused with the first.

OVERSOCIALIZATION

Frequently conflicts can be minimized and replaced by competition only at a cost. Objects of desire must be made available
for sharing directly, or by alternation of exclusive possession
over time. Duration or exclusiveness of possession thus no longer
can be secure or unlimited. If objects are to be shared and
transferred, the intensity of attachment to them must be mod-
erated. They must be regarded to begin with as fairly exchangeable and replaceable. When this becomes true for too many
objectives, the outcome may be a society with little conflict,
with moderate desires—and with a flat and empty style of living.
In such a society, no one would dare to want anything (even
himself) entirely for himself or to regard anything (even himself) as unique. Everyone would want to be an exchangeable,
acceptable, common man by stressing what he has in common
with everyone else. Everything would be psychologically social-
ized and made accessible to everyone—even if it had to be
cheapened. Since everything is available for a price, nothing
is thought worth risking all and perhaps dying for. And since
nothing is of transcending importance, there remains little to
live for. Yet even though they may reject any other end, life
untranscended, life as an end in itself seems to bore people
into desperate or silly actions. Competition, rather than any
of its apparent objects, may become the universal passion in
which all share. Finally, out of sheer boredom and in the hope
of experiencing the thrill that might relieve it, people will

climb mountains, or sit on flagpoles, or kill each other.

Possibly in an oversocialized group where everything is marketable, and nothing has value which is not marketable—where market value, i.e., the value to others, is the overridingly felt value—social stability is purchased at the cost of personal instability and rootlessness. For rootedness is a personal rather than impersonal (market) relationship to things and people, a relationship that cannot be transferred, that itself grows cumulatively and cannot be manufactured. When market values prevail, grandeur, nobility, passion, any end transcending comfort and success fall by the wayside. Paradoxically this may be conducive to *anomy*—essentially an indifference to rules, because of indifference to their purpose, and finally to any purpose.

Indeed, the nature of our desires and gratifications may be be affected and the frustration of thwarted desires replaced by the futility of feeling no desires to be thwarted. For no desperation is deeper than that of aimlessness which leaves us destitute even of desire. In turn, this desperation may lead to social instability, finally to a violent desire for an inhibiting and directing authority which, if it does not fulfill desires, at least makes us feel them.

As mentioned, conflict may be avoided in the opposite way, by assigning to each one a fixed place in the social structure, by conditioning his desires, and directing them mainly to objects which do not permit competitive ranking of achievement. Slavery, or a caste organization such as that of Brahman India, is a way of reducing both competition and conflict within society. The cost seems to be stagnation and the condemnation of part of humanity to utter degradation. Certainly, whatever excuse there may have been in the past, modern industry does make it possible to avoid such extreme measures. But does industry condemn us to the extreme competitive solution we have adumbrated?

If we want some equality of opportunity, and do not wish to train ourselves to stifle all our desires beyond creature comforts, or, which is almost the same, if we do not regard all objects of desire as subject to sharing, conflict cannot be wholly avoided. Once a desire for full possession is felt, and its object is thought to be unique and indivisible, conflict is almost unavoidable. Two men who wish to marry the same woman are in conflict. No compromise is possible. Whether objects, including men and women, are conceived of as unique, and whether intense desires are felt, depends in part on social institutions and the sentiments they cultivate. (Certainly the institution of divorce has replaced much conflict with competition. But by making the market once more available to the married pair, and returning them to it, divorce also changes the nature of the marital relation.) But much depends also on the nature of the object desired. One may have exclusive possession of a garden, or share it, or alternate possession. But whether ancient trees are left in the garden or cut down is not a decision that can be alternated or shared. Hence, if one party desires the trees, and the other does not, conflict is unavoidable.

Conflicts about matters that do not seem vital to those concerned, and conflicts that, however vital, concern only relatively few usually can be solved under rules for decision voluntarily accepted or imposed on the parties. This is what happens when two men wish to marry the same woman. For individuals and small groups, the law decides conflicts with minimal damage to society. But when the conflict vitally concerns significant segments of society, it is not easily litigated and decided in accordance with orderly rules. The losing group may not accept an unfavorable decision. It will attack the rules of decision. Thus the conflict soon becomes a conflict about how conflicts are to be decided—a conflict about the system of rules rather than within it. At this point the social order itself—at least large parts of it—is at stake.

COOPERATION

Competition requires cooperation in setting and following the rules between the groups playing together. The competitors agree in limiting their hostility and the means by which it is expressed. Competition is a way of making association possible by channeling hostility. In competition as illustrated by games, all parties voluntarily accept the same rules to set goals, to limit the means permitted to achieve them, and to rank competitors. It is by playing under common rules that competing teams oppose each other. The teams often interpret the rules differently. But though grumbling, they will submit to the decision of the umpire or court whose authority is one rule accepted to make the game possible.

When "cooperation" is contrasted with "competition," it is to stress the positive mutual help involved. Such help is part of intragroup relations; indeed in the competition of teams cooperation within each team is indispensable for victory. But intragroup cooperation within a firm, a team, a neighborhood is fostered by intergroup competition or conflict. It is not as though we might choose in general between competition and cooperation. They live and die together. We can choose at most where, when, and with whom to engage in which. Indeed, in intergroup relations, cooperation occurs mainly when otherwise distinct groups feel as one in the face of a third group. Wartime coalitions are an instance.

CONFLICT WITHIN AND ABOUT A SYSTEM: DEMOCRACY

If a society is to hold together, all its groups must accept rules limiting the means and ends of competition among them. When societal rules are regarded as important and not self-enforcing, they are usually formulated as laws. People are constrained to conform, and punished if they don't, by governmental organizations which take the place of umpires. Group rules may be inconsistent with societal rules: for instance, those accepted by thieves, or gangs of wayward juveniles. Hence a person in observing the (informal) rules of his (deviant) group may break the law. The motivation and personality of this type of law violator differ from those of the deviant individual who does *not* observe a group rule in violating the law.

Societal rules often provide for replacing conflict with competition. Many types of legal litigation are instances, as are elections, and the regulations governing collective bargaining or strikes. In contrast, the rules for marriage and divorce control conflict. They regulate the means that can legitimately be used in conflict and limit the ends which the winner may attain. Conflict can be controlled by societal rules if only a small part of society is involved, or if neither antagonist can expect to win by resorting to outlawed means, or, if the antagonists do not feel that the issues at stake warrant an all-out effort.

Democracy illustrates the possibility of transforming, by means of societal rules, into relatively peaceful competition what otherwise might be a rending conflict: the struggle for political power. For what is democracy, if not a system of rules regulating competition for governmental power, and sometimes conflicts over particular uses thereof? Trial and error replace trial by terror, and ballots do for bullets. Political power is shared by democratic rules, or at least renewed competition for it is required at intervals. To the defeated, hope of future legitimate victory is always held out. Hence they accept as legitimate the system of rules under which they were (temporarily) rebuffed. The victors may resist the temptation to frustrate such a hope illegally, since their victory shows their ability to win without violating the rules. And the risks of violating the rules are great if there is a tradition of continuous peaceful competition for power.

However, the democratic rules are not likely to be accepted when a major group feels that it has no chance for victory within a period not exceeding its patience; or when a beaten party feels that the victors needlessly use their power to decide, irreversibly, issues of vital importance. Under these circumstances, competition within the rules will be replaced by conflict over the rules themselves. Though the rules may still give their initial form to the conflict, they now function only as does the music which drowns out the cries of a man being murdered. It will not be the music that stays the murderer's hand.

Society can control conflicts about its rules to decide conflicts and regulate competition only if the party opposed to the rules is too weak (and not concentrated territorially) to challenge them illegally. Otherwise a struggle about the rules may take place. Victory will go to whichever group proves stronger extra-legally, whether defending the law or attacking it. The victorious party then will impose new rules arranged to prevent its future defeat.

In the United States only small marginal groups oppose the rules of competition for political power. Major groups accept them. They feel identified with the parties which have a chance to win by competing under these rules. Losing competitors accept defeat gracefully, since the government exercises only a moderate power in a democracy. And others may stand aside from the competition altogether.

The knowledge that the outcome of the political competition does not necessarily affect one's life greatly, that one may safely be unconcerned, may well be one of the greatest advantages of a democratic system over one in which the government exercises such power over its subjects that they cannot be indifferent to politics.

In the United States there is agreement not only on the rules for achieving power but also on the policies that power holders sponsored by either major party may pursue in terms of ends and means. Differences, apart from personnel, are matters of emphasis. The major groups are reasonably united also on the basic principles which regulate economic activity. In contrast, in England the Labor party, one of two major parties, intends to change basic economic rules. But it does not wish to change the rules of political competition, believing that it can win under these rules and use the power it wins gradually to change the economic rules.

Things are rather different in most of the democratic countrie of the Continent, particularly in France and Italy, where the followers of Communist parties are a major segment of the population. These parties attract their following by advocating changes in the system of social and economic rules. They claim that they want to share wealth and power alleged to be "monopolized."

But the followers of Communist doctrine are convinced that either they cannot win under the rules of democracy or that the political power they could legitimately gain under these rules would not enable them to change the social and economic rules as they desire, just because of the limitations imposed by the rules of democracy on the power of any government. No doubt this conviction is related to the fact that in French and Italian societies cultural class differences for many centuries have been very great and, in contrast to England, there are few institutions and traditions exercising a cohesive influence.

The Communist parties then merely use the democratic rules of competition to attract and organize followers so as to strike down the rules and replace them by their own dictatorship. They participate in competition only in preparation for the conflict in which they hope to win a victory to end competition and to replace it by their monopoly. Whether they want this monopoly of power for its own sake or, as their followers believe, only to undertake the economic changes felt to be required is a moot point. Possibly they convince themselves almost as well as they convince their adherents.

Needless to say, the game is not easily played when a major team does not accept the rules but merely uses them to obstruct the playing for a purpose inconsistent with the rules which the others observe. And the question arises whether those who repudiate the rules should be allowed to play. Competition is possible only when the competitors follow the rules of the game; they will not, unless each is convinced that the others will, too. A football team will obey the umpire if the opposing team does. However, if a defeated team must expect to be completely "liquidated," it cannot be expected to play within the rules of competition. You do not play games nicely, according to the rules, when you know that the opponent wants to kill you and is ready to violate the rules as soon as it is to his advantage. The spirit of these rules has already been broken by the prospect of "liquidation"; competition can continue only when matters are of less than vital importance to the competitors. Otherwise conflict replaces competition.

Competition is best set in motion when there are no issues that appear vital to those involved. Continued competition then tends to reduce the importance of the objects that might give rise to conflict in the minds of those involved. Thus, democracy works best when the voters are not divided by disagreements which they regard as vital, when they do not regard affairs of state as overly important. Once it is working, democracy can help to reduce the importance of issues enough to make them amenable to decision through the competitive process—in this case, through competition for votes. Thus the competition for votes can do in the political arena what the competition for money does in the economic area—replace conflict and violence by peaceful ways of transferring power and possessions.

CHAPTER X
Leadership, Authority, and Power

The importance of members within a group necessarily varies with the importance of their functions and with the scarcity of the talent needed to carry them out. Besides, in achieving their own aims and in making and carrying out group decisions, not all group members prove equally able and influential. The most important group members become leaders. They hold under their sway groups of greater or lesser size and lead strongly or weakly in general or in specific activities. The greater their influence on the over-all policies of the group, the more important the leaders.

Leaders have authority: the ability to control the behavior and thoughts of others without either persuading them rationally or compelling them physically to carry out orders. By contrast, wherever it is argument that persuades, or physical force, or the direct threat of physical force (or of other direct reprisal), authority has not sufficed or it has not been used. Pure authority often suffices to form or supersede the individual views of those subjected to it. And pure authority can take the place of individual decisions. Views are accepted or orders carried out merely because of faith in authority.

The subordinates of a military officer unquestioningly carry out his orders because of his authority. Since the military group must be created artificially and subordination is not voluntary,

145

stern training is required to establish authority. Thus training must accustom soldiers to accept unquestioningly the authority of officers—however inept they may be personally—merely because of the rank which endows them with it; and to carry out unquestioningly orders that may seem unreasonable, merely because they come from officers. Strong military authority is functionally indispensable, for the orders soldiers must carry out in battle are unlikely to be persuasive and an army that would have to argue or to force its soldiers to obey would have little energy to spare for the enemy.

Similarly, a nurse carries out the physician's orders and other employees the manager's. Father Divine's followers accept his views, the followers of Stalin followed his, and, if advertisers are right, whiskey drinkers follow the views of men of distinction.

In most groups, however, the authority of the leader is limited and exercised largely through his ability to persuade followers, unless the discipline of a common group task imposes clearly assigned functions and lines of authority. The element of authority resides in the greater readiness of followers to be persuaded by communications of a leader. The same communications coming from someone else would be less convincing. By contrast, a person is not influenced by authority if he comes to decisions and views independently, regardless of those of the leaders, and if he appraises an argument exclusively in terms of its intrinsic merit, regardless of the source—provided also that he disregards any appeal to authority within the argument.

Society (and any social task) requires authority for the sake of order—economy of operation. Individually we often subject ourselves to authority for the sake of psychological economy. And we always follow authority in matters which we do not care to question because we feel they do not concern us much. Culture is cumulative. The heritage of beliefs accumulated by other persons through history is accepted because of the authority of its bearers. We might want to question some element of this heritage, some custom or belief. Culture need not be frozen. We can arrive at independent views and decisions on what we feel to be a problem or a question. But we must accept most of our beliefs on authority, chiefly the collective authority of society rather than that of an individual leader. In effect, we say: "This is what others do, or believe, and I do not care to question it." Even scholars, specialists in independent investigation, must accept a great part of their data, beliefs, and methods on the authority of other scholars. *Ars longa vita brevis*—the things to learn are many, and life is short.

We would be left without references in which to frame tentative answers if we did not rely on authority. To ask, "When does water boil—or, does it really boil at a temperature of 212° F. when the air pressure is 14.7 pounds?" makes sense only if we accept on authority the theories on which temperature and air-pressure measurement are based. We can later question in turn what we accepted before. But we must then provisionally accept what we questioned before. We could never come up with fruitful and testable answers if we did not question one thing at a time so as to use knowledge for the time being un-questioned—the knowledge accepted on authority—to help find and formulate the answer.

Even so, we may question some, but must accept most knowledge on authority; otherwise we would have to start as if no one had investigated the world before us. And we would not go much further than the predecessors whose steps we would be retracing. We would forego much of the very advantage that led the human race, more than any other, to master its environment: the ability to store, accumulate, and transmit knowledge from person to person and generation to generation by means of oral and written language. In the words of the twelfth century Saint Bernard of Chartres: "We are as dwarfs mounted on the shoulders of giants so that we can see more and further than they . . . because we are raised and borne aloft . . . [by our ancestors]."

The transmission of knowledge through education must be based on authority first, much as education may aim to foster independent inquiry in the end. To be able to form his own views with competence, the student must first accept facts, interpretations, methods, and conclusions on the authority of his instructor. Only in this framework can he raise fruitful questions and perhaps independently reject or change some part of our total knowledge. Some teachers, vague in their own minds, perhaps also fearful of seeming "authoritarian" and of quelling the healthy independence of their students, understress the role of authority while overstressing that of independence. But the learning process can lead to true independence only through provisional recognition of authority and ultimate discrimination between warranted and unwarranted authority. Unbounded doubt is not a fruitful method, but rather a sign of personality disorder and muddleheadedness. If we do not want to drown, we can rebuild only plank by plank the vessel on which we are traveling. Since the tendency to doubt seems as prominent in most young people as the tendency to accept authority, much of the educational task consists in limiting and disciplining both without extinguishing either.

The authority which influences our views in the learning process is likely to grow from our respect for the specialized training that the person bearing it has undergone, as well as from our confidence in his ability and inclination to make use of this training in our interest. Similarly, the authority of a physician over his patients rests in the first place on the authority of those who trained and certified him. This authority is then strengthened (or weakened) by the patients' faith in the physician's personal ability and disposition to utilize his skill to their advantage.

The authority of the physician over his patients gets them to take the prescribed medicines without independently investigating. His authority over the nurse differs from his authority over his patients because it is part of their official relationship, rather than the authoritative element in the physician's personal ability to persuade patients who do not submit *ex officio*.

AUTHORITY AND LEADERSHIP

Authority may be acquired either by winning an office vested with it or by establishing personal leadership. A man may lead the faithful because of the saintly qualities attributed to him. The leadership of an influential man—a Gandhi, or a Girolamo Savonarola, and, for that matter, of a Hitler, or a Father Divine—is first informally recognized by his followers. If he assumes an office, it is because of the personal authority he already has.

Some personal leaders even create an office to transfer their personal authority to, and bequeath it to succeeding incumbents. Usually, however, by adding official to personal authority, leaders reinforce both. Like Gandhi, a personal leader may shun office; but personal authority so great that an office can add nothing to it is rare.

Personal authority is called "leadership" by sociologists who define (official) authority as legitimate power of office (status) independent of personal qualities and skills. "Authority" thus defined requires obedience and subordination and rests on power derived from institutionalized consent, whereas "leadership" is defined as influence depending on personal qualities and skills resting on spontaneous consent and causing submission. In this definition, "authority" becomes a social characteristic of group organization and "leadership" a psychological relation between leader and followers regardless of formal organization. These definitions have the merit of stressing the independence of "authority" from persons—the freezing of a personal role into an impersonal social status or office. This bureaucratization characterizes social organization. However, these definitions separate organization entirely from the persons involved in it— they obscure the relationship between the social and the psychological, and make it harder to see how leadership is transformed into authority, and why authority, though exacting obedience, usually also acquires influence and achieves consent beyond its jurisdiction.

ACQUISITION AND SCOPE OF AUTHORITY

Authority comes from the office to the incumbent more often than vice versa. A bishop usually acquires authority only when named to the office clothed with it. He exercises authority, but it is not attached to his person. Without the office he might not have any authority or be able to acquire it. He wins office because he is formally named by other officeholders who, by the authority of their offices, invest him with episcopal authority— if they find him qualified according to the rules and customs limiting their discretion. By similar procedures, physicians are licensed, officers commissioned or promoted, judges named. The

qualities that win office must fit specific rules as well as appeal
to the nominating officeholders. Leadership, in contrast, does not
depend on rules or appeal to specific officeholders. It is a
spontaneous social relationship, arising from psychological rather
than organizational relations.

The qualifications demanded for office vary. If the required
competence is specific and measurable, proficiency can be
established. Examinations are required for physicians, seniority
or examinations for civil servants. Where the skills needed are
not so tangible, access to office cannot depend on formal certification of skill. The office may be vested once and for all in the
firstborn male of the dynastic family. He becomes king regardless of personal qualities. Or, as long as the required skills are
unspecific, the citizens may have the power to judge the qualifications of candidates for office. A governor or prime minister wins
official authority by winning elections—often by displaying his
leadership. In turn, his office gives him authority to name other
officials. Finally, a legal power to dismiss subordinates who are
insubordinate endows employers with authority. Most authority
combines personal and official elements. Episcopal authority,
officially the same regardless of the bishop's person, nevertheless
varies with personal authority. And the United States has
known "strong" as well as "weak" presidents. (Richard E. Neu-
stadt's *Presidential Power* ably describes how the authority of
the presidential office becomes effective through the personal
leadership of the incumbent. The status [office] casts the man
into the rôle. What he makes of it depends largely on his own
ability.)

The scope of official authority can be specified, usually by
laws and the authority of other offices, just as the avenues of
access to office can be specified. But the ways in which the
office itself was clothed with authority are manifold. The functional need for the official authority of physicians and captains
is quite clear, though the vicissitudes through which the office
acquired authority, and its extent, have varied in different
cultures. Functional needs are a necessary but not a sufficient
element in the history of the authority of the offices of President, Justice of the Supreme Court, Sultan, or Pope. The
authority would not have remained attached to the office if it

had not served a function in the group's organization. But other distributions of official authority might have done as well. The degree of concentration of authority in particular offices, the division of jurisdictions, the total scope of official authority in the regulation of social activities, cannot be understood without paying heed to the history of the culture which generated them. Official authority grows up in continuous traditions. It is often justified by derivation from ancient and unquestioned authority. The official authority of the monarch was frequently derived from divine authority, as is the official authority of the priest. The authorities are held responsible for whatever happens, regardless of their actual ability to control events. Thus the emperor of China was officially responsible for the weather; and the fate of an American President may unofficially depend on it, via the harvest. We do expect authority to control or propitiate cosmic forces, as children expect fathers to be omnipotent.

Unlike the avenues that lead to office, the qualities that lead to personal leadership are difficult to specify. Some persons have the gift, the grace, the Orphic charm which attracts others to follow them. Sociologists use the Greek word *charisma* for the gift of personal authority; anthropologists prefer the term *mana*, which refers to the same thing among contemporary primitive tribes in the Pacific.

This gift cannot be reduced to intelligence and training, though it can be supported by both. It was not intelligence, knowledge, or training that made Hitler, or Father Divine, or the Mormon Joseph Smith undisputed leader among his followers. What melodies were piped at Hamelin? Were they sweet or were they shrill? We only know that, to the ears attuned to them, they were seductive. But the personalities of the pied pipers and the situations in which they worked their charm are too diverse to be reduced to a formula. The source of the appeal, and the reason for the response of some people at all times, and of nearly all at some times, are not clear. We do not know beforehand who will be entranced by what music when, or who will produce it.

The degree to which anybody is disposed to submit to personal authority seems to depend on how innate propensities are shaped by early experience in the family. But external situations and cultural traditions contribute. The relationships involved are still too obscure to permit even a fruitful classification. At most we can restrict the range of possibilities a little. For instance, it is doubtful whether austere personalities such as Gandhi or George Washington would acquire, in present-day America, the personal authority which they had in their time and place. Further, in groups with a long tradition of subordination to official authority, and with few discontinuities or violent redistributions, the chances for extensive use of personal leadership are usually small in the body social—except by way of, and within the limits of office.

But even predictions as modest as these must be highly qualified. Most types of leaders and followers are available in some degree in most populations most of the time. What brings whom to the fore in what situation? and how much authority will he have? (Note the influence different types of popular singers acquire with their teen-age followings.) We can only say vaguely that any weakening of official authority—from within through disunity, corruption, or dissatisfaction of the governed; or from an external cause, such as a lost or shakily won war; or from a depression—opens the possibility of replacement first by personal and then, sometimes, by renewed and redistributed official authority. (Senator McCarthy in the U.S.—though more feared than powerful—and Charles de Gaulle in France illustrate these possibilities.) Once official authority is weakened, people become more responsive to personal leadership. The most responsive ones come to the fore. And people who have personal authority use it outside the official hierarchy, mainly in politics. In times of great stress they may advocate radical innovations—freeing the slaves or enslaving the free—and take society on a course that makes it depend on their navigational skills.

The official authority of a bishop is specified, its source and scope are determinate, its use and occurrence predictable. But the personal authority of a St. Francis is unspecific. Neither its occurrence nor its use can be predicted. (Since every creator of the future is also a creature of the past, prediction—the establishment of precise relationships between past and future—is possible in principle. But the elements involved and their relationships may be too many, the possible combinations too manifold, recurrence too rare, the chances for observation too few to allow actual predictions.) Again, the origin of the official authority of the husband is clear; he is invested with it by a formal marriage, and its scope is determinate. But the personal authority of a lover varies in each case and neither the qualities that led to its acquisition nor its beginning and end are easily definable. The fact that romance, too, is often standardized—though the duties and rights of lovers are not usually codified as stringently as those of marriage—bears witness to man's need for order and to the rarity of true personal authority.

That there be authority matters more than how it is exercised. The vesting of offices rather than persons with authority makes sure that the group is led continuously in a reasonably integrated way. When the office of captain is endowed with ready-made authority, the struggle through which the dominant personality on the ship would set the course is avoided. Navigation becomes less dependent on the mercurial elements of personal leadership. Moreover, a man who owes his authority to his office will carry out its mandate and recognize the authorities above him, unlike the personal leader who will follow his inspiration. Since the authority of every office is limited and controlled by that of other offices, there is some protection against abuse. An additional advantage is that access to office can be made to depend on training and demonstration of objective competence. Personal authority need not be related to any objective skill or ability. Medical quacks, for instance, often combine great personal authority, great "human relations skill," with minimal competence.

Because the origin and effects of personal authority are so unpredictable, successful organization of a permanent secondary group requires rather strict subordination to official authority, or else the group is soon divided into splinters led in different directions by different personal leaders. The very function of official authority is to call forth standard impersonal responses to its orders: to be obeyed regardless of the personalities of the superior and his subordinates. The authority of his office is respected by loyal subjects of even a knavish and incompetent king; and the absolution given by an unworthy priest is considered valid by the faithful as long as his official authority has not been revoked. The authority of the official depends on and is limited and regulated by the office rather than by his person. Thus according to rules accepted beforehand, it can be kept and handed from one person to the other, become nearly independent of the competence of the incumbent, and continue nearly unchanged after his demise or misbehavior. However, the transference of authority from person to office is usually a slow and uneasy process. For instance, the Donatists—so called after their leader, Bishop Donatus of Carthage (c. 400 A.D.)— insisted that sacraments tended by unworthy priests were invalid, and the church had some trouble ridding itself of this impractical notion.

If they are united in one person, personal and official authority reinforce each other. But if they are borne by different persons, they may be used against each other. Clearly, if the authority of husband (official) and of lover (personal) belong to different persons with regard to the same woman, discord is likely. Discord between the hierarchy of offices vested with authority and the personal authority of the saint has been rampant in the history of all churches. New sects or parties are usually led by men of personal authority when they can neither be quashed nor reconciled by grant of office.

Yet personal authority is by no means inherently antisocial. It is clearly indispensable in the *formation* of groups in the process of organization—which end by dispensing with it—and in important transformations. The leadership of Joseph Smith was as indispensable to the formation of the Mormon group as that of Brigham Young to its migration. But now the authority that Mormon leaders hold by virtue of their *office* suffices to continue the group. Indeed, groups could not continue without routinized official authority transmitted by rules accepted independently of personality. Strong personal leadership easily becomes disruptive once the group is formed, though without strong personal leaders the group might not have come into existence or be preserved through calamities. The initial success of many organized groups, as well as their ultimate failure, may be explained in these terms. Numerous religious and utopian colonies in the United States were successful while held together

by the personality of their leaders. Without offices bearing
their authority, the colonies disappeared with the demise of the
leaders. On the other hand, surviving groups usually had created
a continuous authority of office. Such an authority may take
various forms. In at least one case—that of the Jews—the un-
contested authority of the sacred scriptures in bindingly specifying rules of behavior and of ritual preserved the group as such.
Group cohesion was helped further by strong external pressures.
Usually, a more concrete and personal embodiment of authority
is needed.

Secondary groups that have persisted usually have found
ways of absorbing into office persons gifted with personal
authority. Otherwise these persons contest official authority too
frequently. Yet the very gifts that make for personal leadership
also hinder promotion to office because of bureaucratic rules
tailored to bureaucratic personalities. Moreover, the officeholders
who apply the rules are apt to be fearful, perhaps jealous, of
"born leaders." Absorption of gifted persons is helped when
there are many types of official authority and many avenues to
it. Political parties or groups within a state, monastic orders
within a church, or new business firms within an economy
illustrate this possibility. The chances of those with gifts for
leadership are multiplied, making it less necessary for them to be
in conflict with the existing pattern of distribution of authority,
and easier to compete with it.

Authority, whether personal or official, whether that of Joan
of Arc or of the Dauphin, later Charles VII, is always a social
relationship. (Nothing illustrates the contrast between official
authority and personal leadership in both church and state—
as well as the unpredictable appearance of personal leaders—more
incisively than the life and death of the Maid of Orleans.) Even
though the bearer of personal authority holds no formal office,
he holds his authority by social consent, as does the bearer of
official authority. The saint can equal or even defy the authority
of the bishop because his personal qualities lend him no less
authority in a Christian society than the office gives the bishop.
Among heathens he may be slaughtered, and among nonreligious
people treated as a sick person. The lover holds authority over
the beloved inasmuch as he corresponds to her ideas of love,

which have a largely social origin. All authority requires respect for the person or the office; respect necessarily grows from social traditions, from experiences, and from accordance with social ideals; and it is always bounded by the communication of these social elements. Authority can go further only by organizing and commanding power.

AUTHORITY AND POWER

Authority is a type of communication which may command power and use it to reinforce itself. Power, in general, is the ability to achieve intended effects. In social relations, power is the ability to use force to reduce the independence of other persons—to impose one's wishes on them.

Power may be possessed without authority. And it is as often a cause as it is an effect of authority. A man may be able to curtail the independence of others by physically compelling them to do his bidding. If his power becomes known, he will acquire some authority. Hence a small boy may bully his way into authority through his ability to punish members of his group. A man in a bar may do the same. But if he has to resort to physical force each time he gives an order, he has not acquired authority through his power. Authority is a recognized (legitimate) right to be obeyed, and a legitimate right to command power against those who refuse to recognize it. Unless it is widely and voluntarily obeyed, authority is not effective, and power replaces or reestablishes it.

Most power in organized society comes from authority rather than the reverse. But there are many combinations. A policeman has the authority of the law. He is authorized to use force to exact obedience. But he will resort to force only against those who do not respond to his authority. A criminal, on the other hand, may hold power, but rarely authority. Noncriminals obey him only because of his power: his use of force or his threat of immediate forceful reprisal. There is no consent, and no legitimacy.

Though authority may be generated by power, though it may increase power and be increased by it, authority seldom springs from power alone. The office or person wielding it must be respected, loved, and feared, and felt to hold and wield authority legitimately, if it is to last beyond transient situations.

To authority we transfer the feelings and relationships which characterized our earliest social experience, within our families. To persist, any authority must be considered just, justified, and powerful, like parental authority. It must be feared and loved by its subjects who must feel loved and cared for by it, and be convinced that the hardships and restrictions imposed are ultimately necessary. The vigor and wisdom of official authority in its commissions and omissions are of surpassing importance for the freedom and the security of the members of any society. But, unlike power, official authority is effective only when accepted as legitimate. Only when it is felt to be exercised rightly and by rights does authority bind men's consciences.

In the long run, the acceptance of authority as legitimate depends on the philosophical convictions of society. The image that man forms of himself and of the good society ultimately determines how society is ordered and how authority is exercised and distributed. The feeling of legitimacy is immeasurably strengthened when authority is believed limited by and derived from a superior authority not subject to human weakness. In the words of Shakespeare's king in *Hamlet:*

> *In the corrupted currents of this world*
> *Offence's gilded hand may shove by justice,*
> *And oft 'tis seen the wicked prize itself*
> *Buys out the law; but 'tis not so above;*
> *There is no shuffling, there the action lies*
> *In his true nature. . . .*

SOME CAUSES AND EFFECTS OF AUTHORITY AND POWER

By guile, propaganda, and organizational means, a leader may go far in acquiring and retaining power. But to be a leader he must have influence first over at least as many people as are needed to enforce his power on the rest. Leadership thus must precede power, which can only extend it. In the long run, his minions will remain loyal to the leader only if they are relatively well treated, and if they feel that his actions are necessary. They must feel that his authority is legitimate and justified by higher ends.

It is hard to imagine a leader convincing his followers of the ultimate justice of his cause without convincing himself. But the conviction of justice in the leader and his followers need not be well founded or shared by others. It is easier, then, for cunning and self-righteously inspired madmen than for intelligent but self-conscious scoundrels to become leaders. Unfortunately, men too honest and reasonable to convince themselves of the justice and feasibility of visionary social reforms also have a hard time competing with madmen.

Yet dangerous as visionary leaders are, at times they are needed. Authority and power could probably not be organized initially without the ruthlessness which a "mission" inspires. On the' other hand, the visionary leader always endangers an existing social order, an existing distribution of authority. He comes to the fore when "the time is out of joint"; but he may cause it to remain or become more so.

The effects of power on those holding it are often described in Lord Acton's phrase: "Power tends to corrupt, and absolute power corrupts absolutely." Despite its air of profundity, this is only a variant of Jean Jacques Rousseau's naïve presumption: vicious social institutions corrupt our originally good nature. The reverse—good institutions are corrupted by our wickedness (or weakness)—is at least as true. To assume that power corrupts those who wield it is like assuming that a tiger freed from his cage is corrupted by his power to eat people. Surely the newly won power gives him the possibility, not the appetite. Most of us, like the caged tiger, do not lack the appetite but the power to satisfy it.

To avoid frustration, we more often learn to restrain than to renounce this appetite. Power mostly causes us to reveal and to satisfy appetites which we seldom display, even to ourselves, as long as we are hemmed in by the power of others. Power must be distinguished, of course, from lust for power which, like any intense craving, can corrode personalities. Also, it is possible that unrestrained satisfaction may develop the power holder's appetites. In this sense, power may help in corrupting him.

The actual problem is not that power corrupts, but that it attracts most, if not exclusively, those persons who have least renounced their antisocial impulses. They need power to satisfy themselves at the expense of others. Yet power is best not entrusted to those who crave it so much; though, of course, they seldom reveal their motive or, indeed, are aware of it. Usually they are convinced that they need power only to benefit others. Sometimes the mere holding of power satisfies them enough so that they do just that.

Beyond tangible rational functions, leadership has psychological ones. Colin G. Butler (in *The World of the Honeybee*) has described how queen bees exude a substance—the "queen substance"—which appears essential for the cohesion of the bee colony. This is also one of the functions of leadership in human groups. To be sure, no organic substance is exuded by our leaders. But human society generally is distinguished from insect societies because it replaces by cultural institutions many of the patterns inborn in insects. Yet human groups need leaders just as insect groups do, even though human authorities, powers, and functions are socially created, transmitted, and destroyed, rather than designated by nature and transmitted biologically. Our system of leadership—the degree of authority of our leaders and their activities, as well as those of each of us—depends on our culture and individuality, varying widely within the broad range nature gives us. Instinct determines the behavior of insects far more inflexibly and narrowly than tradition and custom limit our behavior.

Just as the solidarity of an insect society is maintained through a "queen substance" through which members of a bee colony identify with each other and differentiate themselves from other colonies, so human groups keep their identity and solidarity through common allegiance to images, aspirations, beliefs, and symbols. Of these, the leaders are custodians and sometimes embodiments. It is their function to manipulate these group symbols so as to make the group follow and the members cooperate. Such symbols may take a material form: the scepter, the orb, the crown, the seal of state, the mace, the standard have been among the symbols of the institutes of the political community in Western society.

Abstract ideas, or ideologies, and myths also may serve. People may rally behind such ideals as "democracy," "communism," or "master race." In the past, political symbols were more often derived from religious ones. (Religious as well as political symbols may be embodied in persons, for instance, monarchs.)

To function, a permanent secondary group must not only divide and assign tasks, it must also cultivate psychological ties among the members performing them. Symbols are needed, and leaders, through which group members identify with each other. Emotions alone can be stirred into passions to motivate the sacrifices that mold individuals into a society. These sacrifices are not always mutual. Rational hopes of reciprocity are not enough to create the solidarity of a group. Unrequited services dedicated to the divinities or to the ideals of society are needed. To be charitable to the poor, to give one's life for country or cause, to do one's duty when it is disagreeable and un-rewarded, to forego crimes that would pay—these actions can be buttressed by argument, but motivated only by passion and devotion beyond reason. Ultimately, love for an ideal underlying the social bond is required. The ideal must be felt as sacred to inspire sacri-fice (from the Latin *sacer* and *facere*: to do that which is holy) to him who holds it so. In the Christian con-ception of society, for instance, men are brothers inasmuch as they believe themselves all children of God the Father. They are admonished to love each other for the sake of Christ's universal love and sacrifice and also because they all love Christ.

Modern societies seem to function without explicitly sacra-mental bonds, and often nearly without outstanding leaders and revered permanent symbols through which the group members are tied to each other. And while the symbols and even the leaders of most past societies represented ideals transcending the lives of their members, we find that in modern societies they frequently embody the common patterns and the common man of the society they lead.

When this has happened in the past—for instance, during the decline of the Roman Empire—it has indicated decadence, vul-garization, and ultimately loss of cohesion. When the masses, rather than insisting on leaders superior to the led, wished the leaders to identify with them by demonstrating that they were possessed of no superiority whatever, they lost leadership and direction altogether. The historic parallel does invite reflection on contemporary society. But too many elements differ to permit drawing direct inferences from the past.

Possibly new psychological bonds have grown to replace or supplement traditional ones. As Freud point out in *Civilization and Its Discontents*, "the state of civilization in America offers a good opportunity for studying" what happens "when the social forces of cohesion consist predominately of identifications of individuals in the group with one another," and not shared love for something beyond them. The cohesion of American society, indeed, rests largely on direct mutual identification. We feel equal and identify only with equals. Possibly this is enough. Perhaps this pervasive egalitarianism has its positive aspects, too. But it presages a transformation of culture.

CHAPTER XI   *Culture, Passion,*
and Affectations

A society includes all the people who share a common culture. However, parts of the culture may be diffused beyond the society; and not all its members share all its culture. They are members by sharing essentials. "Culture" includes everything in the environment which is not in the form originally given it by nature: control and transformation of the environment is a cumulative cultural activity learned by each generation. "Culture" further includes all the acquired traits which the members of a society share, but none of the inborn ones. It includes institutions, language, ideas, ideals, emotional and behavioral patterns, and the abiding expectations we place on each other to associate, communicate, cooperate, and compete. Many of these we inherit, but only by learning them individually: our cultural heritage is not innate, though we may think so because we are usually unaware of the informal processes through which we learn to master it.

The society circumscribed by its culture should not be confused with political units such as states or countries. A society may include fewer or more members than are organized in its political institutions. Political institutions may assemble parts of several nations under one roof as Switzerland does. (Nations are subsocieties.) Indeed, few countries comprise all the territory settled by a society or even a nation. Some political institutions,

162

on the other hand, such as the British Empire, comprise the main territories of a number of societies which retain their own cultures.

Each society has a distinctive culture. Variations, which amount to subcultures if they modify a great deal of behavior, distinguish the subgroups which compose large societies. The relationship is like that between a language and dialects. Regional subgroups speak dialects; occupational, age, and other subgroups and social "sets" develop their own "lingo"—modifications of the language and additions to it usually indicative of the sub-group's attitudes. Language is used sometimes spontaneously, sometimes willfully to circumscribe subgroups. Thus, linguistic peculiarities often suggest regional origin, occupation, education, and social class. And children, as well as people who feel the need to belong to a distinct group, may deliberately invent linguistic peculiarities intelligible only to insiders, thereby distinguishing themselves from outsiders ("squares" or "cornballs").

Large societies differ in stability or in fluidity of relationships and patterns. The relationship of groups to each other, their composition, size, and their subcultures may be stable. Or, the relationship and size of groups may change rapidly; members may move frequently from one group to the other. Such mobility shortens the continuity of identifiable subcultures.

THE SCOPE OF CULTURE: ITS INFLUENCE ON INDIVIDUALS

Grammar tempts all and seduces some of us to "reify" culture: to treat it as a thing. Actually "culture" is the name for man-made things, and for what is learned and therefore social, in human conduct. "Culture" merely refers to these aspects of things and conduct and has no existence separate from them. When we say "culture does such and such," it is only a short way of saying "people do such and such because influenced by a group of others and by the customs of the past."

People are always part of a society and therefore always share a distinctive culture. Two related aspects can be distinguished in every culture. Each society selects different materials from the natural environment to create in its own way a man-made environment which provides shelter, food, clothing, ritual objects, weapons, and many other implements. This utilization of the natural environment always depends on the second aspect of culture which we carry within us: the patterns of thought, ambition, and behavior which we acquire from our social past. American territory now is used differently from the way it was used by the Indians before us. Our European tradition and training led to a very different culture, though our innate impulses are not basically different from those of the Indians.

Of man's inborn capacities, each culture picks different ones to stunt or develop. Each culture modifies, channels, elaborates, restricts, and trains them in its own way, though control of aggressive impulses sufficient to enable society to continue must be part of all social training. Each subculture further stresses, elaborates, or restricts some human abilities. Language illustrates how each culture selects and discards from the gamut of possibilities. The whole human race speaks with the same kind of mouth, yet there is an almost infinite variety of tongues. How different are the frequency, the meaning, and the patterns of sounds which English and Chinese cultures cause the same physical apparatus to produce! Yet language is only one form of communication, and communication only one of the many acquired habits in which cultural differences appear.

Each culture narrows the wide range of action and feeling allowed by human nature and the natural environment, to establish an approved smaller range of patterns. The range of some cultures is narrow with rigid boundaries and sharply defined focus; there is a confluence of major preferences and disdain for deviations. In other cultures, the range of choice is wide, the boundaries are flexible and perhaps easily changed, and preferences are distributed over the whole range. Cultures differ further by centering on different segments of the range of human potentialities. In each case, however, the range selected from nature is believed to be the range granted or willed by nature. Thus each culture somewhat narrows down the choice of sexual relationships and stresses a few of them. One culture may foster and approve homosexual impulses while another repudiates them; in both cultures people feel that nature sanctions and dictates what is actually their (cumulative and unconscious) choice.

For individuals, the cultural limitation of the range of selection comes about in two ways: first, culture guides the social influences on the formation of individual preferences and personalities. These influences, transmitted and modified through the family and other primary groups, affect the individual starting at birth. Later, culture continues to guide through social approval or disapproval of the preferences they have developed. Behavior that is out of bounds incurs penalties such as conspicuousness, contempt, ostracism, or even legal punishment. Approved behavior is rewarded by success, popularity, power, or other advancements, as the case may be. Since approved behavior includes a whole range of patterns capable of nearly infinite variation, and since the patterns we develop individually are not by any means always sure of approval beforehand, there is scope for risk and innovation. How much scope depends on the culture, and within each culture, on the field of activity and the subgroup to which one belongs.

Society does not tell Americans to dislike blubber or other Eskimo delicacies, but our tastes are so formed that Eskimo food appeals to us no more than Chinese music. Chinese ears and Eskimo taste buds do not differ from ours; but those cultures do. Again, no formal rule compels a stockbroker to wear trousers rather than leotards. And no law prevents him from doing his hair in pigtails. But a male who wears what his society considers to be badly chosen for the occasion, or fit only for women, soon learns that he must move within the range bounded by his culture. That range may vary with sex, age, social station, and occasion. In a culture that stresses difference between the sexes, the range of approved behavior will be quite different for each sex. In another culture, differences among social stations or age groups may be stressed more. A third culture might minimize all differences, and confront most people with the same range of choices on most occasions.

In every human activity, culturally produced boundaries and ideals limit and direct individual choice, without eliminating it altogether. People do business, amuse themselves, create art, associate, perform rituals, and appraise conduct and things according to their preferences—within these bounds. Moral and aesthetic judgments are culturally conditioned—at least influenced, at most determined, by the paths that others have trod—just as is our taste in clothing. However, "conditioned" does not imply a deliberate, purposeful influence but describes the impact on the individual mind of what surrounds it, whether actively directed at it or not. Even speculation about the cosmos and human destiny, religious and philosophical thought and feeling are culturally bounded and focused.

Culture also directs our perceptions. It sharpens our sensitivity in some ways and dulls it in others. Whether people strike us as black and white, or pre-eminently as men and women, or as rich and poor depends on the socially influenced focus of our attention. Culture strongly affects how we evaluate what we see. Whether we find Gothic cathedrals ugly, as they were thought to be in the eighteenth century, or admirable as today (the very word "Gothic"—in the style of the Goths—was applied by the humanists of the Renaissance as a term of disapproval to the medieval art which struck their classical sense as barbarous); whether our respect for a person depends on age, color, sex, wealth, education, entertainment ability, physical strength, or individual character; whether the ideal woman is slender or, as in former times, full-bodied—all this is influenced by socially formed aesthetic, moral, and erotic ideals. Just compare the women painted by Rubens, Botticelli, and Matisse. We easily distinguish Chinese from Italian, and Renaissance from medieval painting, just because each is informed by different cultural ideals and painted in a style developed as part of a specific culture. The style and the ideal are related. Both are cumulatively developed through many individual contributions of different magnitude.

Social ideals may even influence the actual human physique, not only by encouraging us to paint our lips, or to extend them, or to deform our heads, but also by preferential selective breeding (not to be confused with planned selective breeding). Thus the Chinese, Burmese, and others for centuries have preferred to mate with and hence to breed flat-chested women—a preference we never shared long enough to breed flat-chestedness (*Deo gratias*). Culturally formed ideals go a long way to explain the prevalence of different physical types among various ethnic groups.

The conduct of others, learned and reproduced by us since childhood, also helps determine the expression or repression of such feelings as respect or contempt, hate or love. It suggests the form in which they are expressed (if at all), the occasion, the intensity, and the objects to which they may be attached. Notice, for instance, how emotional and sensual the heroes of Homer are compared to modern conceptions of heroism. (Rival ideals of heroism came to the fore as Greek society developed. Plato disapproved of the Homeric behavior.) Culture even influences the range and depth of feelings which we experience individually. Our self-perception is influenced by the way others see us: even for ourselves we often act the roles into which society has cast us. Last but not least, culture includes the division of labor, the prevailing techniques of production, and the distribution and valuation of products; finally, the production, distribution, and use of political power. If the natural order makes work and human associations necessary, the social order—part of culture—determines how they are organized.

Culture dogs our steps from the cradle to the grave. Our personality greatly depends on the way we are cradled, fondled, nourished, taught control over our bowels, disciplined, and indulged as infants. In all this, our parents follow the patterns of the culture to which they belong. Later, what we learn comes from the social store distributed by education. Throughout life, custom continues to whisper and sometimes to shout cues to us suggesting how to behave. Finally, custom helps to mourn and bury us with proper ceremony, even telling the bereaved how to mark the grave.

Yet culture should not be conceived of as a strait jacket. Its patterns are only one element affecting individual fate. Though society limits the ability of individuals to choose, and stresses some decisions as more desirable than others, it does not deprive us of choice altogether. It could not be otherwise, for culture is seldom transmitted in a uniform and unchanged way, nor does it consist of a homogeneous mass. The cake of custom scarcely resembles a pudding. It consists of different materials loosely arranged in many patterns. Each of us is

lodged throughout his life in many groups which circumscribe
and color his view. But no two individuals have exactly the
same pattern of group affiliations. Their affiliations locate individuals like a system of co-ordinates; the groups intersect in
individuals. Each defines himself by reference to the groups of
which he is a member and by reference to the groups which
are within his purview. And thus each individual is differently
located and uniquely defined within his culture.

HOW WE BECOME AWARE OF CULTURAL PATTERNS

History cumulates customs, ideas, and institutions into a network, culture, which molded individual attitudes before we
were born and continues after we die. Like a sieve, culture strains
our perceptions of internal and external stimuli. It suggests
and channels reactions: "Notice this!" "Ignore that!" "Imitate
this action!" "Shun that other!" "Act on this!" "Discard that
impulse!" "This road is dangerous!" "That way to respectability!" Mostly these signals are so deeply internalized in each
of us that we do not feel controlled and directed by them. On
the contrary, they enter our awareness as an inner ambition or
block, or as a "natural" expectation. Culture, after all, not only
directs and controls the expression of our personalities, but from
the very beginning takes a hand in shaping them.

We become aware of the directional and "stop" and "go"
signals of culture mainly when they are inconsistent, or when
they are in conflict with very strong congenital impulses which
cannot be satisfied without overriding a signal. Discord arises also
when we are unprepared for a change of signals. Such a change
may occur owing to developments within the culture or through
contact between cultures. When we transfer from one group
to another, as frequently happens in fluid cultures, friction
and disorientation may also result. We become aware then of
culture as the external source of directions and limitations. For
we find ourselves confronted no longer with one "natural" set
of customs but with several alternative ones.

Conflicts themselves may be internalized if early conditioning
was inconsistent, perhaps because it came from persons who had

not themselves sufficiently resolved their conflicts, or because it came from different persons with incompatible views and attitudes, or simply from too great a variety of environments. We might then grow up torn by incompatible desires and inconsistent signals which seem to come from within (unlike inconsistent cultural patterns). Even under the best conditions, conflicts between the demands of any culture and some of our impulses are unavoidable, as Freud pointed out. Nor does a socially acceptable and individually bearable resolution always depend only on conditioning. However they arise, conflicts always enhance awareness of cultural boundaries; they permit us or compel us to see our life as a problem. Hence they are also productive of people who throw these boundaries into relief and change them— artists, philosophers, and sometimes scholars.

No one experiences his culture in the same way anyone else does. Each of us acquires and develops his ways from his own models among his family, his friends, the books he reads, the things he sees. And each individual pattern is a new synthesis of old ones. Culture gives us many materials, but we each build according to our own design, a design influenced by tradition but also by our originality. Culture does not provide patterns for all circumstances. At most, there is a cue for the more usual circumstances and often more than one, at that. In creating their future, men do more than reproduce the past which produced them. They learn from the experiences accumulated by past generations and weave old strands into new patterns. Else the changes, which make history so fascinating, could not be explained. Of course the new patterns need not be better than the old ones. (The need to guard against such an implication arises in a society as keen on change as ours, which often makes the very word "new" connote "better.")

CAN WE ASSESS CULTURES?

Different cultures offer different ranges of choice and sometimes incompatible aesthetic and moral ideals. This, however, entitles us neither to the "sophisticated" view that one culture is as good as the other—held by some "relativists"—nor to the naïve "ethnocentric" theory which justifies the superiority of our own culture. There is no objective intercultural criterion by which to judge that one culture is as good as, or better than another. Judgments on the relative value of a culture must rest on subjective preferences. There is nothing wrong with this. Without ultimately subjective value judgments, life would be valueness in every sense.

To say that something is relative, far from making it subjective, merely is to say that comparison is involved. Objective measurement is always comparison—always "relative." "The distance between New York and Boston is greater than that between New York and Philadelphia" is a relative statement, as is any measurement. The difficulty with value statements is not that they are relative; it is that they cannot be tested in the same way most "relative" statements within the sciences can be. One can investigate which values are held, how they are arrived at, how consistent they are, and what their social and psychological function is. But one cannot prove objectively whether they are "right" or "true" or even "good."

The general judgment "all cultures are equally good" is motivated by an attempt to escape making subjective value judgments. But the attempt does not succeed, to say that one thing is equal to another requires judging its value as much as to say that one thing is superior to another. We lack objective criteria for either judgment. As a subjective preference, to say that all cultures are equally valuable bespeaks as little sensitivity as to say that all music is equally good. Of course, one may abstain from judgment. But to abstain from judgment is very different from making the judgment that things are equal.

Finally, one may judge cultural patterns by their usefulness in helping society to survive. Survival value might be established objectively—but not the value of survival: survival cannot itself be shown to be objectively preferable to other values. For instance, moral worth, or beauty, however defined, are unlikely always to coincide with survival. Yet they might be preferred as criteria for judging the value of a culture.

THE ETHOS OF CULTURE AND THE HUMAN PREDICAMENT

The essence of culture—its *ethos* (Greek for "character")—is more elusive than its various patterns. The characteristics are so much more readily measured and described objectively than the character of a society that one is tempted to neglect the latter. But a culture, like a person, is more than the sum of its parts: it includes norms and values which meaningfully relate patterns into a living, uniquely structured whole. "Culture" comes from the Latin *cultus:* ritual cult of the ethos, affirmation of the bonds of society which invest with value one's pursuits and thereby one's life. Culture originally centered around the cult of the spirit who was thought to *inspire* (literally, to breathe life into) society and its members from the outside. The ethos of culture was articulated as religion. Religion was the bond which bound together the members of society by common sacrifice and by worship of the power on which they felt dependent. ("Religion" derives from *re-ligare:* to bind strongly.) However elusive, the ethos of a culture is its very *raison d'être*—though it is less like a *raison* (reason) than like a feeling which breathes life into the culture, giving it purpose and moral unity and motivating its bearers. The Latin word *anima* (soul) could well be used for *ethos:* it animates the culture originating before and continuing after the individual life span. That much is also believed about the individual soul.

Anima (unlike *animus*) is feeling rather than conscious thought. (The Roman grammarian Nonius said: *"Animus est quo sapimus, anima qua vivimus."*—*"Animus* is what we know, *anima* what we live.") Widespread critical scrutiny of the ethos, the soul of culture, its basic spring of action, is not without danger. It reduces awe and, as critical dissection nearly always does, weakens the emotional power and binding force of what is felt. If familiarity does not "breed contempt" (the saying comes to us from the ancients, was current through the Middle Ages, and was given an American twist by Mark Twain: "Familiarity breeds contempt—and children.") it "doth diminish reverent fear," as Sir Philip Sidney said. The spontaneous vigor of the ethos is lessened when it is eyed with scientific coldness rather than felt with spontaneous faith. The *anima* may disappear, vanish as Eurydice vanished from Orpheus's look. For we look behind us when we are no longer quite sure. And our doubt helps produce what it fears as it did in the myth: Orpheus, whose song could melt stones, was allowed to rescue his dead wife, Eurydice, from Hades, the nether world of memory and of desire, provided that he would not turn around to make sure that she followed him on his return to earth; he was unable to resist, and on turning around he caught but a glimpse of her vanishing.

Yet, though it be man's undoing, the desire for intellectual scrutiny is as much part of his condition as the need to suspend it for more ardent vision. In the opinion of his fellow Athenians, Socrates went dangerously far in indulging this desire. According to Plato, he defended it (in his *Apology*) by saying that the unexamined life is not worth living. Nonetheless, to paraphrase Hegel: the owl of Minerva takes flight only when dusk is falling —and people often think it causes the shadows to fall. William Butler Yeats wrote in "Meru":

> Civilisation is hooped together, brought
> Under a rule, under the semblance of peace
> By manifold illusion; but man's life is thought,
> And he, despite his terror, cannot cease
> Ravening through century after century,
> Ravening, raging, and uprooting that he may come
> Into the desolation of reality:

And he commented in a letter: "Science is the criticism of Myths . . . and when the criticism is finished there is not even a drift of ashes on the pyre. Sexual desire dies because every touch consumes the myth, and yet a myth that cannot be so consumed becomes a spectre. . . . We free ourselves from obsession that we may be nothing. The last kiss is given to the void."

As Yeats intimates, the life of individuals and groups must be lived in the tension between aspiration and fulfillment, between myth and its consummation through knowledge, achievement, and expression. Sex has furnished the paradigm for the conflict between passion and knowledge (myth and criticism, in Yeats's words; the poet uses myth to refer not to deception, but to what is unproved, though felt to be true) since biblical times. In sex, enchantment and disenchantment are most acutely and, above all, most universally felt. There vision and knowledge most directly can destroy, or sustain each other. Love and marriage, and many other social utilizations of the sexual impulse, aptly symbolize the contribution culture can make to the conflict, and to its resolution.

Cultures, like individuals, must deal with all the elements of the conflict and must balance them; they must allow passions to be instilled as well as sated. The intellect must be used to guide them, to shelter the flame, and to control it so that it warms men's hearts without consuming them—though passion may consume some hearts to warm others. Cold reason must not be allowed to smother the burning fires. David Hume went too far, however, in saying: "The intellect is, and ought to be, the slave of the passions." Desire no doubt must motivate us. But the intellect does more than find means to carry out desire. It moderates, controls, and guides the fulfillment, consummation, sublimation, renunciation, displacement, or suppression of desire, and partakes in molding it. Only in pathological cases is the intellect permanently a "slave of passions" (or vice versa).

Intellectual exploration is itself a desire. Men want to feel and also to be intellectually aware of their experiences. The human task is to integrate these basic wants—not to extinguish one and leave the other unchecked. Each must help and guide the other without stifling or enslaving it.

MAN'S FALL: FROM JOHN MILTON TO SIGMUND FREUD

Man's plight underlies the cultures of all societies, however differently they deal with it. The human condition is outlined in the biblical tale of Genesis, some variation of which is told in most cultures: you have elected to leave behind innocence; you have eaten "of the tree of knowledge of good and evil"; you must now discipline and control your appetites, select some, discard or transform others at the risk of dampening them through intellectual control. To live in society, and yet to be oneself; to live in the moment and yet continuously; to feel and to think so that one deepens the other, yet does not replace it; in short, to be human, is to carry this burden. None of us is spared learning to bear it as he grows from childhood into manhood, unless he is spared maturation.

The craving to eat from the tree which makes us wise is in all of us. We spend our life longing for, and digesting, as well as cursing its fruits. Theologians have long interpreted Adam's *felix culpa*, his "fortunate fall," as a metaphor of human nature and culture—and of human tragedy. John Milton imagines Adam as saying:

> *Full of doubt I stand*
> *Whether I should repent men now of sin*
> *By me done or occasioned, or rejoice*
> *Much more that much more good thereof shall spring—*

Milton's view is not far from that of Yeats or Freud. The wide acceptance of what is apparently a misunderstanding of Isaiah 14:12 (also Luke 10:18) which led to the appellation of Satan, the prince of darkness, as "Lucifer" (bringer of light) suggests the ambivalence with which knowledge has been regarded through the ages.

Among the fruits from the fateful tree, according to the biblical account, were consciousness and death. They are intimately related. Without consciousness, nothing is known to die; and actually nothing much disappears. At bottom, to die means to lose the distinctive experience one has of oneself experiencing—consciousness. Only the individual structure of which one is conscious disappears from the world. It "returns unto dust." The dust, the materials from which we are built, remains. Nothing falls out of the cosmos. The structure of the particles, their relationship—form—changes; one's experience of it is lost in death, at least in the sense in which science can prove and grasp experience.

Incidentally, to insist that the individual need not vanish from the consciousness of others, that he survives in their memory and enriches the culture is, at most, to prove that others and that the culture survive, not that he does. For to live is to experience, not to be experienced. When the Roman poet Horace said *"non omnis moriar"* ("I shall not wholly die"), he took what from the pre-Christian viewpoint could only be poetic license: others, not he, make his poetry their own and live by it. Perhaps the notion of an eternal soul originated with the contemplation of the continuity, the survival of culture. (The French sociologist Emile Durkheim thought so.) To lead it back to this origin, however, is to deny and not—as some "humanists" believe—to affirm individual survival.

Ultimately cultures, too, die—the distinctive character, the ethos of a society, its style, disappear into the mists of the past. Though an aggregate of people survive, their institutions, their relationships, their world are so transformed that the society as an entity identified by its culture is lost, remembered, at most, as part of the tapestry of history by other societies, which have rewoven the strands into new designs.

In *Essays on the Depopulation of Melanesia*, W. H. R. Rivers many years ago pointed out that, when the British destroyed the ethos of the culture of that Pacific archipelago—when they imposed British cultural norms and prohibited head-hunting— Melanesian culture was left destitute of its organizing principle, of the passion that had clothed with meaning the daily activities of the natives. Head-hunting had given, or had symbolized, a social and individual ambition to the Melanesians, from which sprang the values of life and ultimately the value of life itself, as well as the cohesion of their society. Depopulation followed the destruction of the ethos of the culture. Melanesians died out because of a sense of futility and boredom. They had nothing to live for. The ethos of a culture can be quite literally that which makes life worth living. The Bible is entirely realistic in asserting "Man doth not live by bread only," (Deuteronomy 8:3) and in predicting "Man shall not live by bread alone," (Matthew 4:4).

Americans need not go all the way to Melanesia for an instance of disastrous social disorganization resulting from a destruction of native ethos: we have the American Indians. (A word of caution is in order, though. Professor Harry Shapiro found that the population of the Marquesas declined after conquest from nearly 100,000 to 16,000, owing not to lack of interest in propagation but to spontaneous abortions—an effect of venereal diseases introduced by the conquerors. As soon as clinics started to cure these diseases, repopulation also started. Though

there is no doubt that destruction of the ethos leads to destruction of native culture, depopulation, at least in this rather similar
case, was due to more direct causes.)

The reader might consider this quandary: were the English
right in abolishing a native practice because it was abhorred in
England? Even if more people die because of the prohibition of
headhunting than were killed by it? The answers, of course, depend on one's philosophical views. Facts—here, depopulation—
can be relevant, though not alone decisive, for such answers.

The ethos of Melanesian culture is easily identified since it is
universally shared within that culture; many Melanesian activities and institutions depend directly on the central achievement
in which it was embodied. According to Rivers:

> The actual head-hunting expedition only lasted a few weeks,
> and the actual fighting often only a few hours, but this was
> only the culminating point of a process lasting over years. It
> was the rule that new canoes should be made for an expedition
> to obtain heads, and the manufacture of these meant work of an
> interesting kind lasting certainly for many months, probably
> for years. The process of canoe-building was accompanied
> throughout by rites and feasts which not only excited the live-
> liest interest but also acted as stimuli to various activities of
> horticulture and pig-breeding. As the date fixed for the expedi-
> tion approached, other rites and feasts were held, and these were
> still more frequent and on a large scale after the return of a
> successful expedition.

The Melanesian ethos was destroyed abruptly from the outside.
Perhaps this is why social disorganization was so total and led to
actual depopulation. The operation meant to transform the patient
caused his death from shock. Other societies have been able to
adapt themselves to the cultural norms of conquerors, enough, at
least, to survive as aggregates. Not infrequently the cultures of
conquered and conquerors were fused. History is replete with
instances, from Roman, Islamic, and Turkish conquests down to
our day. But deep changes imposed suddenly can lead to collapse
of the social fabric beyond renewal.

We can cultivate the ethos of a culture or hinder or even destroy it, but we cannot create it. It grows spontaneously or not

at all. We can manufacture it no more than we can a flower or a human being.

The ethos not only sets the course of society, it infuses motivation into individuals as well. Its values are poured into us with (though not in) our mother's milk. Later on, the ideals of the culture, its heroes and counterheroes, its signposts, and its roads to success and failure dominate the landscape in which we must find our way.

Individuals are microcosms of culture. Given congenital characteristics, the integration of personalities depends above all on the intensity, the consistency, and the binding power of the ethos in which the culture is steeped, on the harmony and direction it is able to impart to the institutions and norms of society. To relish life and be gratified by it, we must be animated by ideals. We must be lured on by a set of goals which gives us direction, which instills and sustains the aspirations on which civilization rests. We escape a sense of futility and desperate emptiness—the fertile ground in which grow boredom, alcoholism, and even crime and suicide—to the degree to which we feel that our life is part of an intelligible order which gives it purpose.

We can live thoughtlessly only when the struggle for physical existence is very severe. But to have time, and yet to be without confident and high ambitions, is to be unspeakably bored. Aims that carry conviction and confer value on our achievements must be drawn from the ethos of culture. Ultimately only the culture can inspire what individuals can aspire to, what binds together their personalities and links them to society. Once shared purpose disappears, we become alienated from society, from life and, finally, from ourselves. We sink into bottomless boredom. Individual attempts to escape from it lead more often to frenzy than to success.

Without some aspiration, personalities remain inchoate and disintegrate. But they can be organized around manifold aspirations. The ethos may inspire all sorts of values to bear fruit in ideals, passions, and actions. They differ intrinsically, and in the degree to which they involve the personality and organize society; finally, in the quality and centrality of the devotion they inspire. When endorsed by culture, many types of aspiration can organize individuals. In the United States, gathering of money or of popularity has given some meaning to many lives.

AFFECTATIONS AND PASSIONS

Even minor affectations ranging from collecting (stamps or anything else) to gadgeteering, pipe smoking, baseball, keeping one's car shipshape, connoisseurship of this or that, picture snapping, or automobile racing may help individuals to integrate their personalities tolerably well. Indeed, personalities might be organized around a series of affectations as ivy is trained around a trellis. *"Nous ne sommes que ceremonie"* ("we are but ceremonies"), said Montaigne. However, the less universal the ideal, and the more nearly it is reduced to a series of affections, the less its binding and guiding effect.

Affectations are habits which those who have them do not regard as major values; or habits which are not justifiable as ends within any system acceptable to them; above all, convictions and passions one wishes to have, but does not actually feel. The confusion of the wish with its fulfillment leads to affectation. These habits, nevertheless, replace values. Actual values—for example, religious ones—can also become affectations when they are affected habitually rather than felt. Though they differ, these meanings of "affectation" have in common what concerns us here: the absence of felt values and the presence of surrogates. Affectations usually help to hide a lack of affect and affection, or an unsatisfactory displacement. If they do not fill emptiness, they conceal it.

Just as some things cannot be more than affectations, some people cannot have more than affectations. Philosophy, love, or art, all become affectations when they enter a mind incapable of feeling them. There is nothing wrong with affectations. To be bare of them would be like being unclothed. But they cannot replace values and convictions. Alone, affectations can at best distract from the experience of life—they might help to bear but not to face it.

Dedication to transcending matters is more dangerous to society than affectation; it can lead to more intensive conflicts. But such dedication organizes personalities and groups more thoroughly. Affectations, such as devotion to juke boxes, soap operas, or even public housing, are too soon exhausted. Though they might help organize personality, they do not last in serious trials. They divert, but do not give much strength. Without felt and intellectually shored-up conviction, the motive power wanes and so does the morale of society.

Generalized emotion and habitual morality can carry us for a while. But some underlying devotion to things transcending everyday living is necessary if its strivings and its order are to retain meaning and worthwhileness. And greatness requires more. In Gustave Flaubert's words: "Nothing great is ever done without fanaticism . . . the creative impulse is essentially fanatical. . . ." What is done, of course, depends on the gifts one has and the task to which they are dedicated. But without intense dedication, nothing great can ever be done. Without conviction, intense dedication is impossible. And conviction must ultimately rest on cultural ideals, which in turn must draw strength from a transcending ethos.

ETHOS AND PERSONAL CHARACTER

The type of personal integration and adjustment that takes place depends on the kind of ethos that pervades society. Though a society must have a viable culture to survive, it need not be an optimal one. Between impossible and optimal norms and arrangements there are many which, though permitting survival, do not foster the most advantageous organization of society. Analogously, if any animal species survives, it is proof of sufficient but not of optimal adaptation. The demands of culture, for instance, might be unnecessarily hard so as to impair the psychological health of many members of society. Or cultural norms may be inconsistent so that they cannot all be followed, and the attempt to fulfill them disorganizes individual or social life.

The reports of Bronislaw Malinowski, Ruth Benedict, Margaret Mead, and many others indicate that both the type and the amount of maladjustment can be related to the ethos of culture. Malinowski writes in *Sex and Repression in Savage Society:*

> In the Trobriands . . . I could not name a single man or woman who was hysterical or even neurasthenic. Nervous tics, compulsory actions or obsessive ideas were not to be found. . . . During my few months' stay in the [neighboring] Amphletts, [I was] among a community of people distrustful of the new-comer, impatient in work, arrogant in their claims, though easily cowed and extremely nervous when tackled more ener-getically . . . they would either lie in some sort of fear, or else become excited and offended. . . .

Thomas Hobbes, in *Leviathan,* finds "the life of man to be solitary, poor, nasty, brutish and short" in the "state of nature." His image fits some primitive tribes well, and others not at all. However, it is a mistake to believe that savages are bereft of any culture; they may have little government and a "nasty and brut-ish" culture. But groups always have some social control—cul-turally shaped—over their members. This is what makes them groups. The "state of nature" is impossible. The idea is useful, however, to suggest the importance of social order and the ex-tent to which individual life depends on its pervasiveness and type.

Unfavorable social norms not only produce psychological maladjustments. Other irksome or destructive effects might fol-low. For instance, some sectors of society might be mistreated in ways considered normal within the society, which strike out-siders as unjust; or crime, as defined within the culture itself, might be frequent. The natives of the central highlands of New Guinea, for instance, have managed to create a culture. They survive, though without comfort. Tribal warfare is incessant. Although it gets quite cold at night, they do not produce any clothing. They warm their huts and the boats in which they fish the lakes with huge fires. But they take few precautions, and perish when the hut or boat catches fire, which is often. For this they blame evil spirits. And they have more concrete ways of venting their frustration. Women, once bought from their fathers, become the property of their husbands who beat them, or shoot arrows into their legs, or even kill them when they are displeased. Women are also expected to cut off one of their fingers whenever a mistfortune befalls the husband—for example, when a pig dies—and at least one of his wives is killed by the tribe when a man dies. These arrangements are by no means exceptional. Many societies have engaged in slavery, human sacrifices, mistreatment of some of their groups, or impractical arrangements for which evil spirits were blamed.

Although social norms, by definition, are the source of social injustice, they are not the only, or necessarily the decisive, source of character defects, neuroses, psychoses, and other personality disorders, or of crime. Some types of personality disorders and crimes occur only in certain societies and obviously are related to the culture. But unless they affect everyone in a similarly situated group, such disorders must also be related to congenital divergences among individuals and to differences in their individual histories for which the culture is not responsible. Other personal maladjustments hardly vary from society to society, though the expression they find depends on cultural arrangements. Still other maladjustments occur in practically all cultures in quite identical ways, though apparently more often in one than in another. (Statistical information does not suffice for comparison, particularly since definitions are not standardized.) We must conclude that culture is only one factor in crime and personality disorders. Its importance varies, but few maladjustments are wholly dependent or wholly independent of the culture in which they occur.

Even when a culture imposes only necessary burdens, there are individual deviants. Not everyone is able to follow even very lenient norms. A few people can follow none. And some people cannot be happy in one culture, though they might have done well in another. No cultural process is wholly able to avoid production of personality types which do not fit its ethos. Nor can social arrangements forestall all varieties of personal misfortune that might lead to personality disorders or to crimes.

CHAPTER XII

The Conflict between Economic Progress and Social Well-Being

Perşonal behavior is influenced by the kind of ethos that suffuses society, and by its binding force. The particular kind influences the character traits of individuals; its binding force, the cohesion both of the individual and of his society.

But the ethos may change. Its hold on society may be weakened chronically or by transitional processes. Wars and revolutions often weaken the ethos temporarily. Urbanization and industrialization, which we have experienced for one hundred and fifty years, are long-run trends which might loosen social norms permanently. But the end is not yet. Will a new ethos emerge? Will the old one be reestablished? Or will our society disintegrate, its old ethos destroyed and not replaced? We cannot predict the end, but we can observe the process.

ANOMY AND DELINQUENCY

The process of weakening, and the weakness of the ethos which results, are both called "anomy." Literal "anomy" (from the Greek for norm- or rule-lessness) is a limiting case. But partial anomy is not infrequent. Its main symptom is social disorganization. Among its many forms, the frequency of law violations is most easily recorded. Bernhard Lander, in *Towards an*

Understanding of Juvenile Delinquency, relates the spatial and temporal distribution of juvenile delinquency in Baltimore to it. He found no permanent relationship between delinquency rates and national orgin, for whereas "the 1903 Federal Slum Survey found delinquency concentrated primarily in sections populated by the foreign-born in 1940, delinquency was a characteristic of areas inhabited by the native-born." Nor is delinquency caused by the slum conditions so dear to social workers. ". . . The delinquency rate is fundamentally related only to anomie and not to the socio-economic conditions of an area. The delinquency rate in a stable community will be low in spite of bad housing, poverty and propinquity to the city center." (Anyway, it is easier to see that lack of bathrooms should prevent cleanliness than that it should cause crime. And most of the foreign-born slum residents had still fewer bathrooms in their countries of origin—and a lower crime rate.)

No permanent relationship between delinquency rates and ethnic origin was found, either. The Negroes, a native-born group, contributed a large proportion of Baltimore's recorded crime and delinquency; but,

> . . . The Negro delinquency rate increases from 8% in areas in which the Negro population . . . is less than 10% of the total population to . . . 14% in tracts with . . . 30-40.9% Negro population. However, as the Negro population . . . increases beyond 50%, the Negro delinquency rate decreases to 7% in areas with 90% or more Negro population. . . . A similar pattern . . . also characterizes the white group. . . . As the Negro proportion increases to 50%, the delinquency rate increases. As the percentage of Negroes increases beyond 50%, the delinquency rate . . . decreases. Thus, when other factors are held constant, delinquency rates in Baltimore are highest in areas of maximum racial heterogeneity. In areas of total Negro occupancy the delinquency rate is no higher than in similar areas of total white occupancy. . . .

As in Baltimore, the binding force of group norms can be weakened when groups with distinct subcultures enter each other's residential areas. Here anomy results from the contact of the groups, not from developments within each. The relatively high crime rate among immigrant populations might be similarly explained. Through emigration the binding force of the norms of the culture of origin is weakened. Further, these norms are seldom adapted to the new society. At the same time, the immigrants often are not able to understand fully and to follow the norms of their new culture which they did not absorb as children. They are not themselves completely accepted. The second generation, in closer contact with the surrounding society, usually suffers most severely in acculturation (assimilation to a culture different from their own). They find themselves between parental and social values which are inconsistent. Their situation is aggravated by strained relations with their elders, whose values they cannot accept and who cannot accept theirs. Once acculturation is achieved, anomic difficulties may disappear.

Only when they remain isolated from the surrounding culture are immigrant communities immune from anomy. The Amish and some other religious communities illustrate this.

Delinquency also might spring from something more positive than increased contact with foreign groups: new, deviant norms may achieve the cohesion of small groups—gangs—at the expense of the flagging vitality of the larger ones. If the cohesion of these products of the decomposition of the old groups is strong and the enforcement of the over-all societal norms not overly severe, they can become a permanent part of society. Then deviant groups might continue to live in the interstices of the social structure even after it has become stable again. Anomic processes coming from within the group are not necessarily transitional: we cannot be sure of the acceptance of new, or the re-establishment of old norms, as we can when anomy is traceable to immigration.

When it is the effect of a long-run trend, religious and, above all, political movements may rise as reactions to the threat of anomy. This response is perhaps most likely when the whole society undergoes a shock dislocating entrenched classes. (It is less likely when the society is subject to cumulative modifications, as was the case in the United States. Possibly the reaction in this case is withdrawal, or reform, rather than revolution.) It is as though when belief in the received framework of values wanes, people hastily grasp some new conviction to replace their eroded traditions. Frequently the new creeds are felt before they are intellectually elaborated. Therefore, they are vehemently as-

severated against the claims of reason. Reason anyway has little
to do with conviction. People are far more easily persuaded to die
for a dogma than to stir for a conclusion. The ethos springs from
emotion—faith—not reason. And faith, not reason, effectively
controls anomy—though sometimes at the expense of the very
culture it defends.

ANOMY AND PERSONALITY DISINTEGRATION

The French sociologist Emile Durkheim reestablished "anomy"
—a concept which goes back to the ancients—mainly to explain
acts of individual desperation. Durkheim noted that the rate of
suicide increased with prosperity and is lowest in the poorest
countries. He related this to the difference in the strength of
social bonds. In the poorest countries, the Industrial Revolution
had not yet weakened cultural norms. Durkheim's data, later sup-
plemented by his successor Maurice Halbwachs, do not prove
that differences among groups in the frequency of suicide are
related exclusively to the degree of anomy. Nor can differences
in rates of alcoholism, personality disorders, or homicide be
shown to spring exclusively from anomy. However, statistics
suggest a positive relationship. Durkheim, aware of the difficulties, tried to distinguish anomic from other motivations of, for
instance, suicide. The ritual suicide of a Hindu widow (suttee)
or of a Japanese samurai (harakiri) suggests the strength rather
than the weakness of social norms. But it is often not clear into
which class a given suicide might fall. More important, it is often
not clear whether a death is a suicide.

If a man, drunk or sober, smashes his car against a telephone
pole, is it a traffic accident, a suicide, or a case of alcoholism?
How much suicidal intent was there in taking that "overdose of
sleeping pills"? How accidental was this "death by drowning"?
To know for certain, one must know the circumstances and,
above all, the person involved; and often his motivation is mixed
and conflicting and he could not himself say whether he is attempting suicide. The bare statistical data are not very enlighten-
ing. Further, alcoholism and some types of crime can be forms
of self-destruction—slow, unacknowledged suicide. Suicidal moti-

vation might play a role in some types of overeating and many other types of behavior. On the other hand, they might be alternatives to suicide, or forms of control of suicidal inclinations. Their relationship to anomy is no clearer than their motivation.

Still other difficulties arise from ignorance not of motivation, but of what actually happened—did he fall or jump out of the window?—and from different ways of recording what happened. Disapproving relatives might be more inclined to disguise suicides in a religious nation than in a nonreligious one. Perhaps the actual suicide rate in, say, Ireland is higher than the recorded one. On the other hand, a Roman Catholic group may have a lower suicide rate because suicide, considered sinful, is infrequent: the religious convictions of the members might actually prevent this desperate expression of anomy. But there may be no less anomy, even though expressed in alternative forms. Finally the ethos might be strong enough to forestall anomy in this group altogether. Statistical compilations at most give hints; they do not prove any theory.

The same sort of difficulty is encountered in measuring the frequency of alcoholism, or of psychosis. Official statistics might measure not whether there is more or less, but whether more or less is acknowledged. Even if the data are correct, they are not necessarily meaningful. Possibly one pathological phenomenon is frequent because it is preferred (unconsciously) to other equally noxious ones which, though arising from similar pathological motivation, are less measurable. Fewer drunkards, perhaps, and more coldly nagging husbands. There are still other difficulties. A change in the statistical frequency of psychosis might be due to a change in the age composition of the group, or to a change from (unrecorded) home care to institutional care, owing to changes in the organization of the family.

Careful statistical methods might help to isolate the anomic factor. But so far we have no data fully isolating the role of chronic anomy trends in personal disorganization. Nevertheless the available data, here adapted from Erich Fromm's *The Sane Society*, are suggestive enough to be considered. (Contrary to Fromm's view, the different homicide and suicide rates in different countries do not "contradict Freud's assumption of the comparative constancy of destructiveness . . ." since it is an assumption of *comparative* (i.e., all other things being equal) constancy. Moreover, destructiveness can be expressed in many ways. Homicide and suicide may be alternatives, and there are many others. Which is chosen depends on cultural factors.)

SUICIDE, HOMICIDE, AND ALCOHOLISM RATES, SELECTED COUNTRIES
(per 100,000 of adult population)

COUNTRY	SUICIDE		HOMICIDE	ALCOHOLISM
	1946	*1953*	*1946*	
Denmark	35.09	24.1	0.67	1,950(1948)
Switzerland	33.72	21.8	1.42	2,385(1947)
Finland	23.35	17.4	6.45	1,430(1947)
Sweden	19.74	18.6	1.01	2,580(1946)
United States	15.52	10.1	8.50	3,952(1948)
France	14.83	15.3	1.53	2,850(1945)
Norway	7.84	7.7	0.38	1,560(1947)
Spain	7.71	5.9	2.88	unavailable
Italy	7.67	6.4	7.38	500(1942)
Ireland	3.70	2.3	0.54	unavailable

The data presented are actually no more than educated guesses. One is struck, though, by the high suicide, homicide, and alcoholism rates in countries with comparatively high living standards. Possibly these three rates are high owing to the same cause—or perhaps the suicide rate is high as an alternative to a high homicide rate (Denmark?) or vice versa (United States?). There is clinical evidence indicating that either can be the case.

It is startling that the countries with the lowest living standards usually have very low suicide and homicide rates. Higher living standards or, more precisely, the industrialism that produces them, may cause anomy manifested in symptoms of destructiveness. The data suggest but do not prove as much.

ECONOMIC PROGRESS AND SOCIAL WELL-BEING

In the twentieth century, America has run a little ahead of most of the world. The cumulative transformation of society was accomplished more rapidly and thoroughly than in most of the world because the developments which underlie it met less resistance in a new country not much encumbered with pre-industrial ways of doing things.

Industrialization has made more goods available to more people with less work and less individual craftsmanship. Almost everybody, often as a part of a vast impersonal organization, produces for a vast anonymous market. The market system leads us to change occupation, residence, and associations with unprecedented frequency. Most of us live in cities now. Improved techniques have made it possible for an ever-decreasing proportion of the population to produce all the food required by society, even though *per capita* consumption has risen. Education, newspapers and magazines, radio and television, movies, and automobiles link rural life more closely than ever to city life. Urbanization, and the unceasing relocations required by the economic system, increase the frequency of contact with strangers and decrease the continuity of all contacts. There are more people and fewer persons in most lives.

The rise of scientific mentality, its spread through education, and its technological applications rapidly uprooted group traditions and structures. Groups were blended, their members jolted from one to the other, their norms fused and confused.

As groups became more fluid and accessible, feelings became more egalitarian and undifferentiated; relationships became discontinuous, temporary, and, above all, less intimate. Most social and religious bonds were extended, blurred, dissociated from each other, and often weakened. Individuals seem quite eager to "belong," but they find little to belong to. Perhaps, though the longing remains, the capacity to suffer fulfillment no longer matches it.

For many, life now is at once externally crowded and internally isolated. There is more freedom for all: ambition and opportunity are less limited than ever; the confining walls have been torn down, and our view is wide. But there is less shelter, the wind blows raw, and we are fearful, at times, of being swept into the vastness swirling around us.

The roots of the process should be sought in the Renaissance and the Enlightenment. The Industrial Revolution provided the material base for lack of which the analogous developments aborted in antiquity. The development itself was noted by Alexis de Tocqueville both in America and France, and it was lamented a hundred years ago in England by John Stuart Mill in *On Liberty* (a great champion of many of the things that led to industrialization, Mill can scarcely be suspected of much romantic longing for the past):

> The circumstances which surround different classes and individuals, and shape their characters, are daily becoming more assimilated. Formerly, different ranks, different neighbourhoods, different trades and professions, lived in what might be called different worlds; at present to a great degree in the same. Comparatively speaking, they now read the same things, see the same things, go to the same places, have their hopes and fears directed to the same objects, have the same rights and liberties, and the same means of asserting them. Great as are the differences of position which remain, they are nothing to those which have ceased. And the assimilation is still proceeding. All the political changes of the age promote it, since they all tend to raise the low and to lower the high. Every extension of education promotes it, because education brings people under common influences, and gives them access to the general stock of facts and sentiments. Improvement in the means of communication promotes it, by bringing the inhabitants of distant places into personal contact, and keeping up a rapid flow of changes of residence between one place and another. The increase of commerce and manufactures promotes it, by diffusing more widely the advantages of easy circumstances, and opening all objects of ambition, even the highest, to general competition, whereby the desire of rising becomes no longer the character of a particular class, but of all classes. A more powerful agency than even all these, in bringing about a general similarity among mankind, is the complete establishment, in this and other free countries, of the ascendancy of public opinion in the State. As the various social eminences which enabled persons entrenched on them to disregard the opinion of the multitude gradually

become levelled; as the very idea of resisting the will of the public, when it is positively known that they have a will, disappears more and more from the minds of practical politicians; there ceases to be any social support for nonconformity—the substantive power in society which, itself opposed to the ascendancy of numbers, is interested in taking under its protection opinions and tendencies at variance with those of the public.

No doubt, since Mill wrote the social landscape has been flattened further. The leveling of all potential obstacles to the winds of public opinion, and the uprooting of the institutions that kept the soil in place, abet political and cultural mass movements which, like dust storms, sweep the loosened soil hither and thither. Ultimately the bleak mass shelter of totalitarianism might attract the homeless.

Yet the homogenization which Mill laments is a nearly unavoidable effect of the industrial system which also brought us the unprecedented economic prosperity which Karl Marx described in such glowing colors in his *Communist Manifesto*. Marx clearly went wrong in prophesying that capitalism could not continue to create prosperity: standards of living have risen ever more rapidly since he wrote, particularly those of the lower income groups. Yet Marx's followers continue to complain about the "economic misery" caused by the capitalist system. What really ails us, however, is the revolutionary impact of prosperity and the awesomely vulgar vistas it revealed.

In our economic system the effect of prices on profits and losses motivates people and guides activities; both are relocated and reorganized whenever more value can be created at less cost thereby, and this is often. Each change leads to re-evaluation of people, groups, activities, and customs. Technological changes, changes in the pattern of demand, and many other factors cause whole industries and occupations to disappear (for instance, the candlemakers or the harness makers). New industries take their place: lightbulb and electricity or automobile production, television, plastics, electronics, and nuclear fission. Technological progress and shifting patterns of demand also cause the products of each firm, as well as its techniques of production and marketing, to change swiftly and often. Hence the usefulness of each skill we acquire, the demand for the work we do, and the position we have established—all may disappear overnight. Each of us may change, more than once in his lifetime, his residence, his occupation, his social environment, his prestige and income rank—his whole social position may be altered. Such changes used to be rare and affect few people over several generations. Moreover, the characteristics of the various groups and social ranks, the attitudes they foster, the positions they occupy are themselves far from stable now. All this is necessarily inherent in our economic system. Without this high degree of mobility, we cannot hope to reap its advantages.

But the economic advantages of our system have social disadvantages. For the social mobility, the ceaseless reorganization and reintegration of our economic functions in the service of greater efficiency unavoidably bring some measure of normative disintegration. The *social* optimum may require a degree of stability inconsistent with the *economic* optimum. Thus, at some point, we may have to choose between alternative optima.

Choice, when social trends are at stake, is only seldom and episodically a matter of deliberate decision. Rather it involves a movement in one of several directions open at one time. The implications of such a movement usually are not at all clear when it takes place, even to those who actually lead it. And in America this choice has been made. Indeed, there were hardly any alternatives to choose from. The stable traditional groups which might have opposed market-oriented mobility were easily overwhelmed by waves of new arrivals. Elsewhere in the world the trend is in the same direction, though slower and less thorough, because it has to overcome more entrenched obstacles.

FLUIDITY AND HETEROGENEITY

Despite its manifold origins, American society is characterized today not so much by heterogeneity as by fluidity. Differences among groups actually do not amount to much, comparatively speaking, for mobility and mass media of communication have reduced divergences, as Mill saw clearly. Yet, because there is so much movement from one group to another, the remaining differences are experienced more often and by more people. Hence the dissimilarities, though small, loom large and often in our experience. Further, owing to their smallness, these dissimilarities are more striking: the hill in our way is more irksome than faraway Mount Everest. Finally, since small differences are our main identification tags, pride clings to them.

Because of our high mobility, subcultures seldom have time to take hold and pervade a group thoroughly. Composition, location, and size of the group change too fast. Moreover, homogenizing influences such as education, mass media, and automobiles reach inside most groups. Therefore, group patterns themselves also change rapidly; and they are usually derived from heterogeneous elements. The pattern to which people are conditioned in the first place is not likely to be consistent; in the second place, it is not likely to be the one that will govern the behavior expected from them throughout their lives.

No society is wholly without subgroups. Even the most homogeneous societies tend to elaborate the differences between men and women into differential behavior patterns beyond the requirements of the difference in physiological function. But in an immobile culture the customs which govern intra- and intersexual relations are generally shared. People know what to expect. In a fluid society, such as our own, the actual difference between the patterns of the sexes, and among group patterns in general, may be less; but the expectations that groups place on each other are less stable, less generally shared, or less firmly localized, and, therefore, less often fulfilled. Some may have "Victorian," others "modern" attitudes. Some may follow the precepts of one religion, some of another, some of none. Still other groups may follow *True Confessions* magazine, or ways learned informally in college fraternities, or in a popular course in "Courtship and Marriage." Since our mobility leads each of us into new groups quite often, we must adapt ourselves quite often to different outlooks and behavior patterns. And, unlike people in a less fluid society, we do not necessarily move in regular sequence from one group to the next. Hence the frequency of disappointment, and, on the other hand, the readiness to change. There is, for each of us, more experience of social differences than if we were moored firmly in a society with greater differences. And to get along in so fluid a society we seek our cues in the way others act, rather than within ourselves. No wonder customs are not firmly embedded but hang loosely about us, like actors' costumes.

All this might suggest that ours must be a very unstable society, hardly able to hold the loyalty of its members. Yet it does not seem to be so. Indeed, some of the very forces that are disintegrative in one sense—mobility, change, and the confusing variety of patterns that melt into each other—seem also to make for an integration and stability of sorts. Mobility, as well as our elaborate systems of communication which reach everywhere—radio, TV, movies, newspapers, schools—tend continuously toward homogenization of differentiations, new or old. We are able to move so much with an impunity of sorts because the change we experience in moving is not great. Differences are temporary rather than rooted, and they are comminuted before they are crystallized into definite and persistent patterns. They seldom last long enough to be deeply internalized. They need only be erased, not eradicated. Americans, conditioned to change, are adaptable. Groups rather welcome newcomers, new things, and new patterns. Though not without ambivalence, we are, comparatively speaking, a nation of neophiles. Since there is not enough common past for all to draw sustenance from, American culture does not grow much on the humus of traditions. We grow, artificially fertilized (formal education), by means of transplantations and hybridizations (mobility), and in an environment so free of hereditary ease and disease (leisure classes) that one might almost call it sterile.

We have grown well and sturdily in many respects. Our society is more stable as a whole than many a less mobile society. The prospect of altering their personal life chances by their own effort—with social reforms or revolution—seems to help Americans to overcome whatever difficulty is caused by the fluidity of their society. They devote themselves to changing their personal situation rather than the social system. As experience up to now shows, political and economic stability seem to thrive on the low priority public affairs have in most lives—though this low priority drives revolutionaries to despair. However, the effects of fluidity on intellectual and aesthetic creation may be evaluated as detrimental so far. Other effects—on the integration of personalities, for instance—undoubtedly occur, but it is too early to tell to what extent these are permanently connected with the type of cultural heterogeneity just described. Possibly these effects occur in all industrialized societies and will become apparent elsewhere with further industrialization.

SCIENCE AND SCIENTISM (ERSATZ RELIGION)

Unlike the Melanesians, we are bereft of a clear central core of social life. The ethos of a society as mixed and as fluid as ours is difficult to ascertain. It is not universally shared, nor as specifically or concretely embodied in social life as the Melanesian ethos; neither does it occupy so large and obvious a place in the lives of individuals. The rules we are to follow, and the goals we are to achieve, the measure and evaluation of our achievements are far from uniform or immutable. The ability to make money and to make oneself popular play major roles in our estimates of success. But the meaning of "success" remains vague. And the relationship of the traditional religions, as they are interpreted by their ministers, to this modern ethos is puzzling. They appear to offer both an alternative ethos—that of the Scriptures—and, inconsistently enough, to support striving for our very different goals—for which they offer themselves as means.

In past societies cultural and social diversifications were linked. We have greatly reduced cultural diversification and divorced it from social stratification: different patterns and degree of cultural refinement are no longer much associated with different strata of society. They occur individually, if at all. This might lessen the chance to breed varieties and paradigms, as Mill feared. In past societies also, the ethos of culture was officially and effectively cultivated in special institutions (churches, universities, princely courts) and by specialized groups. Only in modern times have religious and civil bonds been wholly dissociated. Men can now reject the cult of an official religion without placing themselves outside society. Institutions have been shorn of their sacramental inviolability. The sacramental bonds of society are loosened by mobility and by the corrosive impact of scientific rationality.

Unbound, we benefit from enormous economic advances generated by the application of scientific discoveries. Yet these economic advances themselves make most painful the loss of the bonds destroyed for their sake; it is when we have leisure and comfort that we most need an ethos to give meaning to our freedom. Yet the means we use to free ourselves from material necessity weaken the ethos we need to employ our freedom purposefully.

There is no way of weighing our material gain against the loss of moral unity. Nor can we balance the rise of intellectual freedom and its spread against the loss of diversity and reverence, the weakening of the ethos of culture, and the difficulties of personality integration. Where some will see losses others will find gains. Personalities that find it difficult to conform to the official ethos gain by not being closely bound to it; others are disoriented by being unbound.

The scientific spirit itself might create new bonds to replace those it corroded, or the old ones might re-emerge. Prediction would have to take into account many matters as yet unexplored. We should bear in mind also that some gains have proved more apparent than real. Nazism and Marxism were not due to lack of freedom. They seem more nearly reactions against the emptiness freedom revealed. To liberate is not yet to make people free. In the words of Gilbert Murray (in *Five Stages of Greek Religion*):

> . . . Man cannot be enlightened permanently by merely teaching him to reject some particular set of superstitions. There is an infinite supply of other superstitions always at hand; and the mind that desires such things—that is, the mind that has not trained itself to the hard discipline of reasonableness and honesty—will, as soon as its devils are cast out, proceed to fill itself with their relations. Here then the disappearance of the old bonds merely led to new bondage.

Science was not directly responsible for the disappearance of the old authority nor for the tyranny of the new. The discoveries of science are logically irrelevant to the core of the myths around which the ethos is formed, and even to the essence of religion—indeed, to any but the most naïve and literal interpretation of Scriptures. It was the *psychological* impact of science, not its logical or empirical contents, that corroded religious faith. Scientists were molded by this impact and formed others after their image. They often developed a faith no more justified by science than religious faith, and no less destructive when unbridled: a belief that the cosmos is so arranged that its total magnitude and contents cannot exceed the grasp of scientific method—that nothing can exist which cannot be known intersubjectively and explained scientifically. Values, then, either can be proved right objectively, pragmatically, scientifically—which they cannot—or the universe is valueless.

Yet it is difficult to see any reason beyond the nature of scientific method itself, and the exigencies of its practice, for confining truth to what can be proved. To say that nothing can be known that cannot be known by science is but to give a special meaning to the verb "to know"—to make it synonymous with "to demonstrate intersubjectively." Yet although science is the only method we have to make testable predictions it is pure superstition to say that only things subject to testable prediction exist. If only what is true can be proved, it does not follow that only what can be proved is true. Demonstrability and existence need not be identical. Scientific demonstrability is sufficient, but certainly not necessary for existence.

"Scientific faith" is a contradiction in terms: faith is belief in what has not been or cannot be proved—"the evidence of things not seen"—while science is belief in what has been or can be proved. At best scientific faith means faith in the ability of science to catch the cosmos by the tail. This faith seems as mystical as religious faith and much less attractive.

Scientism simply reverses the errors committed by churchmen in the past. Churchmen had thought that scientific questions—for instance, in geology and biology—were continuous with theological ones, and that therefore they could be solved by experts in theology. Some of today's scientists insist, so it seems, that religious and moral problems are continuous with scientific ones. Hence they feel that experts in say, psychology or anthropology, can solve theological or moral problems. Actually, though the methods involved have much in common—for instance, logic—much more divides them. This must be so, because religion and science are not rival ways of answering the same set of questions. They answer different questions which require different methods. Science is concerned with predictions based on observations, and tested by further observations. Religion is concerned with the ends for which science can only offer means, and with a future and past which are not testable but accepted ultimately on the basis of faith and reason.

Of course, it is desirable to prove things, when possible, and essential to distinguish what can from what cannot be proved. But this surely need not imply discarding or disdaining very important segments of experience in which science might be relevant, even necessary, but never sufficient or alone decisive: man's and society's moral and aesthetic dimension, the life of the soul, the kingdom of ends.

The effect of vulgarized "scientific faith" has been disastrous. The fanatic intensity that faith sometimes inspires was displaced to matters that require no more than detached reasoning. People still kill each other, but they believe now that it is for the comfort of their bodies rather than the salvation of their souls. And they accept as scientific truth ideas far more obviously untrue than those held by the most otherwordly of religions, from which scientific faith detached their belief. How sadly have we proved right Goethe's thought: "Anything that emancipates the spirit without a corresponding growth of self-mastery is pernicious"!

At the eve of the Industrial Revolution, the Western world gave a great sigh of relief. Reason seemed fulfilled. Infinite progress—the religion of the future—would liberate men from the bondage of material misery. The promise was kept—and yet we long once more for some liberation. Now we realize—and the heart sinks—that man's plight is not fully relieved by relieving misery; it is only freed from irrelevancies and more clearly defined.

Even at the dawn of the industrial era the difficulties it would bring were perceived. Thus William Wordsworth ("England, 1802"):

> *Perpetual emptiness! unceasing change!*
> *No single volume paramount, no code,*
> *No master spirit, no determined road; . . .*

In his twentieth century "Waste Land," T. S. Eliot scathingly expressed the emptying of our lives. Society has undergone

rending changes, and there is, among the most sensitive, a sense
of loss evoked by W. B. Yeats in "The Second Coming":

> *Things fall apart; the centre cannot hold;*
> *Mere anarchy is loosed upon the world,*
> *The blood-dimmed tide is loosed, and everywhere*
> *The ceremony of innocence is drowned;*
> *The best lack all conviction, while the worst*
> *Are full of passionate intensity.*

A sense of futility, of social boredom, of meaninglessness—
a wish for meaningful social association not fulfilled by merely
gregarious or functional assemblies seems rampant. One feels as
though society is coming unstrung. The mind boggles at predicting the future. But George Orwell (in *1984*) has painted
one possibility which contemporary China appears to approach.
Aldous Huxley in *Brave New World*, Evelyn Waugh in *The
Loved One*, and Nathaniel West in *The Day of the Locust* and
Miss Lonelyhearts have depicted more ludicrous but no less
gruesome possibilities. Perhaps it is not too late to take notice
of Lord Keynes's rueful comment:

> . . . We repudiated all versions of the doctrine of original sin,
> of there being insane and irrational springs of wickedness in
> most men. We were not aware that civilization was a thin and
> precarious crust erected by the personality and the will of a
> very few, and only maintained by rules and conventions skilfully
> put across and guilefully preserved. We had no respect for
> traditional wisdom or the restraints of custom. We lacked
> reverence. . . .

CHAPTER XIII   *Class, Estate, and Caste*

THE UNAVOIDABILITY OF INEQUALITY

In every society there is a wide variety of tasks. Government, religion, law, defense, agriculture (or hunting and fishing), and industry (or crafts), medicine, building, art, science, and other activities are present in all societies in more or less specialized form; and there are such familiar tasks as bringing up children and preparing food. Some of these services are more important than others; some are more attractive; some require few persons, some many; some finally require special aptitudes which are not scarce (e.g., childbearing), while others require special aptitudes that are scarce (e.g., managerial or mathematical talent, or martial prowess), while still others can be performed by everybody. Often the services which require scarce talent also demand skill which the talented acquire through training.

Every society must make reasonably sure that enough persons are attracted to each task—or forced, or permitted to perform it—but not too many; and that the persons most adapted to it perform it; and that they have the means to render the services required—training, power, or implements—and enough incentive to use them. (The incentive can be negative—punishment, or positive—reward.) Societies have found many ways to make sure that essential services will be rendered; they have been more or less successful. If they failed altogether, they did not survive.

In the main, performance of tasks is assured by distributing prestige, power, and income so as to make the performance possible and to serve as incentive for it. (Withdrawal serves as negative incentive—punishment.) Most services necessarily involve an unequal distribution of these incentives. Political and military tasks—government and war—imply an unequal distribution of power: subordination to officials and officers. Judges must have authority to control litigants and those suspected, or guilty, of law violations—an unequal distribution of authority. Production leads to unequal control over goods and services—an unequal distribution of income. Prestige, finally, consists of the unequal deference, respect, and admiration enjoyed by people—it is by definition a form of differentiation. (In a sense, this is true of power, too; but unlike prestige, power need not be an end in itself. And inequality of income is enjoyed only because higher—as distinguished from high—income yields more prestige than low.) Power, income, and prestige tend to coincide to some extent in all societies. But in no society are they identical or coextensive.

Though occasionally awarded directly to individuals, power, income, and prestige are usually attached to the services which people—selected on a hereditary basis, or by individual qualifications—are expected to perform. The activities which inherently require it, as well as those that are important or demand rare talents and skills, are usually invested with more power or prestige or income than others. Thus, in each society, groups can be distinguished according to the power, prestige, and income they have, by virtue of the activities they engage in—by virtue of the social stations they occupy. The classification of groups in these terms is called stratification, and the groups are called strata (layers).

Stratification seems as unavoidable as the division of labor. To some extent the latter is biologically given. The immature and the old cannot work as effectively as the mature. Women, because of childbearing, are more homebound than men. People have different abilities and disabilities. But neither the dictates of nature nor of economic rationality require the specific elaboration

that the division of labor receives, or the specific power and
prestige distribution among age and sex groups that characterizes
each society. Similarly with stratification, which is closely allied
to the division of labor. Historical developments, which might
have been different without impairing the functioning of the
society, account for many special features of the social system.
In all societies stratification is required by the nature of the tasks
performed and as an incentive to their performance. Further,
where personnel is not allocated to various activities on a hereditary basis, stratification helps to attract the right persons in the
right numbers to the tasks they can best perform. It does not
follow that any given system of stratification is indispensable, but
stratification is.

POSSIBILITIES OF CHANGE

Societies have considerable leeway in cultivating or minimizing
differences of position and the numberless privileges and ameni-
ties that go with them. The rank assigned to each position also
may vary from society to society, although similar tasks tend
to lead to similar rankings of positions. Finally, access to positions
in the social hierarchy—the way people are selected for them—
may be made to depend on a variety of personal qualifications,
or parental rank may be inherited. Since there is leeway in all
these matters, one may properly consider whether and how
any given system of stratification should be changed. Yet from
the possibility of abolishing any single rank order, it cannot be
inferred that all rank orders can be abolished. This is a fallacy
many leftists who feel uneasy about inequality—including Marxists (in their eschatological moods) and anarchists—are loath to
abandon. Rightists, on the other hand, are inclined to argue as
though the impossibility of abolishing *all* rank orders proves
the impossibility of abolishing *any* rank order. There is no
evidence to show that sizable societies can exist without stratification. None has. But there also is no evidence to show that any
particular system is indispensable. The most diverse kinds have
existed. Naive defenders and opponents of the *status quo* also
confuse the question, "Should a change be made?" with the
question, "Can a change be made?" Yet change may be possible

without being advantageous, or advantageous without being
possible. And inequality may be unjust without being unnecessary, or just without being necessary.

Membership in a stratum comprehensively influences one's
life chances. The more permanent the membership, and the
greater the rank differentiation, the more important it is, of
course. The higher one's stratum, the better ordinarily the
life chances. One's chance to stay alive in one's first year, the
length of the life span, nourishment, health, physical appearance,
attire, abode, comfort, leisure, ability to communicate, chances
of becoming a criminal and of receiving an education, in short,
the duration, enjoyment, achievement, and style of life—all are
influenced by the privileges and characteristics of the stratum
to which one belongs. A man's friends usually belong to his
stratum. And strata are always somewhat endogamous. Even
when exogamy is legally permitted, people, in fact, mostly marry
within their own stratum.

Persons of equal, or near equal rank in the social hierarchy
form a stratum which is also the stratum of their families. The
family is the basic constituent of strata. Regardless of whether
a family's position has been achieved by its current head or is
inherited, one belongs, at least until adulthood, to the stratum of
one's family. In some systems, offspring remain permanently in
the parental stratum. But even when rank is not inherited, family
membership influences what stratum one can belong to in later
life—what opportunity for achievement one has—by providing
or not providing the required qualifying characteristics such as
education.

In very primitive and in very well-developed societies, inheritance of parental rank can be unimportant. In very primitive
societies, skills are few and easily learned. In very advanced
societies schools, rather than families, serve to transmit skills.
Hence it is possible, in very primitive and in very advanced societies, to take up occupations and social positions not transmitted
by the family. But a society which has skills to be learned and no

schools to teach them must, perforce, rely on transmission within the family. Families cultivate and transmit skills to their members and with these skills they transmit their own position in the stratification system.

Unless the rank of the family into which one is born has some fairly enduring and pervasive influence on life chances and style of life, we do not speak of stratification. Stratification involves not only an enduring rank order of social positions but also a tendency—greater than chance—for people to remain in the strata into which they are born. This is in the nature of stratification and not necessarily due to selfish defense of their position by the upper strata. Logically, a stratified society in which rank is entirely independent of family and does not necessarily last a lifetime is possible. (Plato's utopian *Republic* is a case in point.) But it is a fallacy to infer existence from logical possibility. Else the chances of meeting a mermaid would not be as slim as they are.

The demarcation lines of strata may be quite fluid. And subjective feelings of belonging need not be strictly correlated to objective lines. Nonetheless, objective inclusion—through, for instance, legal privileges, or wealth—influences behavior and subjective outlook and generates subjective solidarity in each stratum. The members feel united to each other in certain ways and separated from other strata—the more so the less the individual members expect to move up vertically. On the other hand, a common fear of being pushed down may strengthen solidarity within a stratum. However, position in the social hierarchy is only one of many influences leading to only one of many group memberships. Hence its importance for the individual outlook varies. All group memberships together (including membership in a stratum) do not *exhaustively* explain individual behavior: sociology adds to but does not replace psychology.

When social positions are highly and rigidly differentiated and people do not expect to change frequently from one into the other—when stratification is objectively at a maximum— invidious subjective perception of stratification is far from intense. Antagonism among strata is inactive because society is split into non-competing segments. People identify with people in their own stratum and not with people in other strata. They are not anxious to rise. They do not form expectations which can be frustrated. Resentment grows when the ambition to change position is cultivated, though, unavoidably, it is often disappointed. People fret also when differentiation of positions, though real, is de-emphasized by an egalitarian ideology. In short, as stratification becomes less steep and more fluid, resentment rises. People compete strenuously, and are necessarily invidious of each other, since all run in the same race for positions that only a few can reach. And since they have learned that men should be equal—at least when equally gifted—those in the lower positions are left to conclude either that their own gifts are inferior or that those who have superior positions do not deserve them. Untold elements combine with the stratification system to determine whether these difficulties are handled through political action or expressed merely in individual dissatisfaction.

CASTES, ESTATES, CLASSES

Three main types of stratification may be distinguished. Strata are castes, estates, or classes, according to the way people are selected to occupy ranks. In caste and estate systems, the ranks are distinguished formally in law and custom. Each stratum has different rights and obligations in all respects. In a class system, differences of strata are not recognized in law. Except in the performance of occupational tasks, citizens, regardless of class, are entitled to equal legal rights.

In a caste system, rank is ascribed by birth and retained through life. Vertical mobility is stunted. Individuals do not change caste by personal activities in this most rigid system of social stratification. People marry within the same caste, and numerous precautions are taken to minimize intercaste associations. Contact with the lowest caste (or outcast) is regarded as polluting particularly with regard to bodily orifices: thus, common eating, defecating, and bathing are particularly feared. The system is rationalized in religious beliefs which hold that imperishable souls migrate from body to body (metempsychosis), and that the souls which have reached higher stages of purification are embodied in the higher castes, whereas those in the lower castes have still a long way to go. Mobility thus occurs—but the movement takes place in an invisible sphere. Analogous systems exist on a biological basis among many social insects, such as termites and bees. Among human societies, the caste system has existed for three thousand years in Hindu India and for varying periods elsewhere, though, of course, it has never been quite as rigid as among the social insects.

Although the Indian caste system was, and still is, much more rigid than our own class system, we tend to overlook what flexibility there is. Each caste is divided into numerous subcastes, and the division changes over time and differs from region to region. So does the ranking of castes, within limits. Over 2000 main castes were counted in India, and some of these are divided into 1000-2000 subcastes. So complex a system, of course, cannot remain altogether the same over a period of time, and does give some opportunity for change—though certainly most people are led to expect to remain and do remain where they are born.

In an estate system, ordinarily part of the social system of feudalism, each individual inherits his rank. Even his attire may be regulated by the estate to which he belongs; the wife of an artisan may not be allowed to dress like the wife of a nobleman, even when she can afford to. However, the idea characteristic of a caste system, that a person of high rank is polluted by contact with a person of low rank, is alien to the estate system. Legally recognized rank depends on ownership of land and on occupation, also largely inherited. But in an estate system, though stratification is rigid, there is some vertical mobility. The king may endow a subject with land and make him a member of the noble estate. Military and, particularly, ecclesiastical careers are not closed to the members of the lower estates who may thus rise. But mobility is scant.

Compared with caste and estate systems, the position one achieves in a class system depends least on inherited rank or parental position. Therefore, it depends most on one's ability. Legal, customary, and material barriers to mobility are minimized. Social strata are ranked essentially by their income, however earned. (Classes may be defined and ranked by many criteria other than income. Certainly income, though usually included, is not always the only criterion considered. But for our present purpose income will do.) Legally, we are all peers, subjected to the same laws. And outside occupational spheres, there is little social recognition of rank. Political, military, judicial, and priestly positions are not inherited, though wealth is. This system, developed in Europe after the fall of the estate system, is the only one the United States has ever known, and it is replacing all others through the world. (Karl Marx distinguished classes not according to income but according to ownership of means of production, such as land or capital. Some Marxists allege, therefore, that where private ownership of means of production is abolished, as in the Soviet Union, there is no class system. But this is a quibble over words. Differences in income, power, and prestige— in life chances—have not been abolished. The important class differences persist. Stratification in the Soviet Union clearly proves that Marx was wrong in believing that class differences originate exclusively with private ownership of means of production and are automatically abolished by socialization. The elimination of private ownership merely eliminates private ownership, one of many sources of income, one of many possible ways of achieving or inheriting rank.)

Though in a class system income and rank are personally achieved, the achievement is by no means independent of the class membership of one's parents. For on parental position depends the ease of access to acquisitions—knowledge, skills, friendships—which facilitate achievement. Life chances are never independent of one's early youth, and the kind of youth experienced is not independent of the parental stratum. (Furthermore, income may be directly inherited in a class system.)

In a caste system, people sit still and remain in the stratum into which they were born. They are trained accordingly and expect nothing else. In an estate system, only a few rather exceptional people move. But in a class system everyone by rights may enter the race for high rank; most people do, and many change their position. Yet most people must start out on foot, though some people inherit bicycles, some automobiles, and a few airplanes.

Actual systems of stratification are never as pure as the theoretical constructs which help us to analyze them, just as the pure elements of chemistry are seldom found unmixed in nature. Though the American system has always been prevalently a class system, slavery was obviously a caste element. Its reverberations are not exhausted. There are still caste elements in our treatment of ethnic groups, particularly the ex-slaves: Negroes. In Europe, there are many remnants of the estate system. Hereditary nobility, including monarchy, is the most obvious. The systems become mixed through contacts or historical developments. Further, each contains some elements of the others to begin with. Even a caste system does not altogether exclude social mobility. In the course of time, some individual "passing" from one caste to the other occurs, and the ranking of castes changes. Since the caste system, like any system of social stratification, is based on socially recognized values on the one hand, and linked to economic and political matters on the other, it is likely to be affected by religious, technological, and political changes. But mobility in a caste system is minimized.

Logically, the system by which positions are ranked is independent of the means used to select people who enter the various positions. One can imagine a system in which ranks are inherited and nevertheless not highly differentiated. And a society is logically possible in which people can achieve rank individually and yet rank differences are great and people of differing rank do not mix. To some extent, the mandarin system of ancient China came near illustrating this possibility. However, experience indicates that when ranks are inherited, they also are highly differentiated. Each stratum keeps to itself; each has rigidly prescribed obligations and privileges. On the other hand, in a class society where rank is achieved individually, social strata ordinarily feel far less differentiated from each other, and, indeed, their ways of life are far less differentiated. As was pointed out, differences may be resented more. But the differences are less steep.

A general theory of stratification can do no more than indicate the functions stratification can fulfill, and the functions that cannot be fulfilled without stratification. But to explain a particular system of stratification, historical elements must be added to the general theory. Each particular system will have elements which, though serving some function in it, need not have been there or could have been replaced by others without interfering with the survival of society. And elements which could have helped the society to survive might be missing. This point may be generalized as follows: no analysis by the methods of any one social science exhausts all aspects of a social problem. The other social sciences are needed; no analysis by the methods of all social sciences exhausts a social problem. Its historical setting and development must be considered. The problems of society are like those confronting the physician. Like each human organism, each society is a multidimensional historical system with intensive relationships among the parts. And there are idiomorphic elements in all societies.

CHAPTER XIV

Expansion, Mobility, and the Class System

PURE VERTICAL MOBILITY

Assume now a class system, a system without legal or forbidding customary obstacles to movement from one stratum to another, and without direct rank inheritance. For simplicity assume only three ranks. Let 5 per cent of the total population hold top rank, let 40 per cent be in the middle, and 55 per cent in the lowest stratum. Assume that these proportions—the structure—remain unchanged over the period; and that people in all strata have the same life span and produce just enough offspring for replacement. Any vertical movement up or down of the children of any stratum then depends entirely on the manner in which people are selected to enter each rank. Let us call the resulting rate of rise or fall the pure rate of vertical mobility. This rate depends (1) on the characteristics, such as intelligence, or skill, on which access to each position is made to depend; (2) on the distribution in the population of the characteristics which qualify for promotion or demotion; (3) on the effectiveness with which people are selected for positions according to their actual qualifications.

Let us call conditions (1) and (3) together the selective system. The selective system may be implemented formally as in the military or civil service, or in academic hierarchies. But it need not be; fitness may be demonstrated and rank achieved, as in the business or entertainment world, by the test of action, by success, without official certification.

In the structure of the system, longevity, and fertility remain unchanged, the pure rate of vertical mobility can vary only if the distribution of valued characteristics or the selective system does. If the distribution of characteristics required for access to positions is constant, the pure rate can change only when the selective system does.

Even with the most favorable selective system, *pure* vertical mobility must be narrowly limited. It would be highest if the talents and skills qualifying for high rank are uniformly possessed by the offspring of the lowest stratum to a greater degree than by the offspring of the higher strata and if the system of selection gives equal opportunity to the offspring of all strata. (Actually, milder assumptions would suffice to assure 100 per cent intergenerational replacement of the top stratum from below.)

Conditions could not be more favorable. If, for the time being, we disregard the middle stratum, the entire top stratum would rise from the bottom stratum in each generation. Nonetheless, less than 10 per cent of the bottom could move into the top stratum in each generation to replace 100 per cent of the top stratum.

The conclusion is obvious: in the absence of structural change, or expansion, upward mobility is narrowly limited by the simple fact that there are fewer positions at the top than at the bottom of the social pyramid. Hence a 100 per cent replacement of the top ranks advances only a few people from the lower ranks. To be sure, the upward movement would be greater if we consider promotion from low to middle rank, which certainly is more frequent than promotions to the top. But we meant to illustrate the factors constricting upward mobility when it is pure (when the structure of stratification is unchanged and there is no expansion)—not to depict the movement in an actual society. The illustration shows not that *revolutions*, but that the *dreams* of most revolutionaries must fail because the factors which limit promotion are more often dictated by external circumstances than by the "unjust" selective system usually held responsible. The number of officers in an army, managers in business—in short, the proportion of chiefs to Indians—cannot be reversed. Nor can the social structure.

If we make slightly more realistic assumptions, the rate of pure vertical mobility will be nearly halved, even in a society which minimizes inheritance of rank. There is, after all, no reason to assume that the children of the lower stratum are uniformly possessed of superior talent. At best, on the average they have as much talent as those of the upper strata. And no selective system can be 100 per cent effective: opportunity can never be quite the same for the offspring of all strata. Even if, as in an ideal class system, only personal talent is considered relevant, the rank of the parents influences the development of talent and its recognition. Hence, opportunities for the offspring of the upper stratum will be better, ordinarily, than opportunities for the children of lower strata. (Indeed, otherwise one can scarcely speak of stratification at all.) Thus, even if access to formal education and inheritance of wealth were entirely equalized, children in the top stratum would still have the advantage of early training in better surroundings and of better connections. These advantages can be minimized, but they cannot be nullified.

More is known about the distribution of opportunity than of talent. Possibly some hereditary talents are more concentrated in the upper strata. Yet, even if inborn talent were proportionately less frequent in the offspring of the lower stratum, there would be more talent among them, since they are so much greater a proportion of the total population. Enough is known to suggest that pure vertical mobility in the United States would be greater than it is now if intelligence and talent alone counted. A sizable percentage of lower stratum children do not go to college, even though they have higher intelligence quotients than some upper stratum children who do. Probably their initial opportunities are inferior to those of upper stratum children and do prejudice their further opportunities. Possibly their inclination to go to college is less pronounced, but surely not enough to account for the difference. Moreover, this weaker inclination may itself be an effect of parental position.

However favorable to mobility the selective system is, we cannot realistically expect less than about half of the top stratum to retain the family rank from one generation to the next. Given our assumptions, this would allow only 5 per cent of the bottom stratum to rise into the top stratum. (Actually the top 50 per cent are more likely to be replaced from the middle stratum; members of the bottom stratum are more likely to rise into the middle one.) The power of any government over the conditions we have assumed to be constant—the conditions that make vertical mobility pure—is limited. Yet unless these conditions change, no government can hope greatly to increase the percentage of the bottom stratum able to rise to the top, even though all social barriers to mobility be minimized. In short, the mobility which depends on the selective system—pure vertical mobility—is not likely to help the bottom stratum much.

Some comment is in order. Replacing even half of the top stratum with people from below in each generation has drawbacks. To be sure, society would benefit inasmuch as the best talent would occupy the highest position. But similar benefits might be obtained by intra-stratal mobility. Even though the leading group remain unreplaced, within it leaders may change according to qualifications. Optimum mobility seems to be lower than maximum mobility. Traditions, customs, and norms might be weakened too fast if half of the top stratum in each generation rises from the bottom stratum. The total effect would be unsettling, threatening anomy and strengthening competitiveness intolerably. And it is fairly generally agreed that downward movement—implied in our assumptions and in most pure vertical mobility—is frequently a source of personality disturbance and of undesirable behavior. For instance, persons who display irrational intolerance of social minorities—ethnic, religious, political, moral, aesthetic—are often those who have dropped below the stratum in which they were brought up. The very threat of moving down is an important source of insecurity, of defensiveness, and of desperate efforts to salvage self-esteem and personality integration by doubtful devices. German National Socialism was largely a reaction of the German middle classes—including peasants—to the threat of downward mobility. Workers continued on the whole to vote for leftist parties despite unemployment. (Unemployment, particularly mass unemployment, though demoralizing is not felt to involve downward mobility.) The German middle classes, in contrast, responded to the great depression of the thirties, by switching from the moderate parties to the radical and anti-Semitic right. Electoral statistics clearly show that the radical right gained mainly at the expense of the moderate right. The middle classes felt pushed down.

There is no exact way of comparing the effect of downward movement on the happiness of the children of the top stratum with the effects of upward movement on the offspring of the bottom stratum. But the unhappiness coming from being pushed down is not likely to be less than the happiness generated by rising. On the contrary. Tastes that have been formed and are no longer satisfied probably cause more intense frustration than the nonsatisfaction of tastes that were never formed or were never satisfied. Mobility forms new tastes but it always frustrates those formed before. No doubt the feelings generated depend somewhat on the spirit of the system in which mobility occurs, on the emphasis generally placed on rank matters. If downward mobility is customary and expected, it might be easier to bear than otherwise. But it will never be easy. *"Nessun maggior dolore / che ricordarsi del tempo felice / nella miseria"* ("No greater torment than to remember happiness in unhappy times"), says Dante Alighieri, implying that misery is easier to bear for those who do not have better times to remember. (Dante in the Fifth Canto of his *Inferno* makes Francesca paraphrase Boethius. *In omni adversitate fortunae infelicissimum est genus infortunii fuisse felicem.* Boethius, who wrote his *Consolations of Philosophy* in prison, was indeed flung from the highest to the lowest level of material existence.)

"Carpetbagger," *"nouveau riche,"* "parvenu," and "libertine" (originally, in ancient Rome, a freed slave) were terms applied to persons who have moved up rapidly to indicate that they behave with vulgarity. ("Vulgarity" [from *vulgus:* people] means "commonness." Both words have acquired a pejorative meaning though literally they denote only popular acceptance. It is indicative of the favorable attitude of North Americans toward mobility that, except in the South, we have scarcely a native term with strongly derogatory connotations to apply to upstarts—though other languages have many.) They may use the privileges of their new position without the restraint, the awareness of obligation, and the taste which come with habituation through the family. So much to suggest that the blessings of pure vertical mobility, like all blessings in this world, are mixed.

A high rate of pure vertical mobility is quantitatively insignificant for the lower and very irksome for the upper strata. It is important only because it measures the one kind of vertical mobility which quite directly and visibly depends on the selective system. Other types of vertical mobility depend far less obviously on political decisions. Further, pure vertical mobility offers the one opportunity of rising in a society which is not changing or expanding.

If the selective system allows enough mobility, good leadership—or at least the best possible—is assured. If pure vertical mobility is too restricted, talent is unnecessarily wasted. An ossified, stagnant society may result. This may also occur if the selective system, though permitting a high rate of pure vertical mobility, selects people with talents or training that will incline them to make the stagnation of society their main business. The Chinese mandarin system illustrates this possibility. (Any system entirely based on Civil Service examinations might have like effects.)

In wasting talent, society may not only forego possible gain; it may also suffer positive injury. Intelligence prevented from rising festers functionlessly; it corrodes the bases of the social edifice it could have supported had it been given an opportunity. The stability of the social order may suffer, and turmoil rather than stagnation may be the effect; yet no advance is possible until and unless appropriate provisions for sufficient pure vertical mobility are made. Sufficient pure vertical mobility, on the other hand, by providing talented leadership may further social changes and expansions. These in turn will create additional possibilities of (nonpure) mobility.

NOT-SO-PURE VERTICAL MOBILITY

The time has come to replace our neat but abstract scheme with a more realistically complete one. Let us consider the vertical mobility which results: (1) from changes of structure—of the proportions in which the population is distributed over the ranks;

(2) from changes of the rank order—of the position of each group in the hierarchy of strata; and (3) from expansion of the system as a whole. We shall also pay heed now to intermediate strata and other neglected elements. Vertical mobility seen realistically is a stream with many sources. Pure vertical mobility is but a minor tributary.

Assume initially that the population is distributed as before: 5 per cent in the top stratum, 40 per cent in the middle, and 55 per cent in the bottom stratum. Now suppose this structure changes. The top stratum expands, relative to the other strata, so as to include 10 per cent of the population. The bottom stratum shrinks as much as needed to allow the top to swell. In the process of change there occurs an upward movement additional to the flow included in the pure rate; unlike the pure rate, it is unmatched by downward movement. Total upward mobility from the bottom stratum will double during the change-over. After the change has established the new structure, the rate decreases. But, still, a higher proportion of bottom children must rise to replace the same proportion of an expanded top—the pure rate has been permanently increased. If we assume that 50 per cent of the top stratum is regularly replaced from below, 50 per cent of 10 per cent of the population—the new top stratum—is more than 50 per cent of 5 per cent of the population—the old top stratum. Moreover, the rise is from a slightly shrunken bottom stratum. As a percentage of the top, pure vertical mobility does not change. As a percentage of the bottom, it is higher than before though lower than during the change-over.

Without any change of structure, change in the rate of vertical mobility may also result from population growth (one form of expansion). Suppose population doubles through immigration. Though still only 5 per cent are in the top stratum, the size of each stratum doubles. Now, if the immigrants were stratified in exactly the same rank order and proportions in which the society they join is stratified, no additional mobility need result. But it is more likely that most immigrants were members of the bottom stratum of the society they left. (This is the case when the motive for emigration is economic, but not necessarily when the motive is political persecution.) Since they double the resident population, if proportions remain as they were, either more members of the latter must enter the top stratum or some of the immigrants must move up. In both cases, there is a temporary increase of upward mobility.

If population grows through natural increase, the rate of vertical mobility might change because of different birth rates in different strata. Indeed, if we drop the assumption of equal demographic characteristics of strata, an interstratal differentiation of birth rates or life spans would affect vertical mobility even without an increase of population. Suppose the offspring of the top stratum suffice less than before to replace it and that the offspring of the bottom stratum fill the gap. The rate of vertical mobility will increase first in the process of differentiation. It will fall, but remain higher than before, when the new birth rates or life spans become constant. Hence, there is an increase both of the percentage of the top stratum that is replaced in any period, and of the percentage of the bottom stratum that goes to replace it. (Whether changes in the rate of vertical mobility owed to interstratal birth or death rate differentiation should be considered changes in the pure rate or extrinsic to it is open to doubt. The same may be said for a change in the distribution of talent as distinguished from opportunity.)

Now turn from changes in the upward and downward flow due to variations in the size of the strata, or of replacement rates, to relocation of whole strata in the hierarchy. Individuals may rise or fall not because they have moved from one stratum to the other, but because the stratum as a whole has been re-ranked: all captains take the positions formerly occupied by corporals, who take the rank of captains. Criteria according to which strata are ranked may change. Or though criteria remain unchanged, one stratum may acquire, and another lose, the characteristics that make for high rank. Such changes in the rank order involve a change in structure only if a stratum which is re-ranked as a whole is more (or less) numerous than the stratum it displaces. In a caste system, for instance, the priestly caste may take the first rank previously occupied by the warrior caste. In a class system, generals may temporarily displace top businessmen from the rank they occupy in peacetime. If income remains the criterion of ranking, it is also possible that the top stratum, which drew its income from producing a now obsolete product, may be displaced by another group which draws a higher income from producing a newly invented product. (In developing countries, land owners may be replaced by manufacturers.) New occupations such as journalism, public relations, or airplane piloting often lead to shifted rankings. There are many such possibilities.

The actual rate of vertical mobility is an average of the far from uniform rates characterizing different segments of society. In one college an instructor can hope for promotion only if his superior dies. In another, the proportion of full professors is being increased. In a third, proportions remain the same but the teaching staff expands and everybody is promoted rapidly. Unless faculty members move sedulously from college to college in search of opportunity, and thereby equalize it, the intercollegiate rate of faculty vertical mobility is an abstract average. (Downward mobility within faculties is exceptional.) So it is in society at large. There are regional differences, differences between urban and rural areas, between small and big towns, between new and old industries, and among the countless groups which compose society. These differences are as often a cause of migrations, domestic or international, as they are in effect. Differences in vertical mobility rates among occupations and industries are also a motive for horizontal mobility: changes from one occupa-made because it is hoped that the chance to rise, or to avoid fall-tion to an other within the same stratum. Such changes are often ing, is better in the new occupation.

MEASUREMENT

Vertical mobility occurs over a span of time; hence, the amount found depends on the period selected and on its length. Over a very long period, some mobility is experienced by almost all families; over a very short time, only by a few families. And since in the history of all societies periods of mobility alternate with periods of immobility, it does make a difference which of two periods of equal length are considered.

By considering only top-bottom movements, we have unrealistically simplified matters. Societies do not consist only of privates and generals. Among the innumerable intermediate ranks, much movement, consisting of a step up or down, takes place. Sometimes the strata are so near each other that they are almost continuous. Movement then is scarcely noticeable, unless it is extensive. In other systems the hierarchy is discontinuous, the strata are distant from each other, and interstratal movement is easily noted. But in all systems, top-bottom leaps are exceptional, and therefore striking.

Comparisons of vertical mobility are seldom simple. Data are scant, equivocal, and often incommensurable. The measuring concepts are tangled and difficult to apply. In some societies many people move frequently but to a small extent; in other societies (or periods) fewer people move and perhaps less frequently but more extensively. Which type of society has "more" vertical mobility? The different types of movement which constitute vertical mobility must be assigned weights rather arbitrarily if we are to compare mobility in different societies and periods. A great deal of judgment enters even into our rough and uncertain estimates.

Types of mobility are easier to list separately than to isolate for measurement. Yet an analysis which does not distinguish the manifold types and sources of mobility would be pointless; it could not help us to explain, predict, or control. Let us characterize once more the main types.

When size of population, rank order, and the proportions in which the population is distributed over the ranks are held constant, mobility is pure. It is narrowly limited even under the most favorable selective system. High rates of (mixed) mobility are likely in a society with growing population, or with interstratal birth rate or life span differentiation, or when the rank order changes, or when there is a change of the proportions in which the population is distributed over the ranks of the hierarchy. In short, most mobility occurs while changes of structure and rank order and expansion are going on.

The point may be illustrated by an army, or any hierarchical organization such as a church, a corporation, a university, or a labor union. If the size of the group, the criteria of promotion, and the life span of officers are all constant, promotion usually is slow. Only few can hope to attain high rank even though the system makes promotion dependent on merit alone. After all, many privates are needed, few officers, and only very few generals. But the rate of mobility quickens if, as in war, the size of the army increases, life spans and promotion criteria change, and new commands are founded. Similarly, opportunities for promotion are greater in an expanding corporation, church, or labor union. Likewise the vertical mobility of a society is quickened more by its expansion (and occasional change of promotion criteria) than by any specific promotion system, be it ever so fair to the lower strata.

CAUSES OF MOBILITY

Which of the many possible causes of mobility have actually influenced the rate of mobility in America? Which might do so in the future? Must we expect a decline of mobility?

Most vertical mobility in America (and elsewhere) has come in the last two hundred years from the process of industrialization. The various aspects of industrialization were, of course, related. Let us list a few.

Population Expansion: The over-all death rate declined faster in all industrial countries than the birth rate, but the birth rate of the upper strata declined before that of the lower strata did. Natural increase at differential rates has thus augmented vertical mobility nearly everywhere. In the United States, immigration has added to vertical mobility beyond the addition that natural increase alone would have caused.

Internal migrations, too, have been more significant in the United States than elsewhere. They probably increased vertical mobility because they led to changes in rank order and criteria for selection. The upper stratum of the newly settled frontier may well have consisted of people who might not have risen without migration. Finally, the more widely dispersed a population is, the higher the proportion of the top group in it. Many small ponds have many big frogs. A concentrated population has fewer top leaders—there is only one heap to be topped.

In similar fashion, colonial expansion may have increased upward mobility in Europe. Even when the upper stratum of the colonies came from the upper stratum of the mother country, the places left vacant increased the chances of upward mobility at home (and certainly colonies diminished downward mobility). In general, it seems likely that geographical expansion adds to the vertical mobility of the expanding population beyond any addition that would have resulted from population growth alone. It is, after all, unlikely that new regions are colonized by simple transfer from the old regions of strata in the same order and proportions. New tasks, a new environment of necessity impose selective processes and readjustments leading to additional up and down movements.

Occupational Changes: Rank in a class system is associated with income.

1) The relative income of various occupations has changed and therewith the stratum of the practitioners.

2) The proportion of the labor force needed in various occupations has changed. Since occupations yield different incomes, this involves vertical mobility. In particular, relatively few people work as farmers and far more work in industry than a hundred years ago. And this movement continues. The income of people in industry is generally higher than that of people on farms.

3) Occupational changes also quicken vertical mobility because they are likely to involve changes of selection criteria. A significant number of farmers must have entered into the higher industrial ranks after leaving the lower farming ranks. The top farmers will not necessarily make top industrial workers, nor need the farmers who received the lowest incomes on the farms receive the lowest incomes in industry.

4) Whole new professions have arisen from technological changes. Think of electronic engineers or nuclear physicists or anesthesiologists.

5) The occupational structure changes in response to other factors, as well as technological ones. A changing general income level—in our case, a higher one—alone suffices to change it. For instance, people can afford more physicians or entertainers. Thus we have today a greatly increased proportion of white-collar workers in the population; their total number now exceeds the number of manual workers for the first time in the history of the world. Finally, many previously incidental occupations have become pro-

fessionalized, and the practitioners have risen in rank. Some women ministering to the sick became registered nurses; some bookkeepers became certified public accountants. Whole groups, such as hairdressers, undertakers, cooks, and real estate brokers, aspire to rank as professionals under such names as beauticians, morticians, dieticians, and realtors. In some instances the qualifications have changed; in others, only the name; in still others, though the actually relevant qualifications have not changed, the educational qualifications have. Sometimes, as in the case of dieticians, there has been an effect on mobility. But usually, although the prestige of the occupation may have been increased, the class of the practitioners has not changed.

To sum up, an expanding society has many sources of vertical mobility. A society without economic expansion is thrown back on pure vertical mobility—which is very limited at best. A shrinking society, of course, will have more downward than upward mobility. Finally, much depends on the demographic characteristics of strata, which are related to the phase of social expansion or contraction but not fully determined by it. We have assumed demographic characteristics favorable to high or increasing upward mobility. Other assumptions are possible. For instance, if the members of the top stratum live longer, or have more children surviving into adulthood than the members of the bottom stratum, upward mobility is slowed down. This may well be a first result of economic development likely to be offset by other effects in the end.

A systematic presentation of causes which increase or diminish vertical mobility in either direction would call for a series of models illustrating the many possible combinations of relevant circumstances. Too little is known to tell which are most likely to occur. We can barely hint at the future. The past in the United States is clear. Our population has grown by leaps and bounds; immigration has contributed much to it; westward expansion, industrial and technological change have been nearly unceasing, though occurring in waves. Our income has risen with unbelievable swiftness to an unprecedented level. All this has led to far-reaching changes in the occupational structure, producing a high rate of vertical mobility which sprang from the rapidity and the extent of economic change and expansion. Pure vertical mobility might well have been high, too, but its direct contribution must have been minor.

All the available studies indicate that more sons remain in the paternal occupation than enter any single other one. But about 70 per cent change. More of them move up than down, though ordinarily only slightly: from semi-skilled to skilled or from un-skilled to semi-skilled work. In a survey carried out in Minneapolis in 1950 (see *American Journal of Sociology*, July 1955) it was found that about 30 per cent of the sons remained in the paternal occupation or one ranked the same, 44 per cent rose above, and 24 per cent fell below. These data are what the foregoing discussion should lead us to expect, but they should be considered illustrative rather than probative. Indeed, the authors who present them stress the precariousness of their enterprise.

No satisfactory separate measurement of the vertical mobility of females is available. Married and nonworking ones, of course, are in the stratum in which their husbands are. But little is known about the difference between that stratum and their parental one. Even less is known about the vertical movement of working females, and particularly of those who belong to a different occupational stratum than their husbands.

Mobility within the manual and white-collar occupations exceeds mobility between them, though the gap is by no means insurmountable. One recent survey has found 30 per cent, another 47 per cent of the sons of manual workers entering nonmanual occupations.

Much mobility is owed to changes of the occupational structure. Census data indicate that between 1910 and 1950 the number of farm laborers in the labor force has decreased from 14.5 per cent to 4.3 per cent, that of farmers from 16.5 per cent to 7.3 per cent. It is likely, of course, that the farmers who left the farms they owned or tenanted were the least prosperous, eking out a living not much better than that of their hired hands. Their movement away from the farm probably meant upward mobility. The number of unskilled workers decreased from 21.5 per cent to 16.5 per cent—the proportion of the population in the lowest ranks has greatly decreased. And there are significant increases in the number of persons occupying the higher ranks. Semi-skilled workers increased from 14.7 per cent to 19.8 per cent of the labor force; skilled workers and foremen from 11.7 per cent to 13.8 per cent; clerks from 10.2 per cent to 18.9 per cent; managers, officials, proprietors from 6.5 per cent to 8.6 per cent and professional persons from 4.4 per cent to 8.5 per cent.

STAGNATION AND THE CASTE SYSTEM

Among systems of stratification, the caste system, which minimizes vertical mobility, is usually found in stagnant societies. Its polar opposite, the class system, which maximizes vertical mobility, is characteristic of expanding societies. Let us take a moment to ask: does expansion produce the class system or vice versa? Is one possible without the other? Analogously, do stagnation and contraction produce the caste system or vice versa? No certain and exhaustive answers are possible. Some expansion has taken place without a class system; and stagnation has not always been associated with rigid caste systems. But reasoned guesses are possible.

In a stagnant society, a class system would be out of place. Unless the society expands it might actually fare better with a caste or near caste system (such as the estate system). If the society does not expand, the vertical mobility that could take place under even the most permissive class system would allow only very few members of the lower strata to rise. A large proportion of the top strata would have to move down to permit this. The difficulties are greater than the results could justify. Ambition would make the lower strata restless and, since disappointment would be the lot of most, dissatisfied. Fear and insecurity would make the members of the upper strata ferocious and defensive. They would not have leisure to cultivate traditions. Their major concern would be to keep on top. Nevertheless, in each generation the lower strata would be joined by an embittered group of impoverished people who had lost their top positions. They might give a sharp edge to the frustration of the lower strata and, under favorable circumstances, mold them into a revolutionary movement. Even without such movement, the class system would surely weaken the loyalty of all strata to the institutions of the stagnant society. At length, with a class system, the society could not remain both stagnant and stable.

Besides being a danger to the social order of a stagnant society, the class system would be useless. Its advantage—attraction of the fittest to top positions—becomes a disadvantage. The leaders of a stagnant society must be steeped in tradition and reverence for existing institutions. This, perhaps, is their most important qualification. It is found in the existing upper stratum and fostered by immobility. But those who rise from below in a class system do not rise because they are more steeped in tradition than those they replace. On the contrary. A man who did not inherit his top rank can be relied on to be more inclined to change things than one who is to the manor born. And he inspires less superstitious awe. A stagnant society has much to lose from a class system and little to gain.

Even in an expanding society upward mobility may cause more discontent than it assuages—and discontent may increase with the frequency of upward mobility. The more often they see others advance, the greater the awareness and the pain of those who are left behind. Thus, during World War II it was found that the discontent of the unpromoted was greatest in those military units in which promotion was most frequent. The feeling of *relative deprivation* increases among those who do not advance, because those who do set a *standard of aspiration*. They become a *reference group* with which others identity to ask, "What have they got that I haven't got?" The difference between the standard set by the reference group and the actual situation of those who aspire to it causes and measures their dissatisfaction.

Possibly the discontent of the unpromoted is increased in military groups because the military hierarchy combines caste characteristics—legal rank distinctions, legally distinguished privileges, legally distributed coercive powers, and distinctions of attire—with upward mobility. Our civilian society, in contrast, combines vertical mobility with a class hierarchy. Also, the military unit has only one reference group—the promoted. The unpromoted feel relatively deprived in reference to them. But in civilian society people feel deprived or satisfied relative to a number of reference groups. There are many hierarchies, and many avenues

of advancement leading to many goals. Hence, relative deprivation is less intense.

A QUALIFICATION ILLUSTRATED BY THE ROMAN CATHOLIC CHURCH

In the hierarchy of the Roman Catholic Church, vertical mobility was not accompanied at all times either by expansion or by
excessive discontent in the lower clerical ranks. Yet, even though
top ranks were filled from below, few priests could move up. In
short, the church at times was a nonexpanding group with a class
system and a high rate of pure vertical mobility. Why did the
difficulties we find in this combination fail to occur? Can a whole
society be successfully organized on this model? It seems unlikely.

The ecclesiastical hierarchy consists of people who volunteered
to enter it, forsaking possible alternative careers. Those who might
be dissatisfied by the slow advancement need not enter upon an
ecclesiastical career. Hence, those who do are a selected group
of persons to begin with, less keen on moving up than others
(at least in modern times—in the Middle Ages, when the Church
offered a greater chance than other available institutions, the contrary might well have been true.) But society as a whole cannot
select; and it includes ambitious people unprepared for the hopes
which a class system in a stagnant society would raise and disappoint. The priesthood is far more homogeneous in its occupation, education, and beliefs, and presumably less career-minded,
than a whole society can expect members to be. Further, though
organized in a hierarchy of ranks, priests hold as an article of
faith that what matters is not their earthly advancement, but advancement in the eyes of God. Indeed, it is their occupational task
to persuade others of this. Such a belief surely makes manifestation of dissatisfaction with lagging advancement difficult. Thus,
there is less initial ambition for upward mobility than in society at
large; training reduces or at least limits further the manifestations
of ambition; and finally, priests enjoy special prestige which helps
assuage dissatisfaction with lack of advancement within the
church. All this is possible only for a group within a society and
not for a society as a whole.

But the most relevant difference is that the church hierarchy is celibate. The rise of low-ranking ecclesiastics replacing high-ranking ones who die is not offset by downward mobility of the children of the latter. The ecclesiastical hierarchy has no downward mobility. In a stagnant society with a class system, the children of the poor could rise only by replacing the children of the rich. The church does not have that problem. This alone might explain how the church has succeeded in combining vertical mobility with stability in periods of stagnation, whereas a society probably could not. Besides avoiding downward vertical mobility, celibacy avoids the limitation on mobility that the social inheritance of privilege in families necessarily involves. (Yet even a celibacy rule does not avoid all temptation to family favoritism. The word "nepotism" [literally "nephewism"] was applied first to the ecclesiastical hierarchy—and some of the "nephews" actually were known to be illegitimate offspring of church dignitaries.)

EXPANSION AND THE CLASS SYSTEM

What about an expanding society? Bare listing of the characteristics of expansion suggests that a class system is needed. In expansion, the number and the proportion of people in the upper strata increase. They must be recruited from the lower strata. The main function of the upper strata is to lead toward change and innovation requires readiness to abandon tradition. Often talents different from those that served leaders in the past are needed. These are more likely to be cultivated—or not to have been stunted through trained incapacities—in the lower classes. In short, all the characteristics of rapid expansion discussed before require the vertical mobility which defines a class system.

Surely this brief sketch cannot begin to do justice to the multitude of questions it raises. Its purpose was to suggest more than to answer them. We have not solved our initial problem: which comes first, the class system or expansion, the caste system or stagnation? But we have suggested why they come paired as they usually are. One policy suggestion follows. The class system becomes the more useful the more external circumstances permit expansion; the less that is the case, the more difficult it is to justify and maintain a system that promises a vertical mobility it cannot deliver.

WAR

The vertical mobility caused by war, conquest, disaster, and revolution still wants discussion. Even if these events leave the ranking of positions unchanged, they hurry the rise and fall of occupants and are likely also to change the relative size of strata. Often these events prompt changes in the hierarchy of ranks, sometimes of the whole system of stratification. Such are the temporary, unintended effects of wars, and the temporary effects of revolutions. The war over, the revolution accomplished, the rate of mobility once more depends on the factors already discussed. Mobility changes permanently only if the revolution or war succeeded in changing those factors, that is, if the rate of expansion has been affected.

At least temporarily, war changes the direction and speed of economic expansion by requiring increased production of military goods and by inflation. Inflation, favoring debtors and robbing creditors and holders of money, increases vertical mobility. Usually the middle class suffers. Many of its members are flung from their stratum altogether, retaining but a memory of better times. Often a new group of business leaders leaps up, uncommitted to established channels and ways of doing business. But the old business leaders are not pushed down altogether. Hence the total effect is an increase in size of the top stratum. The economy can support the increased proportion of people in the upper ranks because ordinarily production expands in inflation.

The demographic effects of war also have repercussions on mobility. A higher proportion of officers than of enlisted men is killed, and relatively more come from the upper than from the lower strata. Their replacement in the civilian ranks temporarily increases upward mobility, as would any shortening of the average relative life span of the members of the upper strata. War quickens mobility also by changing career lines and by numerous educational, resident, and occupational dislocations.

The temporary effects of army expansion are not without lasting influence on people's ambitions, which in turn play a major role in upward mobility. The often neglected role of motivation in selection for mobility or immobility may be illustrated by the fate of the European refugees driven to the United States by the Nazi and Soviet regimes. Even though all material circumstances seemed likely to push them down in the social hierarchy, they almost instantly regained their former stratum. Many refugees who fled Hitler's anti-Semitism in Germany were professional men and middle-class businessmen who had to leave behind the businesses, savings, and professional practices which had given them their rank. Except for the effect on motivation, their education can have been of little advantage. Once in this country, an amazingly high proportion rejoined the stratum from which they had come, despite the new language and the uselessness of many of their professional and practical skills. The ambition not to fall below one's past rank may be stronger in Europe; the ambition to rise may be stronger in the United States. However, both in Europe and in America, the effect on one's ambition of being born in a given stratum may be more important than the direct material advantages or disadvantages.

REVOLUTION

In a class society, revolution can maximize the rate of pure vertical mobility, but this has only an insignificant numerical effect on the lower classes. Revolution also can "liquidate" the current top stratum and replace it from below. But once the new top stratum is established, it cannot be replaced at a faster rate than before—unless the "liquidation" is repeated. Thus, unless it can increase the rate of expansion, the effects of revolution on the advancement of the lower strata are temporary or minor. If a class society expands at a rate that cannot be greatly increased, the usual revolutionary promises, whether made in good or bad faith, cannot be kept. What may be achieved instead is more modest; not more persons but different ones will be moved into the higher ranks.

Matters can be otherwise if the revolution occurs in a stagnant society. Beyond "liquidating" and replacing the top strata, under favorable circumstances revolution might also transform the stagnant into an expanding society. The European revolutions which replaced estate by class systems certainly accelerated the rate of pure vertical mobility. They changed the selective system. They also changed rank orders (mainly by demoting nobility and clergy). But it was the effect of the new leadership on the economic development of society which was paramount; society started to expand and the rate of vertical mobility rose with the rate of expansion.

Increasing mobility might have been an effect of revolution or of more general changes that might have taken place anyway. Surely revolution was not always needed. In England industrialization did the trick without violence. But without economic expansion, vertical mobility never did rise permanently. In some countries expansion was achieved under the old leadership. Elsewhere new leadership came to the fore without revolution. But in many countries, political revolutions broke the ground for economic expansion. There is no deciding, at least not in general terms, whether, or to what extent, expanding economic forces stirred up political revolution or were afterwards unbound by it. History in turn casts economics and politics into decisive roles. Historiography bathes now one, now the other in the spotlight, according to the equipment and inclination of historians. But Clio, a flirtatious muse, isn't going steady.

VERTICAL MOBILITY IN EUROPE AND AMERICA

It has long been thought that our rate of vertical mobility exceeds Europe's. Though no hard comparative data are available, the more rapid expansion of American society suggests that this view is basically correct, although the European and American rate of *pure* vertical mobility probably have not differed greatly. Nevertheless, the rate of vertical mobility in the United States was perhaps thought higher than it actually was and that in Europe lower. Psychological reasons might account for this overestimation of the true difference.

1) The income level of nearly all classes has been higher for some time in the United States than in Europe. A farm worker immigrating from Europe, even if he remains in his original stratum, might well feel that he has moved upward in the United States. Further, the income differences among strata are probably smaller in the United States, strengthening this impression.

2) The psychological differences among ranks are smaller. Prerequisites, symbols, and mutual attitudes are undoubtedly less rigid in the United States than in Europe. A man who has not actually moved upward in objective terms may feel he has because he is treated differently and feels differently. The walls to be scaled are lower and the ascent does not seem so forbidding.

3) Upward movement is highly regarded in the United States, where many members of the upper strata have experienced it fairly recently. To emphasize their personal achievement individuals may make their beginnings more humble than they actually were. Not so in Europe, where pride more often rests on the antiquity of the family's wealth and position. Unlike Americans, Europeans who have risen by their own efforts are likely to make their beginnings less humble than they actually were. Hence vertical mobility in Europe is understated, in America overstated, if one goes by the impressions received by visitors.

4) Horizontal mobility in the United States is undoubtedly greater than in Europe. People are much more prepared to change occupations. Since horizontal is not always easily distinguished from vertical mobility and often produces a feeling of having moved up or down, greater horizontal mobility contributes to the impression of greater vertical mobility. Indeed, though not identical with it, horizontal mobility is likely to help vertical mobility. A man prepared to change occupations in general will be far more prepared to climb up or down than one who expects to remain in the occupation of his fathers.

THE OUTLOOK

It is difficult to gauge mobility in the past; to fathom the future is to throw caution to the winds. Nevertheless, there are indications which might tell us whether our speed or direction is changing.

We have seen that much vertical mobility is connected with geographical expansion and population growth. These sources of mobility in time must dry up altogether; even now they contribute less than they did. If all other things were to remain equal, we might expect less vertical mobility then. But we pointed before to additional sources of vertical mobility: technological innovation, general economic expansion, the increase and equalization of income per head—none of these shows signs of declining. On the contrary, it is entirely possible that additional mobility springing from these sources will continue to make up for the slower population and geographical expansion. What measurements we have indicate no decline in the rate of pure vertical mobility, or of total vertical mobility.

Upward mobility now originates more equally in the various segments of the population viewed horizontally. Ethnic, religious, regional, and sex differences affect the opportunity and the motivation to rise less than before, because of ideological changes, and improved means of communication and transmission. A change of motivation also may have occurred, impelling people to seek prestige and popularity more and income less. In other words, it is no longer thought that income alone—and thus high class as we have defined it—gives prestige. It is therefore no longer pursued as the main avenue to advancement. This would mean that people are less interested in belonging to a high stratum and more in having high prestige by other means. Yet material opportunities have been spread more widely and equally than before, particularly through the educational system. This has been both a cause and an effect of the spread of the American ideology which Abraham Lincoln interpreted:

[The authors of the Declaration of Independence] did not mean to say all were equal in color, size, intellect, moral development, or social capacity. They defined with tolerable distinctness in what respects they did consider all men created equal—equal with "certain inalienable rights, among which are life, liberty, and the pursuit of happiness." This they said, and this they meant. They did not mean to assert the obvious untruth that all were then actually enjoying that equality, nor yet that they were about to confer it immediately upon them. In fact, they had no power to confer such a boon. They meant simply to declare the right, so that enforcement of it might follow as fast as circumstances should permit.

They meant to set up a standard maxim for free society, which should be familiar to all, and revered by all; constantly looked to, constantly labored for, and even though never perfectly attained, constantly approximated, and thereby constantly spreading and deepening its influence and augmenting the happiness and value of life to all people of all colors everywhere.

To some, social equality, a nonstratified, a classless society, is a beautiful dream. To others, it is a nightmare. We need not take sides. Be it feared or wanted, total equality is only a dream. But no one, scanning the history of American society, can deny without churlishness that Lincoln's standard has been "constantly spreading and deepening its influence." Has it been "augmenting the happiness and value of life"?

Hitherto we have built a model in layers (strata) extended horizontally throughout society. Vertically, the layers form a society-wide hierarchy of strata which, in a class system, are each defined by the income range of the people included. Class membership influences people's life span and life chances, their chances for health, confort, leisure, knowledge, and achievement, their power over other people, and their prestige. Members of the upper class have money to spend. This facilitates the acquisition of other qualifications for prestige and power. But, even unspent money brings some prestige.

The objective influence of class membership is reflected in subjective feelings of closeness to members of one's own class, of distance and sometimes hostility to members of other classes. Vertical mobility allows people to move upward or downward in the class system of stratification. But in all systems, each person and his immediate family can be a member of only one stratum at one time—one caste, one estate, or one class; and membership is unequivocally determined by objective criteria—in a class system by income.

STRATUM AND STATUS DIFFERENTIATED

However, *class* is often less important than *status*. Unlike class, status is subjective; and each person has multiple statuses. (The plural of the Latin work *status* is *status,* which in English would be confusing. I have followed usage in forming the plural "statuses," though it pains me.) Status refers to *personal* prestige (esteem) in each of many groups, large or small, your family or co-workers, the home town folks, your friends, or the public at large; to the *impersonal* prestige of each position, independent of who occupies it; and to the behavioral expectations held by the occupants about themselves by virtue of the position they occupy, and to what is expected of them by others. The rank of "physician"—the status of the position—differs from that of "janitor." And the prestige of the position is independent of the personal prestige of John, the physician, or Jack, the janitor —though the occupant of each position is affected by, and expected to act in accordance with, the demands of the position. His prestige depends to some extent on how well he fulfills these demands.

Each position is located and ranked in a system of statuses. "System" here means: (a) the basis of ranking (e.g., occupation, color, kinship); (b) the criteria used for the ranking on that basis (e.g., manual, nonmanual work); (c) the actual allocation of ranks (the hierarchy); (d) the nonprestige expectations attached to each occupation. There are many systems. Everybody, without respect for person, is ranked in status systems according to age, sex, kinship, occupation, and so forth, just as everybody is ranked in the class system according to income. But since there are many status systems, everybody occupies many statuses, though lodged in only one class. Age may bring deference regardless of personal merit. The father may be the head of the family regardless of who supports it. Status includes what was described (in Chapter 10) as personal and as official authority. But status goes beyond authority over others, formally estabished or derived from respect and esteem, to comprise all the expectations people place on each other by virtue of office, occupation, age, kinship, and finally by virtue of the regard they have for each other personally.

The conduct expected in each status is called "role." The aged are expected to behave in one way, the young in another; parents play one role, children another. As the individual ages, his status and his role change. But the role associated with each of the statuses he enters and leaves is expected to remain rather stable—though in our society this is less so than in others. Ralph Linton called categories the statuses directly related to biological matters, such as age or parenthood; other social statuses are mostly related to occupation—chief, priest, servant, policeman, merchant, physician. But they are not unrelated to the categories: the priest is "father" and the chief has paternal authority. To hold together, a society must rely on the sentiments that link a family together and are generated by it. Society must foster and then bend these sentiments to social uses.

Status always occurs in a particular group and system; it is seldom the same in all groups, at all times, or in all systems. The prestige of positions, as distinguished from that of the persons occupying them, varies least from group to group when the positions are linked to occupations. Indeed, in industrialized countries, the hierarchies of occupational prestige are quite similar, as Alex Inkeles and Peter H. Rossi have shown. (*The American Journal of Sociology*, January 1956.)

In some hierarchies, the vertical order of statuses is formally established and indicated by standardized symbols. This is the case in the military hierarchy, in some ecclesiastic ones, and less explicitly in many hierarchies organized to perform definite functions. In the most formally organized hierarchies, rank officially defines both one's authority and the respect which others owe, and are expected to pay in standardized ways. Hence "status" sometimes refers to both. But the power and the prestige of positions may diverge: the king (or the President of the German Republic) has less power, yet more prestige than the prime minister. Analogously, the power and prestige of persons may diverge. We shall, therefore, use "status" to refer to prestige ranking (and to role expectations) and otherwise speak of "power"; whereas "class" will be used to refer to income and, occasionally, wealth. Note however that colloquially "status" is used to refer to position on any scale, and "class" to sometimes used to refer to quality or prestige (e.g., "high class"). Unavoidably there is some overlapping also because the role expectations placed on a status may include the exercise of power. Still the fact that power and prestige, though related, do not coincide with each other, or with income, makes separate designations convenient.

In informally organized groups, the status hierarchy is implicit. And when informal groups do not have functions which require a stable rank order, status is highly volatile as well as elusive. It can be descried but it shifts subtly. It depends both on how one behaves and on what criteria others apply to evaluate behavior. Hence the same behavior brings different status in different groups and occasions. And different behavior produces different statuses in the same group.

Class membership does not depend on anyone's opinion; the class hierarchy is ordered according to an objective quantitative criterion—income. In contrast, except for the formal hierarchies mentioned, status hierarchies, being subjective, can be ascertained only by inquiring into people's opinions of each other and their ranking of positions. Everyone's status depends on everyone else's opinion of his occupation, religion, dialect, behavior, race, residence, family, automobile, and so forth. Status changes with the opinion of others. Unlike stratum, status is a segmental matter. You have one standing in a particular group and, possibly, a different status in another group, or according to another system. Your status may be high on the ethnic prestige scale and low on the occupational scale, if you are a white dogcatcher in Alabama; and conversely if you are a Negro physician there. Status is an *ordinal* ranking—higher or lower. Unlike class, status cannot be measured *cardinally*—there is no way to measure the distance between adjacent ranks. Unless handled with great caution, the concept "total social status" (or "socio-economic status") is an average of incommensurables which obscures as much as it enlightens. It is used though, perhaps because most persons themselves feel that they have one society-wide social status—usually the one they have in the group that ranks them highest. To that group they cleave because actually their status in it is higher than the "total social status" would be; and because the ranking (and the group) is meaningful to them; it fits into their self-image and aspiration and involves the activities they are concerned with.

The many systems in which we occupy different statuses and the manifold expectations placed upon us by them were not designed according to a master plan. They grew separately, and unevenly, as society developed. In various periods they proliferated from one institution, sank roots in another, were grafted upon a third. Social institutions themselves do not develop necessarily in a harmonious order, nor do they mesh neatly into each other. On the contrary, since they originate in different parts and groups of society, and develop at different rates of speed, and sometimes in different directions, there is in all societies a need for overarching institutions which have the main task of unifying the others, adapting them to each other, and, where necessary, weeding them out. Religious, political, and economic institutions share this task, though they do not always succeed in it. (The place of religious institutions in the past has now been taken largely by political ones.)

One of the major discomforts felt in modern society is probably caused by the economic change which burst upon us over the last two centuries. It required the sudden adaptation of social institutions developed slowly and painfully before and meant to serve smaller and more isolated societies than ours. Some institutions undoubtedly are being bent to new uses; others are being shattered. But the process of institutional change seems to lag behind the economic changes which require it. This is one cause of friction, social conflict, and possible disorganization. For those caught in functionless institutions, or in non-institutionalized functions, there is uncertainty and status anxiety.

STATUS GROUPS

When several persons have similar status in one or more groups, or systems, they form a status group. A master of ceremonies in a night club, interested only in the degree of celebrity (defined as nondishonorable notoriety) of the customers, may rank Liberace (a famous TV "personality" whose piano playing impresses the nonmusical), Rudolph Serkin (a famous pianist whose playing impresses the musical), Cassius Clay (a boxing champion), Albert Schweitzer (a Nobel prize-

winning humanitarian), Brigitte Bardot (an actress famous for
her sexual allure), and Bernard Baruch (a philanthropist and
symbol of business respectability) as having equal status. For
him they form a status group. But they would not in a system based on criteria other than celebrity: among musicians,
Mr. Serkin and Liberace are ranked very differently. A
status group, then, consists of people occupying similar rank in
the same hierarchy—for instance, a brace of generals; or in
different hierarchies—for instance, a bishop, a corporation vice-
president, and a high judge. A status group may also be constituted by people enjoying equal prestige in the eyes of a third
group, not necessarily their own—the nightclub audience, for
instance.

A status group should not be confused with a class. The
judge and the general might well have a lower income than
the corporation vice president and yet belong to the same status
group. Further, the general may have a lower income, and thus
belong to a lower class, than a private who has lower status. A
person upon misbehavior may lose status but not class. A harem
wife may have low status in Moslem society. But she belongs
to the upper class if her husband does. On becoming a call girl,
a teacher may ascend into a higher class by descending into a
lower status. Albert Einstein had high status (among scientists)
and low class. The status of Bernard Baruch is not that of a
playboy millionaire, even though they both may have the same
income.

Status is not entirely unrelated to class, however. In many
circumstances, groups, and occasions, prestige ranking, particularly in the long run, depends on income, or on what income
enables one to buy—which last means that class can be a helpful, though not a sufficient circumstance of status. Though class
membership ordinarily influences rank on all social scales, it
does not determine social standing. More generally, the values
that people cherish are somewhat agglutinative and can be transformed into each other. Prestige can be monetized, money can
bring some prestige, and power can bring, or be brought, by
both. They are not identical, however, and the possession of one
is never indispensable in our society, and seldom alone sufficient
for the acquisition of the others.

THE SEGMENTAL NATURE OF STATUS

Though never quite the same, the status of a person or position may be similarly ranked by all or most groups and in most systems. A physician may have high status in most groups because of his occupation and a senator because of his political influence. When a formally organized group is entered, such a ranking may be recognized. Thus, physicians and ministers usually enter the army as commissioned officers. It is possible then to construct a society-wide status system or prestige ranking of, for instance, occupations. (Needless to say, since a man cannot be reduced to his occupation, the status of his occupation is only one of his statuses.) One can ask a properly selected sample of the population—one that reflects its age, sex, class, religious, residential, occupational, and educational composition —how it rates each occupation. From their answers may be constructed a society-wide occupational status system.

In this manner, status of occupations the world over can be ranked by averaging the esteem in which they are held by Hottentots, Eskimos, and Englishmen. The usefulness of a system so constructed is limited. For instance, North and Hatt found that in the United States, Supreme Court Justices rank highest, physicians and state governors rank equally high, and bartenders are ranked near the bottom of the scale. (No doubt, this averages the view of temperance and of alcohol addicts.) Do people always respect those who dispense justice more than those who dispense beer? Average men do on average occasions. But average men are so few! Bred by statistics, not by flesh and blood parents, average men have characteristics and views derived from all of us, but not necessarily the views and characteristics of any of us. Statisticians combine our features into shapes which may bear no resemblance to anything on land or sea. Actual beings are particulars. Statistical entities averaging the views of sheep, of wolves, and of shepherds have only statistical existence, which is instructive only as long as its sheerly statistical character is kept firmly in mind.

Behind his bar, the bartender often ranks as high as the

240 PART TWO: SOCIETY

captain on his bridge. While tending bar, he is no less an arbiter of disputes and a paternal authority, who by giving his attention may enhance the customer's self-esteem, than the judge is to those who stand before his bar. And, on the beach among a gaggle of teenagers, the status of the judge and of the bartender may be equal—and below that of the handsome lifeguard. Possibly it is the judicial quality with which these occupations are invested that causes them to have a high status on occasion. This suggests that a prestige rating of occupational *functions* and *powers* is indispensable to make sense of the rating of occupations and to make it more applicable to actual situations.

In the United States at one time, the *success system* prevailed sufficiently to make status and class nearly identical. In the last chapter of his *American Notes*, Charles Dickens caricatured it in the following dialogue:

> "Is it not a very disgraceful circumstance that such a man as So and So should be acquiring a large property by the most infamous and odious means, and notwithstanding all the crimes of which he has been guilty, should be tolerated and abetted by your Citizens? He is a public nuisance, is he not?"
> "Yes, sir."
> "A convicted liar?"
> "Yes, sir."
> "He has been kicked, and cuffed, and caned?"
> "Yes, sir."
> "And he is utterly dishonourable, debased, and profligate?"
> "Yes, sir."
> "In the name of the wonder, then, what is his merit?"
> "Well, sir, he is a smart man."

Some remnants of this use of monetary success, regardless of the means used to achieve it, as criterion for ranking—a bequest of rough and ready frontier days—lingered on into the 1930's. Thus, gangsters had low rank, but big gangsters, such as Al Capone, enjoyed high, if ambiguous, prestige. Yet even in Dickens' time, status was differentiated from class in many groups, and predicated on the use of socially approved means of achievement. And today this is more so.

Since people have many statuses, it stands to reason that they ordinarily prefer situations which grant them high status.

Liberace will be found more often in the company of middle-aged ladies than of musicians. A pretty young thing is seen more often with appreciative swains than in W.C.T.U. meetings. A senator might enjoy the company of people to whom political power is an important status criterion more than a gathering of Egyptologists. A man who has high status in his family, and low status among his business or lodge associates, will prefer to be with his family, and a man for whom the situation is reversed may devote more time to his business or lodge.

A student may have high status among football-loving fellow students and alumni and low status among his professors. His status may differ further in these and other groups according to many elements. Is he colored or white? To what, if any, denomination does he belong? A popular singer may have high status among teenagers, but not, perhaps, among older persons. Some groups (including professors) probably rank the status of tweedy professors above that of pin-striped businessmen. Other groups (including businessmen) may rank them lower. And so it goes with military men or poets. Even within the same physical group, you may occupy more than one status according to whether the group is at a cocktail party, at work, sailing, dancing, or discussing entomology—according, that is, to what *system* is applied.

The fact that each of us has many statuses gives room for maneuver. You may succeed in transferring the high status achieved in one situation to another. The baseball hero or movie star might marry a wife and have children who are baseball or movie fans. Most people try to influence their immediate environment toward appreciation of the activity in which they achieve high status, or to seek an environment in which such appreciation is forthcoming. This is not always easy because private and public views and local and at-large situations differ. (*Nemo propheta in patria*—but, as with so many adages, the opposite is equally true.) There are difficulties, however. The football hero, whose classroom status is low, may not be able to avoid the classroom altogether. The man with high barroom status might have to go home once in a while. Even Socrates, whose status with his wife Xantippe is reported to have been rather low, had to. (Philosophers are suspected of loving wisdom

242

more than wives, which makes home life uncomfortable.)

Finally, though the individual belongs to one class, and has many statuses, he also remains an individual endowed with propensities and characteristics which are prior to his current social rankings, whether they are biologically inherent or the effect of past social situations. These biological and historical factors influence individual behavior as much as status and stratum. A beauty queen may give up the situations in which she enjoyed high status and become a nun rather than marry a man in the status group to which she belongs (and possibly in a higher class). The respected senator, the highly regarded businessman or scholar, occasionally can be seen within a group, or engaged in an activity, in which he will rank low. Sometimes this is done for moral reasons. A powerful prince may become a humble and anonymous monk. Sometimes it is done for non-moral reasons. Grandpa may lose status by chasing the baby sitter, or the King of England by marrying Mrs. Simpson. The conflict between the expectations of behavior placed on a person by virtue of his status and his personal wishes or pyschological needs has always furnished material for comedy—and tragedy.

The segmental nature of status systems and the diversity of criteria for status prevailing in different groups and occasions, offer scope to ambitions left unfulfilled by the race for economic and power rank. Indeed, the growing independence of status from class, on the one hand, and from tradition, on the other, makes it possible now for people to compete for status, even though unsuccessful, or uninterested, or too weary to attempt reaching the top in the class system.

Yet, however different your status is on different occasions and to different people, you may feel it to be constant. This feeling is protected through repudiation (or ignorance) of unwelcome status criteria and by avoiding as much as possible groups that hold them. Thus when we say "Mr. Gallagher has high status," without adding among whom, we mean that he is highly regarded among those with whom he actually associates or among those whom prestige criteria we approve. Since most people move in a limited circle and base their status expectations on selected criteria, we can assign a particular status to them.

We can do so just because of this limitation. The usefulness
of saying "Mr. Gallagher has high status"—and even the meaning of the phrase—becomes doubtful when we refer to society
at large, including groups with very divergent criteria.

DIVERGENT DEFINITIONS OF STATUS

The reason for separating class—economic rank—from status
—prestige rank—is that one ranking is not always identical with
the other. For the same reason, power ranking has not been
included in status. It is not implied that these rankings are always independent of each other. They are related. But their
relationship does not amount to identity. This is why we have
eschewed definitions of "status" as a residual category combining power and prestige ranking and definitions of "status"
as an all-embracing category combining power, prestige, and
economic ranking.

There are other usages. Marxists identify status and class.
Now, there is no denying that class influences rank on all social
scales. It has effects on power and on prestige. But rank on
the prestige and power scale is not automatically given by class
which is only one influence affecting it. The status of the wife
of the president differs from that of other perhaps more wealthy
ladies. A professor of chemistry may belong to a lower class
but have a higher status than another chemist or a carpenter.
More generally, white-collar employees may belong to the same
class but have different status from manual workers. By dog-
matically refusing to recognize that this difference makes a
difference, that class is relevant but not sufficient to establish
status, and that status matters, Marxists have marvelously misled
themselves and rarely attract those to whom their status is important (unless they feel greatly aggrieved).

Some scholars, outstandingly W. Lloyd Warner, have tried
to do away with the multiplicity of systems in which people
are ranked, not by reducing them to the economic one, as Marxists do, but by combining them. Class, to Warner, is a society-
wide status group. The status of the members depends on the
prestige brought by their occupation, source of income, house

type, and dwelling area. Each of these factors is weighed by the importance it has in determining total prestige. In Warner's words, "it is not the house or the job, the income or the neighborhood that is being measured, so much as the evaluations that are in the back of all our heads." The resulting ranking is combined with the rank resulting from an individual's participation in various activities, the prestige of which in turn is ranked by the members of his community. The whole thing gives great scope for questionnaires and statistical calculations. One does not always find it easy to resist believing that complex methods requiring intricate calculations are favored by some sociologists in the unconscious hope of enhancing their status among scientists and laymen. But there is no evidence for this suspicion, and anyway, it would be irrelevant to the validity of the methods.

Many of Warner's investigations were made in a town of six thousand inhabitants, and none in towns of more than seventeen thousand. The high degree of correlation among various status indices in small towns, and their general acceptance within the population, do not hold in big cities. The homogeneous small town evaluations led Warner to neglect the *segmental* nature of prestige ranking—the fact that the ranking of the same person or occupation differs from group to group. Moreover, the most mobile persons, and those least content with the small-town status system, are apt to leave for wider fields. Yet Warner thinks that his system holds for all the United States, and that a decline of vertical mobility (which he did not actually show to occur even in small towns) has taken place throughout American society.

Though Warner's scheme at first sight appears to combine various rating criteria, in the end class is made to depend entirely on prestige "in the thinking of the inhabitants of the community." Thus Warner nearly reverses Marx's reduction. Instead of reducing prestige and power to economic rank, as Marx does, he reduces everything, including economic rank and power, to prestige. Now, to fuse into one scale prestige, power, and income, each of which can be measured separately, is justified only if people ordinarily occupy identical ranks on each of the separate scales or if there is a constant relationship among these rankings. This would be likely if one of these factors determined the others entirely—for instance, economic rank, as Marxists believe—or if all rankings were determined by an outside factor. Neither seems the case. Hence, combination on one scale is largely a mathematical exercise which obscures the independence of these rankings from each other. It also obscures the entirely subjective and segmental character of status (prestige).

Data on stratification may be gathered also by asking people to what class they think they belong, and to what class they think others, within their purview, belong. This indicates how people classify themselves and others verbally and is an interesting reflection of stratification into statuses and classes. But the mirror image is not the object it mirrors. Stratification involves more than conscious and self-conscious classifications. The data gathered in this manner give only a superficial and partial view, reflecting ideology as much as fact, and thought (muddled thought) more than behavior.

Further work may lead to a more general agreement on definitions and methods among sociologists. So far it is obvious that the phenomena observed are important, the concepts helpful, the language in which sociologists talk about them too often ambiguous. Let us turn to another area made hazy by ambiguous definitions.

ELITES

Elite literally means "the elect" (from the Latin *eligere*: to choose). Generally, by "elite" we mean those eligible for leadership—the group of actual and potential leaders. Gaetano Mosca, Roberto Michels, and Vilfredo Pareto pioneered in investigating the political significance of stratification. They believed at first that the ineluctable existence of elites, which they discovered, made democracy impossible. This belief stemmed from misconception of democracy. (Particularly Mosca, but also Michels and Pareto in the end suggest that their discovery excludes only a narrowly conceived egalitarian democracy.) Similar ambiguities led Karl Marx astray in the opposite direction. He believed that elites need occur only in some economic systems. Communism would bring a classless and eliteless society. The Italian authors—who wrote after him—proved the unavoidability of elites in all social systems. Michels, in particular, insisted that "the iron law of oligarchy" controls revolutionary groups as much as it controls the governments they oppose. Michels was right in contending that all political movements have elites, wrong in his belief that these are *necessarily* oligarchic, i.e., independent of those led by them. (Max Weber's work led to similar conclusions, through less directly.) Though overstating the case, these Italian scholars gave much impulse to current studies of power distribution. But with the exception, perhaps, of Mosca, they were addicted to a romanticism which, being disguised as realism, endeared them to the disenchanted, but has little merit otherwise.

If we mean by elites simply the aggregate of persons who hold both highest power and highest prestige in any of the various hierarchies, stratification necessarily, and trivially implies elites. But there need be no single group which holds highest prestige and power in all hierarchies. Prestige and power elites need not even be identical. Nor need elites exist as closed, organized, dominating minorities, i.e., as oligarchies.

Since democracy is a form of government, it involves leaders and led by definition. (The word "democracy" defines their relationship: the leaders depend on the led.) The leaders usually are part of a political elite. Hence, some types of elite are necessarily compatible with democracy, but not all. Much depends on vertical mobility. How easily does one acquire and lose elite membership? By what means? Who selects for membership in the elite, and how? Are there segmental elites or is there one over-all elite *acting as a social group?* What are the relations between elite membership and top class? How important is the elite in deciding matters of concern to others? What does it decide? Does it coerce or does it influence others? These matters, the degree of cohesion among elite members, the degree of concentration of power and prestige in the hands of the elite, and, finally, its *autonomy*, together indicate whether the elite is more or less compatible with democratic government.

Do we then have elites in America? We have income classes and status groups. Among them some are more powerful in making decisions affecting the country and more prestige-bearing than others. But suppose we ask: do the same persons hold high rank as income recipients, prestige bearers, and decision makers? The answer is that high rank on one scale increases the chances of high rank on the others, but does not suffice to establish it. If we ask: where do those who hold high rank on any of these scales come from? how long do they hold it? how cohesive a group do they form? we find that though family position makes a difference, mobility is considerable and shows no signs of declining. Status group solidarity is immensely strengthened if the bishop, the general, and the corporation vice-president each come from high status families and have undergone similar educational experiences. Class solidarity is strengthened equally if the rich have come from rich families. On the whole, this does not seem to be the case in the United States as much as in Europe.

More important still, we have many elites originating and functioning separately and remaining quite independent of each other. There is an artistic elite, an intellectual elite, a political elite, and a military elite. But our generals do not have power over politics and art. Our politicians do not influence the intellectual elite (nor is there much influence the other way around, unfortunately) and so on. In each profession we may speak of an elite more or less narrowly defined. For instance, there is an elite of ophthalmologists and of physicians, of criminal and of corporation lawyers. The artistic elite is important in determining the prevalence of aesthetic fashions and sensibilities, just as the fashion elite is in determining fashions in garments. The elite of geographers plays a major role in originating, approving, vetoing, or spreading new ways of map making. And the political elite exercises influence with regard to government policies. Quite often the exoteric elite—the group that has influence or prestige in various publics—differs from the esoteric elite—the group that has high status among professionals, whether psychoanalysts or politicians.

The existence of many elites, independent of each other, and so constituted that elite status in one hierarchy is not sufficient even for much prestige, and certainly not for power in another hierarchy, means that we do not have a national over-all elite as a self-conscious social group that acts together as such and dominates the others in its own interest. Particular geographical units or professional groups may well be oligarchies. Small and medium-big towns and regions or professional groups may each be dominated by oligarchic elites. But the very plurality and separate existence of elites argue against a national elite. The many elites (plural) do not form an elite (singular) except by arithmetical aggregation. They neither act nor feel as a unit. Even where national over-all leadership necessarily exists—as in national politics—its power over local leadership, and in matters other than national governments, is very limited, as is the influence of the local elites on the national political elite. C. Wright Mills (see *The Power Elite*) thought differently. But his evidence is unconvincing. His method might be used to prove that we are dominated by men wearing glasses. (It was used to prove at various times that we are dominated by Jews.) Basically it consists in pointing to a number of men more powerful than others and implying that this aggregation *ipso facto* proves that they act together as an independent and coercive group in their own interest, and contrary to the interest of the people at large whom they dominate.

ELITES IN A DEMOCRACY

Democracy implies popular influence on the selection of political elite members. If membership in a political elite is inherited without effective popular consultation, and the elite forms a closed, caste-like, cohesive, homogeneous group, concentrating in its hands decisive power over many activities, democracy is ineffective. More important still—and of course in turn dependent mainly on the influence nonmembers have on the selection of the elite and ultimately of leaders from it—is the influence of the people at large on the conduct of the elite. The elite may lead and guide the people. It may govern as a responsive agent of the people, even as its servant—or as its independent master. Influence on the selection of the political elite by nonmembers is indispensable if the government process is to be democratic. Not so, however, in nongovernmental institutions. Professional and ecclesiastical elites are often selected through co-optation by current members. The word "democracy" has no relevance to hospitals—we do not want surgeons selected or treatment prescribed by popular election. Where tests of expertness can be used, popular preferences are irrelevant, or at least not decisive. Democracy is justified in politics because there are no objective, accepted tests of fitness for political leadership.

The process by which the elite is selected also affects the distance of the elite from those it rules or influences. The elite may be the top of a continuous pyramid, or stratification may be discontinuous with great gaps. Finally, the extent of the elite's power over the people and the means of exercising it help determine whether the elite is a democratic one. Power and prestige can be concentrated exclusively in the elite, the people hardly sharing in either. This is most likely when the elite is closed—when nonmembers have little influence on its selection. It is likely, too, when elite membership requires qualifications few can achieve, a special combination of talents, or a degree of education available only to a few. Elites, then, may be classified according to whether (a) membership is hereditary (closed) or not (open). If the elite is open we may further consider (b) vertical mobility, (c) criteria of selection, (d) locus of power to select, (e) extent of power held.

An effective democracy has a political elite selected at least in part by those below, though the range of selectors and of available selectees need not include all adults. The power of the political elite is limited—as is political power itself in a democracy. All power and prestige are shared fairly widely in a democracy, since there are many elites, and non-elite members can both rise into the elite and play an important role in selection. The degree of concentration is comparatively low: the number of persons in the elite is greater, and the extra prestige and power shared among them less, than in nondemocratic organizations. The distance between elite and non-elite is bridged by numerous groups in between. The power exercised by any group over another is limited in a democracy, and the conduct of the elite ultimately depends on the people at large no less than the conduct of the people depends on that of the elite. In short, in a democracy the elite leads with the consent of the led. Its autonomy and coercive power as well as its authority and internal soldiarity are limited and shared among a large number of persons who have made their way up by different means and from various origins.

In some countries, elite groups lead the others. They set the pattern by taking initiatives and by accepting, or vetoing, initiatives coming from elsewhere. This state of affairs was characteristic of democracies in the past, and it seems to be what most of the Founding Fathers of the American Republic had in mind. However, particularly since the presidency of Andrew Jackson, the trend in the United States has been toward curtailing the influence of elites. Elites often become marginal rather than leading groups. Elites are allowed to lead only inasmuch as they embody and heighten common popular tendencies; they do not create, or truly lead, or veto them. To be sure, a single elite member, by definition, has at least in some fields more power and prestige than a single non-elite member. But in most fields in America the elite groups, singly and together, are less powerful than the non-elite groups. Just as landlords as a group are assuredly less powerful than tenants as a group, the elite groups today, rather than initiating or vetoing popular tendencies, express them, justify them, and write footnotes to them. The advantages of this state of affairs are patent. Some drawbacks will be discussed later.

AGGLUTINATION AND TRANSFORMATION OF STATUS

Statuses are highly agglutinative when elite status in *all* groups automatically results from elite status in *one* group, or when all elite statuses depend on each other, even though not dependent pre-eminently on status in a particular hierarchy, or finally when high prestige (status) is automatically linked to (and particularly when it is generated by) high power and income. The first type of agglutination does not occur in a democracy and the second does, although less than in other systems. A rich man, a powerful politician, a famous actor, or baseball player does not automatically have top prestige in different systems. But such men seldom rank at the bottom among astronomers, teenage girls, or biophysicists. They each have higher status in these groups, and more influence, than they would, had they not been respectively rich, politically powerful, or famous.

However, very agglutinative statuses, all depending on political status, are characteristic of totalitarianism. Thus Stalin (and Hitler) was in his lifetime not only political dictator—the head of an organized, oligarchic, political elite—but also the unquestioned head of the hierarchy in any field in which he cared to pull his rank: in music, linguistics, genetics, architecture, law, painting, literature, and what not. And so with other members of the political elite. Both prestige (status) and actual power depended on rank in the political hierarchy. Political status carried over into all fields; no status in any hierarchy was independent of political status. In contrast, the American president and the whole American political elite together have limited political power, and no power whatever—though some prestige —beyond politics. The president's high political status gives him neither top prestige nor power as linguist or geneticist or musician. He scarcely influences which theory of genetics is to prevail or what music should be played. (President Truman's protest against a critic's view of his daughter's musical talent did not change the critic's mind or anyone else's. Of course, the daughter's "singing" attracted a public because of the father's prestige. But this prestige led to curiosity rather than high evaluation of her talents: it gave her no rank whatever in the musical hierarchy.) Characteristically, the many elite groups in a democracy are autonomous. Few persons have elite status in several hierarchies and none automatically.

Status agglutination means that status in one hierarchy and system *automatically* carries over to another; or that the same factors that led to one led to the other. The more or less successful *use* of one status to achieve another may be distinguished from agglutination as *status transformation*.

From time immemorial riches, power, and prestige (sometimes called honor or glory) have been the main social ambitions of men. Usually the achievement of one has permitted the achievement of the others to some degree, by agglutination or by transformation. The relationship of the values longed for may be alternative: a saint does not achieve his power or prestige by riches; nor does he gain riches through them. Or the relation-

252   PART TWO: SOCIETY

ship may be cumulative: prestige may be transformed into power
or wealth and thereby increased. In some societies wealth could
best be transformed into power, and prestige was more easily
transformed into wealth than vice versa. Societies differ also in
the intensity of the ambition they instill for any and all of those
goals and with regard to the means they make available to
fulfill it.

Some opportunity for transformation of statuses exists in all
societies. Few are the societies where great sexual attractiveness—
high status in the sexual prestige (glamour) system—automatically implies high power or wealth by agglutination. But fewer
still are the societies where great sexual attractiveness cannot be
monetized or transformed into power to some degree. When
the mists of prehistory lifted, such transformations were among
the first things recorded. Mistresses exercised royal power by
trading on their charms. Captains and kings traded on their
power and prestige to possess these charms. Through recorded
history, the possibilities of status transformation have changed
but they have never been lost sight of.

Possession of any of the values men cherish gives appropriate
status in some system. In turn, possession of one value can be
used to acquire another, and therewith status in other systems.
(Of course, when status is agglutinative, status in one system
is status in others, too.) The use of sexual attractiveness to acquire power has been mentioned. It is patent that sexual attractiveness can also be monetized—societies only differ in the manner in which this can be done. The reverse procedure is implied in this: money and power can help acquire possession of
what is sexually attractive. Besides, money and power lend
some sexual fascination to the possessor apart from any use. All
other things equal, the powerful or moneyed, and indeed the
bearers of any prestige, are more attractive—however irrelevantly
—than those equally endowed as persons. But then the person,
partly a creature of society anyway, is difficult to disentangle
from the setting.

DEMOCRATIZED—OR COMMERCIALIZED?—TRANSFORMATION

Whereas in the past, sexual attractiveness would lead to the acquisition of riches and power mainly through marriage or other sexual relationships, today the "glamour girl" (or boy) can easily use her attractiveness without becoming dependent on any one owner of wealth or power, and without sexual relationship. For example, by becoming a TV or movie actress, she might directly acquire wealth, power, and prestige. She still monetizes her attractiveness and uses it to acquire prestige. But she no longer has to devote it to a single person, or to a few, who have what she needs to transform what she has into what she wants. Mass media have wrought a triple change: they have multiplied the avenues of transformation; the power of those holding sway over the few avenues previously available has diminished accordingly; and people who have neither glamour to sell, nor the money to buy it, as the wealthy and powerful could in the past, now can purchase some form of participation in glamour through the mass media. Indeed, their purchasing power is likely to exceed that of the richest single person, and so does the prestige they are able to lend collectively.

The easier transformation of values and of status spreads access and possession more widely. But it has drawbacks which become patent when we inquire into the relationship of status and personal behavior.

CHAPTER XVI

Roles and the Prestige of Histrionics

The same person may have the statuses of male, husband, lover, father, son, student, waiter, Methodist, American, baseball fan, patient, bowling club member, dentist, and customer. He may activate additional statuses at any moment. He may become an automobile driver, guest or host at a party, or defendant in a law suit. Status in each situation indicates the rank, both of the position occupied and of the person occupying it. But the esteem in which the incumbent is held depends chiefly on the way in which he fulfills the requirements of the position, the way in which he plays his role. Indeed, status becomes real inasmuch as the bearer plays the role that goes with it, and his performance is accepted. There are differences in the way roles are played. Mr. Smith's personality largely disappears behind his role as a mailman, whereas his role as a mailman may all but disappear behind the forceful expression of Mr. Jones's individuality.

The role implicit in each status includes many aspects of social existence. It determines, or at least limits and influences, the conduct of its bearer on many occasions and the attitudes, values, and behavior expected of all persons occupying the status. Every status is linked with a particular role, but the two things are not the same to the individual. His statuses are ascribed to him on the basis of his age and sex, his birth or marriage into a particular family unit, his occupation, etc. His roles are learned on the basis of his current or anticipated statuses. Although occupying statuses at all times, individuals activate sometimes one status and play its role and sometimes another. Consider Ralph Linton's illustration (paraphrased):

A man spends the day working as clerk in a store. Behind the counter, his active status is that of a clerk. The role associated with this status patterns his relations with customers. The patterns will be well known both to him and to the customers and will enable them to transact business with a minimum of delay or misunderstanding. When he retires to the rest room for a smoke and meets other employees there, his clerk status becomes latent; he assumes another active status based upon his position in the group composed of the store's employees. When closing time comes, he lays aside both his clerk- and store-employee group statuses and, while on the way home, operates simply in terms of his status with respect to the society's age-sex system. Thus, if he is a young man, he will at least feel that he ought to get up and give his seat to a lady, while if he is an old one he will be quite comfortable about keeping it. As soon as he arrives at his house, a new set of statuses will be activated. In pursuance of the roles associated with these family statuses, he will try to be cordial to his mother-in-law, affectionate to his wife, and a stern disciplinarian to Junior, whose report card marks a new low. If it happens to be a lodge night, all his familial statuses will become latent at about eight o'clock. As soon as he enters the lodge room and puts on his uniform as Grand Imperial Lizard in the Ancient Order of Dinosaurs he assumes a new status, which has been latent since the last meeting, and performs in terms of its role until it is time for him to take off his uniform and go home.

Since the individual's various statuses are activated at different times, there can be no head-on collision between the roles associated with them although these may be inconsistent. Usually, however, the roles associated with the statuses within a single system do not conflict. This also holds for statuses within different systems when they normally converge upon the same individuals. Thus the roles of adult male, of father, of craft specialist, of friend, and so on will normally be adjusted to one another. Such adjustments are developed through the experience of individuals who have occupied such series of statuses simultaneously and have gradually eliminated most of the conflicts through a process of trial and error.

In those rare cases in which, through some accident, statuses whose roles are fundamentally incompatible converge upon the same individual, we have the material of high tragedy. The tragedy of the House of Oedipus and the closing episodes of the *Niebelungenlied* are classical examples, while at the level of simpler folklore we have the Scottish story of the man who finds himself host to his brother's murderer. The individual upon whom the incompatible roles converge meets the problem by the familiar pattern of operating in terms of different statuses at different times, even though recognizing that the associated roles will, in their performance, negate each other's performance. Thus in the Scottish story the brother, as host, conducts the murderer safely beyond clan territory and then, as brother to the victim, engages him in combat to the death.

Societies may vary greatly in the sharpness with which they define roles, in the firmness with which the status is attached to the rolebearer, and in the combination of roles which are regarded as permissible. Each society gives us some choice among the callings in which we may work and the ways in which we may live. The range of choice is set by our sex, our age, our inherited physical and psychological endowment, and by the social interpretation placed on all these. It is narrowed further by having parents located in some specific part of the system of social relationships. Since each society elaborates and partly creates its own needs by selectively interpreting and utilizing the potentialities of the human species and its environment, each will open its own choice of opportunities to individuals. Each society must condition individuals to the opportunities offered, or its order will be endangered.

The choice open to individuals is narrow in primitive societies with only few positions to be filled. Almost every man might have to hunt or to cultivate the soil and almost every woman might be expected to prepare the resulting food. In developed societies, choice for individuals is narrow when most functions are "ascribed," and wider when positions can be "achieved." Positions are "ascribed" when they are filled according to birth. They are "achieved" when they are filled according to individual qualifications other than parental position. In many societies a great number of positions are ascribed. It is believed that the required capacities are inherited in a straight line: to the son the abilities of the father are ascribed. In present Western civilization, the position of king is almost the only one which is still wholly ascribed by law. There is no doubt, however, that birth still gives direct advantages to the well-born, and they also have more opportunities to use what talent they have to qualify for the most desirable positions.

Choice is widest for all when there are many positions to fill, when individuals are not bound to them by birth, and when they have many opportunities to acquire the qualifications for the calling of their choice. A more precise definition would confront us with the question: is there more social choice when there is less choice (opportunity) more equally distributed, or when there is more choice less equally distributed? Unfortunately, the most equal distribution is not necessarily the one that distributes most. This problem, overlooked in the utilitarian formula "the greatest happiness for the greatest number," need not worry us with regard to happiness, which anyway is not measurable. But it crops up when we consider the social distribution of any actual quantity—for example, income. Which of the alternatives would make people feel better is still another problem.

THE NEED FOR ROLES

> *All the world's a stage,*
> *And all the men and women merely players:*
> *They have their exits and their entrances;*
> *And one man in his time plays many parts, . . .*
> *Seeking the bubble reputation*
> *Even in the cannon's mouth.*
>
> *(As You Like It)*

Why do men take their many parts with less conviction and more anxiety than in the past? We self-consciously *play* our social roles and do not live them; we change them too often to use the Stanislavsky method. (The famous Russian director, Constantin Stanislavsky, insisted that actors live and feel roles before attempting to play them—wherefrom "the method.")

Modern man must keep fit for ever-new parts, and adjustable. He has neither the time nor disposition to grow into any role. Since there is no regular progression from one status to another, individuals cannot be fully prepared for the variety of roles into which society may cast them. They feel uncertain, therefore, of how their roles should be acted. There is a sense of drift—the suddenly cast actors are trying to understand the play's meaning with little knowledge of the interpretations tradition has left.

Many roles are not only new to the bearers but unprecedented in society and undefined by custom. Even the accustomed, unavoidable roles of women, of parents, of old people, of husband and wife are changing toward new definitions with as yet vague and often inconsistent outlines. We are bemused, therefore, unsure about what is expected from us and about what to expect from others. Yet, to live and work together serenely, people must harbor and fulfill mutual expectations which can come only from stable socially defined and accepted roles. When roles, and his progress through them, are somewhat continuous, the individual's life, too, becomes continuous. If not, life is in danger of being reduced to discontinuous fragments.

The part each of us takes has meaning only when others take theirs. In John Donne's words, the world is "a great and harmonious organ where all parts are played and all play parts." Harmony can flow only from the relation of the parts. Without supporting players there are no cues and established characters. Life without an ethos to organize it becomes inchoate clutter or a tedious jog trot. Greed, horseplay, and smart chatter are all that is left. A lover needs a beloved; a parent, children; an authority, subjects; a hostess, guests; a teacher, students; a minister, a congregation. Props are needed too: directly functional props, such as the teacher's blackboard; and ceremonial props, such as the minister's vestment and the church. They give purpose beyond giving warmth and shelter. This is true for most of the things we wear, live in, and move in. Yet the props have no meaning unless the roles do. And the roles have no meaning unless we have time to grow into them, to make them our own, and through them to relate to others in the conviction that what we are doing is meaningful.

We are each secured to reality and life by social bonds that

tie us to persons, positions, and things. Life is real to us and
meaningful only if we take a part, only if we part-take, only
if we have a role to play. When we each feel but tenuously
linked to our part, social ties easily come undone. Individuals, dis-
affected and disengaged, float freely like specks of dust. It is not
an enjoyable freedom.

Shakespeare's Lear went mad when, having stripped himself
of power, he was shorn of his entourage by his black-hearted
daughters. His entourage had allowed Lear to continue in the
role of king, to keep his status after giving up his kingdom.
When the ungrateful daughters insisted that his courtiers were
functionally unnecessary, a luxury, Lear rightly, though in vain,
entreated:

> *Oh, reason not the need. Our basest beggars*
> *Are in the poorest thing superfluous.*
> *Allow not nature more than nature needs,*
> *Man's life's as cheap as beast's.*

Turning directly to Regan, Lear averred:

> *Thou art a lady.*
> *If only to go warm were gorgeous,*
> *Why, nature needs not what thou gorgeous wear'st,*
> *Which scarcely keeps thee warm.*

No sociologist could stress more tellingly that physically
unneeded "luxury" may be socially indispensable. It is needed
to play a role which in turn may be indispensable to life and
sanity. As Lear says, "our basest beggars" often put their social
before their physical needs. "Nature needs not what thou gorgeous wear'st" (wear for the sake of splendor) is not literally
true. Nature, too, needs the physically unnecessary. The pea-
cock's tail, the lion's mane, and the nightingale's liquid song do
not keep the beasts warm. They serve a social function. They are
as much part of the sexual roles animals play as Regan's costume
is of her female role (except that the gorgeous gown is worn
also to indicate high status). Men differ from beasts not because
they have roles and signify them symbolically, but because they
can slip in and out of raiment and roles. We are not, as animals
are, endowed each by nature with an instinctively fixed role.

We create and we take ours, using and developing the *personae* culture transmits to us. We can thus emancipate ourselves from any role. But not from all roles. We can change, but to do altogether without roles and the props that complement them, far from being natural—or functional—is, and literally brings, madness. Nor can we do without the norms, the rituals, the splendors, and the symbols that signify our roles.

> How but in custom and in ceremony
> Are innocence and beauty born?

Yeats asks in "A Prayer for My Daughter." Not only beauty and innocence—all the humanities, civilization itself, are born in and live by custom and by ceremony, by conventions and symbols which give meaning to roles and to us the conviction that they are lawfully ours. But when our roles change too often, it is as though we were without: we have no role that is quite our own. Meanings and symbols are linked by time. Without tradition, life loses symbols and ultimately meaning.

TRAGEDY AND ROLE CONFLICT

In our society, the frequency of role change, the ambiguity of roles, the mutability and diversity of their definition, and our unavoidable lack of preparation breed much confusion and anxiety, a sense of discomfort and alienation. We feel unable to identify the self with any role. Yet when it is not bounded by status and role and firmly related to a system of expectations that gives orchestral support to its solo performance, the self is hardly identified. It may never take shape, remaining outside of its many activities, ever ready to play new roles but never fully invested in any. In the end, no self is experienced—only impersonations, pseudopersonalities which do not amount to one identifiable person. (The Italian playwright Luigi Pirandello deals with this problem in most of his plays—quite explicitly in *Six Characters in Search of an Author*.)

In times past, tragedy issued from incompatible roles demanded of one individual by his several statuses. Tragedy was bred also when individual needs collided with the demands of a social status. The conflict was transcended by sacrifice not of one or the other—for tragedy becomes tragedy because neither status nor individual needs can be renounced in the end—but of the person in whose breast they clashed. Aristotle's notion of tragedy as caused by a "fatal flaw" in the character of the protagonist applies only to some tragic heroes (to Shakespearean more than to Greek heroes). Even where the difficulty originates in a "flaw," it becomes tragedy only when the flaw includes conflicting personal needs and a strong sense of social duty, be it manifested only in guilt. When the flaw (*hamartia*) is conceived of merely as personal error, or weakness, or avoidable sin, the tragic hero is reduced to a misguided neurotic and tragedy to a case history. The waning of the tragic sense causes us to experience life less deeply and fully and to banalize existence to the point of identifying "tragedy" and "unnecessary pain" (for example, a traffic accident). Tragedy no longer requires a hero or a fate to be transcended—it is painful without being meaningful. In the past, tragedy was sorrow attending greatness of aspiration or conflict of obligations, an examination of meanings and a reflection on fate. Tragedy is possible only when roles are sharply defined and when the statuses with which we are invested are treated as though inexorably given us by a divine or natural order—at least by more than individual convenience. A sense of tragic—that is, justified—incompatibility becomes rare when the sense of status obligation does. Perhaps tragedy in the past, too, existed chiefly in the poet's imagination. No matter. That imagination was produced and accepted then, whereas today we can no more imagine a tragedy than we can design a public monument. Both require a spirit transcending kindness, comfort, and convenience. But these are the virtues—no small virtues at that—our age prizes.

Role conflicts still occur but they seldom issue in tragedy. Edward VIII, King of England, found it impossible to reconcile the role called for by his royal status with the modern ideal of romantic love and individual selection of marriage partners regardless of status. How did he resolve this role conflict? King Edward declined the role into which his birth had cast him. Confronted with a choice between the duties imposed by *raison d'état* and the pleasures of playing husband to a Mrs. Simpson,

on whom he doted, he simply slipped out of his royal status.
Then, without too much delay, the ex-king and the ex-Mrs.
Simpson each published their stories in the newspapers. They
caused a "sensation" but no tragedy. Compare the French trage-
dian, Jean Racine (in his *Berenice*), speaking through the emperor Titus confronted with the same choice:

> *Vous même rougieriez de ma lâche conduite*
> *Vous verriez à regret marche à votre suite*
> *Un indigne empereur sans empire, sans cour,*
> *Vil spectacle aux humains de la faiblesse de l'amour.*

(You would yourself blush at my slackness. You would regret
being followed by an unworthy emperor without empire, or
court, offering to the world a sleazy spectacle of love-weakness.)
So Desdemona today might sue Othello for separate maintenance
—exchanging her status as wife for that of divorcee and delight-
ing the gossip columnists rather than the tragedians. All this makes
life much more comfortable. But we are paying a price, too: the
inconveniences of the past were only an aspect of the depth of
feeling that was then idealized.

For us, the fuss that Rigoletto makes about his daughter's lost
virginity is as hard to understand as the behavior of the elder
Germont, who appeals to the generosity of the courtesan his
son wants to marry to reject the son so as not to harm his sister's
status. The marriages of sister and brother appear unconnected
to us; and the father's role is not to interfere with either. Yet
the roles of father, son, and daughter, the statuses of "courtesan"
and "nice girl," and the institution of the family once were so
defined in the upper bourgeoisie as to make the matter not out-
landish. If today we still feel anything for Alexandre Dumas'
La Dame aux Camélias (dramatized in Italian as *La Traviata*) or
for Victor Hugo's play *Le Roi s'Amuse* (entitled *Rigoletto* in
Italian), it is because we are enchanted by Giuseppe Verdi's
music, which transmutes emotions occasioned by a past social
order into universally experienced feelings of sorrow, love, rage,
and tenderness.

Yet we find it difficult to accept the intensity of these feelings. Not only our definition of particular statuses and roles has
changed; the general meaning of "status" and "role" as we ex-

perience it differs from that of the traditional definition. No status and no role seem to us to require the sacrifice of the individual or to generate the conflicts that issue in tragedy. Statuses are not as polarized and definitive as they were. There are no chasms, no tragic passions. Instead we have maladjustments, anxieties, traffic accidents, and soap operas to celebrate them. Beyond that, we find the grandeur of opera and of tragedy hard to take. It is too uncommon. Man elevated to the height of passion appears unreal and ludicrous. We are accustomed to consider "realistic" only an image of man reduced to squalor, or comfortable triviality. Prose, we believe, is somehow truer than poetry. This notion rests on a confusion of the familiar with the true; nonetheless, it may well drain the mind of its vision and make itself come true. Already aspiration, "idealism," largely aims at more comfort for more people.

Every generation sees the Golden Age at some other time, past or future. Paradise is never here—it is always lost or to be gained. Lest we be unjust to the present, let us note that our way of life has advantages which the grandeur of the past did not have. And we are getting rid of the material misery from which that grandeur rose. Quite possibly the gains offset the losses—or do we think so because the gains are more tangible and obvious than the losses? Since direct experience might not reveal them, it is necessary to stress the losses here.

The old rigid definitions of roles recede slowly. *Life* magazine (November 14, 1955) reported that in Aspromonte, in southernmost Italy, one Giuseppe Calipari surrendered to the police, after living as an outlaw for years because he murdered the murderers of his brother, the brothers of the fiancée his brother had jilted. In Aspromonte, kinship statuses and roles are still defined not only differently but also more seriously than with us. One does not play them; one lives and dies in them.

THE PRESTIGE OF HISTRIONICS

In contrast, we feel that we assume parts temporarily, as actors do. We vest ourselves easily with statuses and divest ourselves easily. But role playing has not lost importance. On the contrary. Nothing is more important to actors than their success in any role. Because we are not quite sure of the demands of the role, we cannot measure our performance by them; we stand in need of constant reassurance and, like actors, we use applause as our main measure of excellence. Success is not governed by specific criteria applying to each role as in the past. The player achieves popularity not so much by playing a role as by displaying what is believed to be his personality in that role. Perhaps the public wishes to learn how to have "personality" from the TV "personalities," actors, and gossip columnists who give the "inside" view of their world. The folks must learn how to be folksy, to invent and exploit their own personalities. Having a personality has become almost a synonym for engaging in histrionics. Many people, wistfully or with awe, refer to those engaged in conventionally unconventional antics as "characters." "Character" is identified with the dramatic, the make-believe, and the conspicuously senseless. Such spectacular "craziness" is usually adopted and admired by persons who are nagged by a feeling of emptiness. They attempt to satisfy the gnawing hunger for self-identity by impersonation—by covering the void with a pseudo-personality implanted by and for the outside. Our yearning to be approved by others may alienate us from ourselves if in making a play for them we only try appealing lines and do not internalize anything but sensitivity to public applause or disapproval.

Yet this ambition engages the attention of the audience as much as the roles acted. There is less interest in *Julius Caesar* convincingly acted than in the way actor X does Julius Caesar. We identify with the actor playing more than with the personage he plays, with role taking more than with the role taken. Actors were outcasts in the past because they impersonated rather than were, because they had substance only in the personalities and the eyes of others. They were considered "secondhand characters." If they are cast in nearly central roles in our society, it is because conscious role playing has become nearly central. We feel cast no more securely, no less arbitrarily and temporarily than they. And they, playing with professional aplomb, have much to teach us. No wonder the prestige of histrionics has been rising.

The high mobility among groups, the looseness with which our social roles sit on us, the uncertain and inconsistent cues roared at us from all directions make for a specific type of anxiety. It stems less from conflicts of well-defined obligations and patterns than from lack of accepted patterns and from disorientation and insecurity. But there is no evidence that total anxiety (if it could be summed) is greater than that generated by societies with people unalterably welded to firmly patterned roles. In such societies, those suffered who would have been better off if they could have changed. In our society, those suffer who find it hard to adapt to sudden and frequent change. Similarly, primitive societies, though they prepare their members well for the few roles and statuses they offer, stunt the capacities of those who might have thrived in roles that do not there exist. With many roles to choose from—though we insist now on a uniform style of playing—we impose the agonies of choice and change.

ROLE CONFUSION AND INCONSISTENCY

Just as tragedy in the past pointed to the importance of role conflicts, so jokes today indicate how important role confusion and inconsistency are to us. "Jokes," the German philosopher-poet Friedrich Nietzsche said rightly, "often are the epitaphs of emotions." They slay them sometimes, too, one may add, or replace one emotion by another, or shrink it to a manageable size. When becoming the subject of jokes, even the devil is reduced to a "poor devil"—clearly a wishful transposition, for it is humans who feel as powerless pawns in his hands.

In the past, vertical status differentiation jokes were more frequent. Obviously in defense and rationalization of the status pretension of the upper groups, the subjects of mirth were immigrants, Negroes, servant girls, and country bumpkins. Our egalitarian views make these jokes unappealing: role confusion jokes have replaced them. And career women, Boy Scout leaders, women drivers are mines for humorists, for they combine sexual roles with activities which seem not quite to fit these roles. *Charlie's Aunt*, a hardy play and prototype of a whole genre, produces in a slightly more elaborate form the sort of merriment with which children react to the archetypical role confusion joke: daddy putting on mommy's hat. Just as the art of tragedy permits us to express our feeling and take some of the sting out of it by re-experiencing it vicariously (as well as deepening and universalizing it), is humor, too, takes the sting out of many a painful and anxious experience, through making it trivial or unreal, or depersonalizing it; often (but not necessarily) by banalizing and vulgarizing it.

In a minor key, role conflicts, too, continue and even inhere in many statuses. A factory foreman, for instance, is charged with enforcing the orders of the management. Yet he may identify himself with those who carry them out. A noncommissioned army officer has a sometimes uncomfortable status between officers and privates.

Other conflicts are due not to ambiguous status, but to the difficulty of separating sharply contrasting roles played by the same person. Career women experience conflicts between their female and career roles. Male roles, in contrast, are traditionally integrated with careers of which they are part. Most children experience some conflict between their roles in the family and among friends. The student member of an honor board experiences a role conflict—owing to conflicting group loyalties— when he discovers a fraternity brother or friend among those he is in duty bound to punish for cheating.

Persistent role confusion or inconsistency can have effects as grave, even though not as dramatic, as those of role conflict. The role confusion of parents, for instance, may wreak havoc on the children. Some types of homosexuality can be regarded as internalized and perpetuated role confusion; the little boy may pattern himself after the mother or sister, rather than the father or brother. He may have been pushed into that role or have found it rewarding. Possibly he escaped into it from a role that, for internal or external reasons, he felt inadequate for or feared to play; or the model patterns may have been confused.

Role inconsistency associated with inconsistent statuses held by the same person, in different systems or groups, can be deeply disturbing to the unfortunate bearer of the statuses. A Negro physician, holding high occupational and low ethnic status, will be treated with the deference paid his occupational status in the hospital. Outside he will be expected to show toward white men of lower occupational status the deference demanded from colored people. He will be vexed much more by this inconsistency, and resent it more, than he would consistent statuses, even if they were lower. The situation of a Jewish businessman ranking high on the income and less high on the ethnic prestige scale; of a clergyman or professor, ranking high on the occupational and low on the income scale, differ only in degree of inconsistency from that of the Negro doctor. It seems likely that status inconsistency is a major source of frustration. Like so many private frustrations, it is expressed in ideas and actions addressed to logically unrelated public issues. "If anything ail a man," said Henry David Thoreau, ". . . if he have a pain in his bowels even . . . he forthwith sets about reforming—the world."

CHAPTER XVII

Snobbery (and the Supreme Court's Prescription)

STATUS AMBITION

Status is mainly a rank on the prestige scale maintained by taking an appropriate role. To raise status is to increase the deference of others. Ordinarily status is changed by means of winning or losing the things by means of which it is legitimately achieved: in Melanesia, enemy heads; in Western society, offices, titles, and occupations. The yearning for higher status, for fame, honor, respect, and deference inspires accomplishments of varying social usefulness, as does the craving for higher income. All societies approve some means of raising status, punish others, and ridicule still others.

When there is a genuine concern for the achievement which changes the status base, status ambition can be of great social benefit. The wish for the lasting esteem of our fellow men— status ambition—has motivated many a deed of war and peace. *Exegi monumentum aere perennius* ("I built a monument more lasting than bronze"), Horace exclaims. His poems shall assure his fame—his status—through the ages. Thus, he comforts himself, *non omnis moriar* ("I shall not wholly die"). And John Milton (in *Lycidas*): "Fame is the spur that the clear spirit doth raise/To scorn delights and live laborious days."

A Japanese samurai committing hara-kiri—ritual suicide—and

an American white-collar employee working hard to make enough to buy expensive Christmas gifts are both motivated by status concern. Competitive gift giving or sometimes destruction of one's own property—often referred to by the Chinook (American Indian) word *potlatch*—is an ancient custom known in most primitive tribes. It survives in manifold ways today. It always includes attempts to raise, demonstrate, or maintain one's status. Thorstein Veblen regarded it as an element of the conspicuous waste which he dourly satirized in his *Theory of the Leisure Class*. (Numerous other elements, chiefly magical, are involved. The French sociologist Marcel Mauss has assembled much evidence indicating that the primitive division of labor was connected with gift exchanges.

"THAT LAST INFIRMITY OF NOBLE MIND"

Prestige (ironically, the word comes from *praestigium*: illusion), the esteem of others, can be gained and lost in countless ways. To acquire "the bubble reputation," people may go quite literally to the length, the height, and the depth Shakespeare suggests. Reputation is found not only "in the cannon's mouth" but in many equally deadly places.

The savage wearing a lion's mane hopes to impress on others that he slew a lion; in a sense he hopes to increase his status by incorporating that of the lion. This is also the aim of the cannibal who eats the slain foe: he hopes to acquire his qualities by incorporation; mainly, he hopes to appropriate the enemy's fame; sometimes literally to appropriate his name, too.

Likewise, a hostess may bag a famous "lionized" man to get some of his reputation and enhance her status, to partake of the deference paid him. She reverses the cannibal's procedure—she usually feeds her man—but she hopes for the same result. Hostess and cannibal have discovered that by association, such as eating or feeding each other, one can take over some of the fame and the *mana* of one's victims or guests. ("Host" has the same Latin root as "hostility.") This is also the belief of many of the faithful who incorporate the religious hero through ritual eating—direct or symbolic—of his body (the host). Totemic feasts and communal meals are part of many religious observances.

Hostesses, however, discovered something primitives did not know: a reputation can be built without achievements or deeds of valor, simply by being associated in the public eye with those who have high status. One can manipulate status without changes in the status base. A cannibal after all has to beat his man before he eats him. The hostess only needs to entice her lion to feed him. With this discovery *snobbery* was born.

Snobbery is an attempt to vest oneself with an undeserved prestige, by striking an attitude sheerly for the sake of the prestige it is to bring, making the attitude therefore spurious; or by presuming on an association entirely because of the prestige it carries. Snobbery may involve more than this but never less. Purely "social" snobbery is perhaps the least harmful. The craving is sated by misusing personal relationships without missing much else. Few of us do anything without an occasional sidelong glance at the effect it will have on our status. From there to doing things—ever so little—for the sake of that effect is a brief step. An element of snobbery inheres in many social actions of nonsnobs. In the snob, that element becomes dominant, and in the pure snob it excludes all others.

Snobbery proliferates in untold ways and occasions. There is literary, intellectual, esthetic, political, sexual snobbery—a baffling multiplicity of forms. Any activity or endeavor can be misused to slake the snob's thirst for unearned glory. He pretends to countless attitudes, feelings, beliefs, or achievements to enhance his status.

To raise his status, a man may seek to associate with famous people or status groups above his own. He can claim to have succeeded by "dropping names" or by indicating participation (even mere presence) at status-conferring events such as exclusive parties or *premières*. Other "firsts," attendances and achievements, or "mosts" serve, too. He may try to be the first man through the newly dug tunnel, or to set foot on the *Jungfrau*, or eat the most pancakes, or sit longest on a flagpole. The quality of the achievement is less important than the renown it brings. The bizarre competes with the great and defeats the unspectacularly good without trying. "Firsts" enhance status perhaps because to be first (*princeps, primus*: whence prince, principal, primary, primate, and so forth) originally meant to lead. And to be presented with something first meant a recognition of leadership status. This is also the origin of the *ius primae noctis* (*droit de seigneur*). However, to go to *premières* or to race through the new tunnel first is neither assumption nor recognition of leadership nor even any longer actual presumption. It expresses at most a yearning, possibly unconscious, to be thought to belong to a high status group. One does, if enough others think one does.

A pining to be publicized above all, or to associate with those who are, is the outstanding peculiarity which marks the *democratization of snobbery* in our time. ("Democratic" is here used in de Tocqueville's sense as nearly synonymous with "egalitarian." There is a social but no logical connection between these two concepts.) To crave the limelight is to want prestige and acceptance not in a distinct or highly regarded group but among the broadest mass of people. The inchoate longing for "popularity" expresses the same craving for indiscriminate acceptance, a wish to be reputed in the largest rather than the highest group; or it reveals identification of these two. The ambition to belong to a high status group, the original ambition of the old-time snob, presumes a stable and acknowledged hierarchy. The contemporary egalitarian snob measures his prestige by the *number* of people who defer to it. Perhaps he knows no other measure; perhaps no other social measure is left.

A negative form of democratized snobbery ought not to go unrecorded. The anxiety generated by the prospect of losing prestige and popularity may lead people to act so as not to distinguish themselves. If the action or inhibition occurs for the sake of avoiding loss of prestige and not as an end in itself, we are faced with democratized snobbery. A little of it is useful as normative cement in the fabric of democratic societies.

Whether democratic or aristocratic, snobbery is a degenerate offspring of status ambition. The snob does not try to achieve a high status by doing what is required—by leading in slaying enemies, making money, or writing poems. He tries to sneak into the high status by associating with those who have it. But even the association is not genuine. The snob does not hope, as the cannibal does, to acquire the famed person's qualities, nor is he moved by admiration for the achievement of the high status group. He does not wish to emulate it for any intrinsic merit he finds in it. The snob craves fame, deference, or reputation, not the qualities that won it. He is not interested in anything he does but for the effect it may have on his status. The object of his ambition is the effect achieving it will have on others, nothing else. Though his ambition be true, any ostensive objects are spurious. Snobbery is based on judgment of one social fact: reputation. All other matters are disregarded; in respect to them the snob at most rationalizes his disregard into prejudice. The pure snob—an ideal type—is interested in objects, achievements, and persons only in terms of their social existence, the prestige they command or may procure for him.

Snobbery is thus the most purely social of relationships. Snobbish association is independent of the personalities of the people, of the qualities of the things, or of the meaning of actions sought after or snubbed. Free of any taint of economic, intellectual, sexual, or political motivation, and of personal preference, it is association for the sake of sheer social effect. Only to that extent is it snobbery.

Though the varieties of snobbery beggar description, we ought not to confuse it with related attitudes. We may disapprove of rudeness and insolence, of ostentatiously displayed superiority, of arrogance and all forms of incivility, even of mere aloofness. But though the snob may be rude to those he snubs, an overbearing, boastful, or aloof person need not be a snob. There are snobs who are not rude and uncivil persons who are not snobs. A general who brags about the battles he has actually fought may be a braggart and tiresome, but not a snob. He wishes to enjoy well earned fame. Even if he exaggerates, he is hardly a snob, though he may be a liar. But the man who cultivates acquaintance with the general only because of his celebrity is a snob. The mere seeking of acquaintance could be due to curiosity. Not however the cultivating. It is not snobbery to eschew things or company one finds vulgar even though they be popular; or to prefer to associate with high status groups or with "highbrow" things. Attachments and slights are snobbish only when spurious and motivated by the wish for prestige, the concern for status, and not by a genuine judgment or a true personal preference. Snobbishness always involves status pretension—

a wish for unearned reputation—or, at least, exclusive concern with others in status terms.

Snobbery may seem a trifling matter. But it is anything but that to those involved and to the student of behavior. The belief —actually a moral judgment—that snobs are interested in petty matters does not make matters petty to them. And the consequences to persons and groups "snubbed" can be far-reaching.

The significance of pure snobbery recedes as concern with differential status bases grows. Pure snobbery comes into its own whenever, wherever, and to whomever the status base is a given fact. Hence snobbery is strong among children and students (whose power to alter the status base is limited), among wives (same reason) and in non-mobile groups. In mobile groups status ambition is more prominent.

None of us is entirely free from snobbery, a motivation difficult to disengage from other, more legitimate forms of status ambition. A man may like a girl; or date her because she is liked. He may read Jean Paul Sartre because he is interested in Sartre's ideas, or because he wishes to appear to be for prestige reasons, or, finally, because he wishes to become interested for prestige reasons. People seldom are interested in the actual qualities of anything without being impressed by its reputed qualities. We think we perceive and admire aesthetic qualities in a famous painting. But our change of attitude, once we are told that the painter was not Leonardo—that the signature was faked—should give food for thought. For the aesthetic qualities of the painting we just admired have not changed—only its reputation. And we do look differently at our neighbor once we learn about his fame—even though he has not changed. Not that this makes us pure snobs. Our judgment is not entirely based on reputation, nor do we look at the painting, or associate with the neighbor only for the sake of our status. Rather, our motives are mixed.

Often something connected with a famed action or person serves to make tangible both the fame and that which brought it. Perhaps we do think that some of it rubs off on whoever or whatever was touched by the famous. Thus, the autographed book, the desk used by a great man, the flag borne aloft in the decisive battle, the shirt worn by a saint have prestige in our eyes from having been there and perhaps having absorbed some of the *mana* of the event or person. So it is also with personal keepsakes. Note how unmaterialistic we are. The flag that witnessed history is more to us than a piece of cloth—it becomes a piece of history. And yet how materialistic: the piece of history is embodied in a piece of cloth as though what memory tells us of the past could be materialized by a piece of cloth—the cloth of history.

The flag is glorious, the shirt a holy relic. Neither is prized for material or symbolic value. (Any other flag would do as symbol.) Though our interest in something because of its fame is akin to snobbery, it need not be entirely snobbish. We may prize the flag or the saint's shirt because of our reverence for the events they witnessed. Our interest in the *fame* of these events, or in the effect of our association with them on our fellow men, need not be primary. Once more, snobbery is exclusive concern with repute, and unconcern or spurious concern with the cause of merit of it—desire for prestige and unwillingness or inability to earn it on one's own merits. Few people want to be president because of sheer snobbery. But many snobs want to have lunch with whoever becomes president.

Molière's *Bourgeois Gentilhomme* was a proper subject for satire because the protagonist did not really like aristocrats better than commoners or care for their way of life. Though he felt far more comfortable behaving as a commoner, he wished to be among noblemen simply because they had a higher status. His wealth should have enabled him to acquire the higher status. Not being genuinely attracted by the aristocratic style of life, his attempts to learn the required role were inept and came to nought.

Status ambition, anxiety, and snobbery, as well as vertical mobility, loom important in the works of many writers such as Stendhal, Balzac, Jane Austen, and Proust. In Proust's work, the contrast and occasional fusion of status ambition, anxiety, and snobbery are supremely drawn. American literature, too, has been concerned with status and snobbery, generally with an air of wonder and fascinated disapproval: for instance, F. Scott Fitzgerald, Sinclair Lewis (in *Babbitt*), and on a more popular level, J. P. Marquand and such comic strips as "Maggie and Jiggs" and "Gasoline Alley."

GROUP SNOBBERY, PREJUDICE, AND DISCRIMINATION

Just as it is snobbish to seek the prestige of high status while indifferent to the merit on which it may be based and to the exigencies of the roles involved, so it is snobbish to snub those who, having parity of merit, are entitled to share one's own status. The desire to keep and raise one's status above that of others, regardless of merit, leads to both upward and downward manifestations of snobbery. The gestures directed upward are ridiculous to all but the snobs (to all, that is, who are not actively involved); the downward gestures present a melancholy spectacle and are painful for those who are snubbed.

Disdain for whole groups because their status is low, and attempts to keep their status below one's own by slighting them, regardless of their qualifications, is a form of snobbery usually served by opinions which rationalize the low esteem in which the slighted group is held and the high esteem one claims for one's own. These opinions are commonly called prejudices. The group against which the prejudice is directed is seen to have disqualifying characteristics which often are imaginary. Sometimes these characteristics exist but are—at least in part—the effect of the low esteem which they are supposed to justify (for example, the comparatively low living and educational standard of Negroes in Alabama). Prejudices often are ideological links in the historical chain that keeps the disdained group bound to its low status.

Generally prejudices are rationalizations of low (or high) esteem based on real but irrelevant characteristics of the object, or on nonexistent characteristics which are presumed to be associated with the real ones, or on a confusion of cultural (hence modifiable) with innate characteristics. Prejudices differ from judgments, which are conclusions derived from a study of actual characteristics relevant to the matter at issue. Prejudices also differ from likes or dislikes. If a man likes (or dislikes) blondes more than brunettes, this liking becomes a prejudice only if he attributes to them characteristics that are not actually associated with blondes (e.g., intelligence or giddiness) more than with brunettes. Similarly, if a man likes (or dislikes) Negroes—people with dark skin color—this becomes a prejudice only if he believes that pigmentation is associated with characteristics with which it is not actually associated (e.g., rhythm or dishonesty). If a man dislikes, (or likes) a cultural characteristic (e.g., certain attitudes of American Negroes) as such—i.e., without confusing it with a "racial" one—such liking (or disliking) is no prejudice; indeed, it is less prejudicial than the denial among "unprejudiced" people of the existence of such cultural group characteristics. Liking is a feeling as legitimate as any; judgment is based on an analysis of relevant data; prejudice rationalizes a feeling—attempts to support it intellectually—by using less than adequate data and reasoning processes.

When the low status of the slighted group is used to inflict material disadvantages on its members, they are "discriminated against." Their common characteristic—such as skin color or nationality—is regarded as sufficient *per se* to deny them the parity of advantages or opportunities they seek, though it be without relevance. That such a common characteristic is perceived and stressed often is an effect of group discrimination, as much as an occasion for it. Thus physical size is not made in our society an occasion for discrimination against groups (or for identification as group members) whereas pigmentation is, though intrinsically it probably is not more relevant to character or capacity. We group people on the basis of schemes which the culture transmits to our minds. It is within these schemes that blue eyes, dark skin, or, as in England, linguistic habits become signs of superiority or inferiority. Sometimes a common characteristic is taken to indicate incapacities—for instance, stupidity—which, were they present, would be truly disqualifying. This implies that the irrelevant common characteristic itself ought not to serve as a basis for discrimination against the group, unless indicative of relevant incapacitating traits—which stands to reason. But, in fact, characteristics such as skin color, white or dark, do not indicate the presence or absence of relevant inborn talents. Those who argue to the contrary reveal by their inconsistency that they merely seek to rationalize status anxiety. For instance, they may maintain that higher education should not be imparted to Negroes because Negroes lack intellectual ability. Were they fully convinced of this, they might allow the deficiency to become apparent through the tests all students must pass. Analogously, it strains one's credulity when people who advocate exclusion of a group from job opportunities insist that the group is unqualified. If the group were incompetent, it would be unable to qualify for the jobs. One might reasonably suspect that what is feared is the group's competition—that is, its competence.

People who wish to give ethnic minorities equal representation in high status occupations, instead of equal opportunity— in the manner of politicians arranging tickets of candidates for public office—are often motivated by generosity. But not much is gained if instead of discriminating against an ethnic group, we discriminate against those relevantly qualified, in favor of those irrelevantly qualified by belonging to the minority to be represented. The criterion of individual qualification is still not used. As long as persons are honored or slighted because they are Negroes or whites, as long as actually irrelevant group characteristics are treated as relevant, we cater to prejudice.

Slighting a group in the merest social sense as well as "discriminating against" a group—placing it at a material disadvantage—is obnoxious only if and when based on an *irrelevant* distinction. If we select girls with shapely legs to dance in a chorus line and girls who believe in God to become missionaries, we discriminate; we reject nonbelievers for the missions and girls with spindly legs for the chorus lines, but the discrimination is relevant. If we were to reject candidate missionaries because of unshapely legs and applicants for the chorus line who do not believe in God, our discrimination would be irrelevant. It would be based, as snobbery is, on the rejection or acceptance of people regardless of their relevant qualifications. Yet atheistic chorus girls and candidate missionaries with unshapely legs would ordinarily be able to find jobs elsewhere. Things become really bad when a group is irrelevantly rejected almost anywhere and thus kept in a permanently inferior position. This has been the experience of Negroes in the United States.

Of course, the matter is regarded as a problem only in a class society. Hereditary allocation of opportunities is the basis of caste and estate societies. It does not appear as irrelevant discrimination, snobbery, or prejudice there. Rather, it is the very principle of that social order. However, in a class society, status based on matters independent of personal efforts, such as race or nationality, is a historical remnant inconsistent with the logic of the class system. Such a status allocation is rationalized by prejudice. Since the class system is most thoroughgoing in America, the remaining hereditary status allocation stands out most incongruously here. It contradicts the ideological bases of our class society and leaves us with a bad conscience—for we believe in "equal opportunity" for all, yet often ascribe status to Negroes.

Consequently we have guilt feelings. They are useful in prompting action against irrelevant discrimination but they also spill over and prompt indiscriminate actions. People hesitate in undertaking relevant discriminations and become reluctant even to discriminate in their social relations according to their personal preferences. The flight from one form of snobbism—unwarranted discrimination—sometimes leads to another: indiscriminate acceptance at least of everything that is socially accepted. The person who refuses to discriminate by insisting that every belief or person is equally acceptable to him is likely to be indifferent to all and not to have a personal relationship to any. (Possibly this hides strongly repressed loves and hates.) Usually he finds an outlet for his hostility by warring against those who do discriminate—who have strong and open likes and dislikes, whether relevant or prejudiced. Thus the idea that everyone has a right to his own preferences and that society must protect this right may be perverted into the idea that all likes and dislikes are equally good, or even that no one has a right to any likes or dislikes.

Whereas individual snobbery is ridiculous, organized snobbery is repulsive in a class society. When it serves the function— barely rationalized by prejudice—of keeping one group in a low status held in the past, thus maintaining the higher status of the prejudiced group, legal remedies are called for. Without such remedies, discrimination against the low status group might inflict material disadvantages which perpetuate the conditions used to justify the discrimination against it. To be sure, legal remedies cannot defeat snobbery or destroy the hankerings which are expressed in prejudice. But the law can forbid the *organization* of snobbery to inflict material disadvantages on the group against which the prejudice is directed. The law may bid for less group snobbery by forbidding the imposition of conditions which perpetuate it.

THE SUPREME COURT AND GROUP SNOBBERY

In the end, the ideological and economic forces of a vigorous and expanding class society tend to defeat discrimination against minority groups. Thus, in the United States, both legal measures and public opinion have reduced discrimination at an unprecedented rate in the last twenty years. We are finally on the way to carrying out the interpretation the Supreme Court placed in 1896 (*Plessy v. Ferguson*) on the "equal protection of the laws" granted to all twenty years earlier in the Fourteenth Amendment to the Constitution: separate *but equal* facilities have been opened to Negroes in increased measure. In 1954, the Supreme Court went much further. It imposed an obligation on public schools to educate colored and white children together. Since then, legal decisions have struck down segregation of races in public facilities such as parks, swimming pools, public carriers, etc. (Privately owned schools and swimming pools and non-public carriers, etc. are not affected but there is a tendency to declare them public when there is any public participation, e.g., tax preference.) The Supreme Court's decision did not deny that segregated facilities, equally good in all material respects, might be offered to all groups. But material equality, the Justices now hold, is not enough. The equal protection clause of the Fourteenth Amendment (in *Brown v. Board of Education*) and the due process clause of the Fifth Amendment (in *Bolling v. Sharpe*) are found violated whenever, by means of segregating the members of a group in public facilities, the government intends to impose (or maintain) an inferior status for the group. The Court had little doubt that this was the intent.

Had the Court outlawed only the compulsory segregation of groups legislated by many Southern states, it would have extended freedom of association hitherto denied those Southerners of both races who wanted their children in mixed public schools. But the 1954 doctrine goes beyond prohibiting *compulsory segregation*, to replace it with *compulsory congregation*. To increase freedom of association, the Court curtailed freedom of dissociation. It might have been possible to increase both by allowing school boards either to have segregated *and* mixed schools or not to have segregated ones. The Court, however, disallowed the first alternative. The Fourteenth Amendment was interpreted to mean that no group has the right to be separated from another on public property when the other's pride is hurt thereby. (That no *material* disadvantage should be inflicted had been granted by all litigants before the Court and was not an issue.)

If the pride of one group is hurt by compulsory segregation, the pride of the other might be hurt by compulsory congregation. The pride of the group resisting congregation, the Court must have felt, is arrogant and snobbish and rests on a feeling of superiority undeserving of public protection, whereas Negroes were found deserving of protection when they resist being stigmatized as inferior, injured in their pride, by segregation. Thus, not only are people equal before the law; the law now actively prevents one group from stamping another as inferior by refusing to open public facilities to common use.

The Court's decision has the defects of its virtues: it attempts to compel equal esteem of groups for each other. This attempt narrows, as well as enlarges, the right we each have to associate with whoever consents to associate with us, and to dissociate from whomever we do not care to associate with. Of course, people can still send their children to private segregated schools. But this makes segregation a privilege of the rich. The snob value of segregation will be increased thus, as well as the resentment of the Southern "poor whites," who must use the public schools and are already a highly prejudiced group. Time will tell whether the Court overshot its mark—whether its generosity exceeded its wisdom.

Though the Court prohibited segregation only in public facilities, many well-meaning people seem ready to go beyond this, to insist that no schooling, and no officially chartered private activity should be allowed unless all races are admitted and actually take part. Thus a New York State Attorney General refused a charter to a bowling club which excludes Negroes. And the New York *Times* reported (December 18, 1954): "Jersey closes all Negro school because it can't get white pupils."

The New York *Times* also reported on November 20, 1956, that the Urban League insisted that, for the sake of integration, "white children [be sent] a few blocks into an all-Negro community." Thus, the judicial mandate not to separate children deliberately by color is transformed into a mandate deliberately to mix them by color. No doubt, Negroes make as good bowling companions as white people—the club members were prejudiced. But should they be denied the right to choose future members as prejudiciously as they wish? We might tell them that they are misinformed and foolish. Should we try to compel them to accept members they don't want? And should we close schools whenever the mixture of races is not complete?

It would be callous and unreasonable not to sympathize with the basic purpose of the 1954 decision: to raise the low status of Negroes by lifting measures designed to perpetuate a superior status for whites. The inferior status of Negroes rests on unjustifiable prejudices and perpetuates an unpleasant form of group snobbery. Snobbery is always a debasing thing. It denies the true (individual) values of those involved, and caters to values they hope will improve or maintain their (social) standing. When a whole group is snubbed, even without suffering material disadvantages, snobbery inflicts an unhealthy mass humiliation. Is compulsory congregation an effective remedy? Those who think so offer three arguments:

First, they insist, whites hold Negroes to be inferior chiefly because of segregation. They will cease to do so once they mix and come to know each other, particularly at an early age. This must be true for those whose prejudice rests on innocent misinformation. But, unfortunately, much serious and active prejudice is the cause rather than the effect of misinformation. It is unaffected by anything that does not affect the psychological *need* to hold it. How little group hostilities depend on segregation is sadly demonstrated by the fate of the Jews in Germany. They were segregated only for the slaughter—segregation was the ultimate effect, not the preceding cause of hostility. Generally, there is no indication that, to arise, race prejudice requires segregation or that it is squelched by congregation. Perhaps it will be spread less widely. On the other hand, where it persists, it might become more intense, particularly when congregation, imposed from the outside, is opposed by large, geographically concentrated segments of society.

The second argument in defense of compulsory congregation is that segregation unavoidably includes discrimination against one group in a material sense. Historically, segregation has often been used as a means to this end or as a screen to hide it. Yet this can be prevented. In a *material* sense, segregation is not inherently discriminatory. That much has been conceded by the Court, and such things as schools segregated according to sex illustrate the possibility of segregating without placing one group at a disadvantage relative to the other. (Moreover, such disadvantages can be—and have been—imposed by schools through restricting acceptances of members of the group discriminated against without segregating those accepted.) We must not confuse a historical *pattern*, which linked segregation with discrimination against one group, with a historical or logical *necessity*.

The third argument offered in favor of the Supreme Court's 1954 decision is the most serious one and essentially was adopted by the Court: segregation in public facilities is humiliating to Negroes because it arises from the belief in their inferiority and is designed to maintain it. Thus segregation is a stigma which, being imposed by public means, deprives the humiliated groups of the equal protection of the laws. Negroes feel, in fact, degraded by segregation. (Individually they may suffer more from rejection by white costudents in mixed schools. But still, the social stigma is removed, and the Court apparently was optimistic on individual adjustment.) The substance of this complaint is undeniable. We have raised doubts on the Court's methods of satisfying it—both as to effectiveness in achieving the desired end and as to undesired effects that might occur. Let us hope that these doubts turn out to be unjustified and that the 1954 decision helps accomplish what so obviously was intended, a less snobbish and prejudiced community. (It is unlikely, rumors to the contrary, that the Court's decision was designed to placate public opinion. The Court would be remiss in its duty were it to pay such heed to public opinion here or abroad. The judicial branch is to interpret the laws. Were the Court subservient to domestic public opinion, it would obliterate the distinction between the judicial and the legislative branches of the government. And, if the Court had catered to public opinion abroad, it would also have had to sanction anti-Semitic laws if people abroad became Nazis.)

PREJUDICE ABOUT PREJUDICE

Whether humiliation through prejudice leaves deep and lasting traces, and whether it increases the incidence of personality disorders among Negroes, we do not know (nor do we know whether congregation would improve matters). Possibly the Court found it enough that there is humiliation attached to segregation—which is common knowledge. Yet lawyers argue as to whether the court did depend on the attempt of the social scientists to detect and prove psychological injuries by "scientific" tests. It would be unfortunate if it did, for the evidence presented is so flimsy as to discredit the conclusion, a conclusion which might be correct nevertheless. Much weight was given to certain "generally accepted tests" which Professor Kenneth B. Clark undertook.

Professor Clark tested sixteen children between the ages of six and nine in Clarendon County, South Carolina, and elsewhere about three hundred children. This number would be too small to test reaction to a new soap, and Professor Clark seems not to have made sure that his sample is unbiased. Reactions to segregation may vary, beyond age and sex, according to type of school and teacher, parental income, parental residence, religion, type of community, and so on. As far as the court knew, no attempt was made to compare the reactions of Negro children in segregated schools with those of Negro children in nonsegregated schools. Suppose their response to the test had not differed; we might still ascribe it to the pressure of prejudice—but no longer to segregation. (To determine whether the reactions in question were due to environmental prejudice, comparison with reactions of children in a nonprejudiced environment would be useful.)

Actually, Professor Clark had undertaken tests in unsegregated schools before he undertook those in South Carolina on which he testified. He found then that the behavior he attributed to segregation in his testimony—rejection of colored dolls by Negro children—occurs more often when children are in *nonsegregated* schools.

It is not hard to guess why in his court testimony Professor Clark did not attempt to compare his tests of Negro children in segregated schools with those in unsegregated schools. If Professor Clark had taken both his "scientific" experiments seriously —a mistake he makes only part of the time, but which a surprising number of social scientists make most of the time—he would have had to tell the Court that his evidence proves *desegregation* harmful to Negro children. Instead he insisted that *segregation* is. He might be right—provided his own evidence is wrong. (For references, quotations, etc., see E. van den Haag, "Social Science Testimony in the Desegregation Cases," *Villanova Law Review*, Fall 1960.) That the Southern lawyers who cross-examined Clark when he appeared as an expert witness did not manage to discover so obvious a discrepancy makes one wonder whether Negroes who want to attend Southern law schools have any motive other than to improve them.

Professor Clark presented drawings of dolls to the children, identical except that some dolls had dark and others white skin color. After making sure that the children had noted the difference, he questioned them as to which dolls were "nice" or "bad"; and as to which dolls were like themselves. The majority of the Negro children found the white dolls "nice." And about half picked the "nice" white doll as being like themselves. Professor Clark concluded that prejudice had led them to identify white and nice; and even to identify with the white dolls despite their own dark color.

Professor Clark does not mention the possibility that once a child identifies "white" with "nice" he will identify himself with white if he thinks of himself as nice. This is remarkable. His general interpretation—that the identification of "white" with "nice" is a result of anti-Negro prejudice—is truly astounding, however. Suppose dark-haired white children were to identify blonde dolls as nice; or suppose, having the choice, they identified Teddy bears as nice rather than any dolls. Would this prove injury owing to (nonexistent) segregation from blondes? or communal prejudice against humans? Professor Clark's logic suggests that it would.

Control tests—which unfortunately were not presented—might have established an alternative explanation for the identification of white with nice, and black with bad: in our own culture and in many others, including cultures where colored people are practically unknown and cultures where white people are unknown, black has traditionally been the color of evil, death, sorrow, and fear. People are called blackguards or blackhearted when considered evil; and children fear darkness. In these same cultures, white is the color of happiness joy, hope, purity, and innocence. We need not speculate on why this is so to assert that it is a fact, and that it seems utterly unlikely that it originated with segregation (though it may have contributed to it). Professor Clark's findings then can be explained without any reference to injury by segregation or by prejudice. The "scientific" evidence for this injury is no more "scientific" than the evidence presented in favor of racial prejudice.

The cause of science as well as the cause of Negroes, is much better served if we simply stick to the facts: prejudice exists, it is painful to those against whom it is directed—we need only ask them—and we call it prejudice because it rests on no respectable argument, scientific, or moral. Let us try to eliminate it then. We need not try "scientifically" to prove that prejudice is clinically injurious. This is fortunate, for we cannot.

PART
THREE
Popular Culture

CHAPTER XVIII

Why Is the Crowd Lonely?

Non ridere non lugere, neque destestari; sed intelligere.
("Do not laugh, weep, or loathe; but understand.")

SPINOZA

Unlike any other type of culture, popular culture—a full-fledged style of living with a distinct pattern of feeling, thinking, believing, and acting—was made possible and in the end necessary by mass production. Unless the requirements and effects of industrialization are fully grasped, popular culture does not become intelligible. Failure to relate the cultural, esthetic, psychological, and social changes in our life fully and specifically to the industrialization which has brought them about has caused even the best studies of popular culture to remain phenomenal (crudely empirical) or to become forensic expressions of taste, distaste, or philosophical predilection. Yet, a theoretical explanation of the genesis, function, and effects of popular culture is needed.

Popular culture is a by-product of industrialization whether under democratic or dictatorial auspices, and regardless of whether the economy is planned or unplanned. Totalitarianism would compel composers to compose in the popular manner. A nontotalitarian industrial system induces them to do so by rewards rather than punishment. In human terms, the difference is immense, but popular culture may be produced either way. However, in a nontotalitarian industrial society, individuals not sharing popular culture can survive physically. Totalitarian industrialism makes survival even in the interstices of society doubtful. (To be sure, the wishes of the totalitarian government rather than those of the consumers must be satisfied in a totalitarian society. But the totalitarian government, unlike the absolute kings of old, is culturally sterile precisely because it governs an industrialized or industrializing country.)

THE INDUSTRIAL SETTING

In the last two centuries, machinery and specialization have immensely increased economic productivity—the amount of goods produced per man-hour—in Europe and America. This process has gone furthest in America, where popular culture, too, has gone furthest. Enrichment led to a vast population increase: between 1800 and 1950 the population of Europe more than tripled, that of the United States rose from less than 6 million to 165 million. (The population of Asia and Africa barely doubled.) In the same period *per capita* production rose stupendously and is still rising. Everybody benefited materially. But the main beneficiaries were the poor. Their incomes rose most. Besides, if the income gap between poor and rich had not narrowed, as it did, an expanded national income distributed in unchanged proportions still would have augmented the welfare of the poor disproportionately: if the income of poor and rich alike increases by 50 per cent, the welfare of the poor is raised far more than that of the rich. Our progressive tax system—which taxes the income of the poor at a lower rate than the income of the rich —is based entirely on this (occasionally and roughly) correct view. (There is no actual proof of the diminishing "utility" of successive additions to income, particularly when the comparison is interpersonal. The idea becomes doubtful indeed once the income of the poor is high enough to satisfy the most compelling needs, and additions to the income of the rich do not increase their consumption. But the idea is popular for obvious reasons.)

Mass production has magnified the power of the poor, as well as their income. The establishment of a progressive tax system itself eloquently testifies to the mounting political power of the lower income groups, unless it be assumed that the upper income group was unable to restrain its generosity and inflicted a "soak the rich" policy on itself. A single tycoon remains more powerful than a single worker. However, industrialists as a group are politically less powerful than workers as a group (thus monopolistic action by the sellers of services is protected, by the sellers of goods outlawed). Similarly, the wealthy *as a group* are less powerful than the poor *as a group*. (In feudal regimes this is not yet so, in totalitarian regimes, it is no longer so.)

Since so much more is produced in less time, more time is left over to spend rather than earn income. Fewer hours per day are spent working than before, fewer days per week, and fewer weeks per year. As a proportion of the life span, worktime has shrunk beyond this. People live longer, but start work later and retire earlier. This, too, probably has benefited the poor most— the work-time of the rich has scarcely declined. Indeed, partly because of inheritance taxation, partly because of loss of prestige, the leisure class which supported the high culture of the past has dwindled as a separate group. The rich, characteristically, are no longer leisured. Indeed, no class is. And although the material need is less, ideological changes have caused the gainfully employed proportion of the population to grow as technology improved.

The increased productivity which bore these fruits also lessened physical toil during the abridged worktime. But drudgery was intensified. Owing to specialization and mechanization, work for most people is standardized and less varied, its pattern and rhythm inflexibly set by machinery, with little scope for individual intelligence or initiative or for spontaneous action. Mass production is distinguished in this respect from work on small farms, and in small firms. (The farm population has dwindled, as has the share of total output produced by small firms and farms. Besides, specialization even in the surviving small units is high.) Assembly lines, which feed machinery and are fed by it, depend on bureaucratic organization, and demand of each worker only a small, endlessly repeated manipulation. Monotony is made more dreary by the vastness of the organization which weakens the relationship of each worker to the end product and, indeed, to production as a meaningful process. Emotional attachment to products also is loosened as each contribution becomes insignificant, and the end products are uniformly bereft of identifying marks of individual skill or imagination. Once the techniques of mass production are highly standardized, they require more self-repression than self-expression of workers. Thus, by helping machines, workers increasingly produce something abstract and shapeless for themselves: money-income and time in which to spend it. Life falls into two compartments: work—a means; and play—an end.

The burden of enjoyment and of personal experience falls heavily then on the extended proportion of life left over from work. But the longest period of time spent on any one activity is still spent on work. And though physically fewer, working hours become psychologically longer through the repetitiveness of tasks. The meaningless drain on energy influences the kind of play-experience sought: though condemned to pleasure, people often find themselves unable to serve the sentence and crave to be "distracted from distraction by distraction" (T. S. Eliot). Monotony depletes people psychologically and makes them weary and restless. The spontaneous imagination needed for recreation seeps out through nonuse during working hours. Thus "recreation" often becomes a search for excitement—vicarious or direct—to offset the monotony of work and give a feeling of "living." But excitement pursued for its own sake only exhausts eagerness and impulse without creating anything. The wish for the creation of personal experience is overwhelmed perhaps, but it is not satisfied, once it has degenerated into greed for sensation.

In addition to shortening worktime and toil, lengthening playtime, and increasing fatigue and income, mass production has accelerated and spread mobility. Popular culture is heterogeneous in its origins but characteristically jells into a smooth blend owing to mobility. This is what makes American society so remarkably homogeneous. Social distances dividing groups horizontally and vertically are smaller than within any European country. The contrary impression comes about because fluidity is great and contacts frequent. Thus individuals experience differences more intensely and more often, though the differences are fewer and less steep than elsewhere. Hence the illusion of great differences shared by many sociologists. (The latter may magnify group differences also because of occupational and ideological bias.)

Population is concentrated in metropolitan areas to an unprecedented degree. Swift and cheap transportation promotes far more frequent and varied contacts than in former times and congestion and crowding as well. Airplanes or buses throw together people from distant areas and groups on their way to distant places. The multiplicity of contacts is compounded by the ubiquity of means of communication. Movies, television programs, newspapers, and magazines link vast heterogeneous publics and establish constant contact among people even if they stay put. They help bring about more uniformity of attitude and a further blending of customs and beliefs. However, most contacts are casual and transitory, or in the case of mass communication media, generalized, vicarious, and abstract. They do not replace personal relationships to things or people but make it harder for them to grow. No man is an island—everybody is at sea, though, and the electrically amplified bell tolls so deafeningly that conversation must often degenerate into shouting.

Mass production not only makes mobility possible, it also makes it necessary. Changing techniques, markets, and products, the expansion and contraction of industries—in short, innovation —cannot proceed unless people can be induced to go from one residence and occupation to another and therewith to exchange one group of friends for another, and sometimes their status, role, and social class.

Industrialization also reduces the autonomy and intensity, the numerical size, the duration, and the functions of primary groups such as the family, and expands the role of fluid secondary groups. The influence of mass media rises correspondingly. The unprecedented spread of formal mass education contributes to the readiness for change. Education brings together the offspring of heterogeneous groups and subjects them to a homogenizing curriculum. The main effect is to weaken any differentiating heritage, and to prepare each generation for mobility in pursuit of ambitions such as success or happiness by means of the newest techniques.

As contacts multiplied and geographical distances shrank, so did social distances. Most of the things produced by modern industry tend to shorten the distance between rich and poor. The poor read, travel, wear nylon stockings, and see the same television programs in their homes as do the rich. With regard to the kinds of things consumed, the monopoly which distinguished the rich has been broken. To be wealthy means chiefly to have more, rather than different things and often only to have more command over things.

Nearly a hundred years ago, John Stuart Mill already saw how industry blurs the contours of society by leveling the elevations and filling in the chasms that formerly divided it into remote, noncompeting segments. (See the passage quoted from *On Liberty* in Chap. 12.) Remaining privilege or even differentiation stimulates resentment the more, for it sticks out on an otherwise level plane. Yet it does not stick out far enough to remove the privileged from invidious comparison: envy and the craving for equality are intensified by their own success.

More income and power and less work for the lower-income groups, mechanization, increased mobility, shortened social distances, weakened and abridged primary groups, and finally the rise of mass communication—all these are direct effects of industrialization and direct causes of the erosion of folk and high culture. Cumulatively, they create the attitudes and ambitions, the sensibilities and insensibilties which prepare the market for popular culture.

"Folk" and "high" cultures flowered simultaneously in different strata of many past societies. But popular culture, when fully developed, penetrates all strata about equally and without significant variation of its main qualities. As society becomes fully industrialized, popular culture becomes the most universally shared type of culture and colors most aspects of individual and social life. High and folk culture retain only marginal influence on private and social life. They become islands lapped at and often swamped by popular culture. They are isolated and dry up in institutions or regions cut off from social development. If they are not isolated, high and folk culture tend to become denatured, although fragments may be preserved and mounted as quaint tourist attractions (for instance, Henry Ford's Green-field Village and the great English country estates).

However much cultures differ, they fall into one or more of these classes: folk, high, or popular (mass). For instance, all American Indian cultures were folk cultures, and Europe had a combination of folk and high cultures in antiquity and from the Middle Ages to the nineteenth century. Whereas folk cultures fall in the first half of the usual dichotomies (Weber's "tradition-alistic-rationalistic"; Tönnies' "community-society"; Redfield's "folk-secular"; Becker's "sacred-secular"), the second half of the dichotomies is *one* characteristic of all popular cultures. High cultures, finally, straddle the dichotomies by growing from the first into the second half, but the process affects only a small stratum of society—unless it is spread through industrialization. When this occurs, popular culture replaces both high and folk culture. Of course, some elements of each culture-type are usu-ally contained in the other. Thus, wherever there was an urban proletariat, or some form of mass production, there also were elements of popular culture. But they did not *prevail* until the machine age came.

THE ECONOMICS OF TASTE

Most of the goods monopolized in the past by the privileged few are now available to the many, not only because they have more time and money but also because the goods themselves are mass produced and have become cheap. Quality has changed, but not necessarily for the worse. Our dental fillings and eyeglasses are better than those available to Nero or Louis XIV. Our food, to judge from the increased life span, is not less nourishing, and it is more plentiful. Lighting, heating, cooling, and transportation are much better. More books are more available to more people, not to speak of television, movies, the radio, and records. Even in live entertainment, George III probably could not get as much as our poor can afford. Surely he had nothing like Radio City Music Hall. The variety of entertainment available to any New Yorker could (and does) arouse the envy of many a prince.

However, only those things—good things or bad things—are

cheap that are demanded by enough people to make mass production feasible. Things that are not mass produced are hard to find and very expensive. Anyone cursed with an unshared taste—be it good or bad taste—must rid himself of it or be prepared to pay an awful price. For the gap between the cost of an article which must be custom-made to supply an unshared taste and that of an article which can be mass produced to supply a widely shared taste is steadily widening.

The *real* income of a consumer who cleaves to an individual taste has declined precipitously, and is much lower than that of a person who never formed one. Though the material and workmanship of his specially made suits, china, furniture, or house need be no better than the material and workmanship of mass-produced ones, the person who sticks to an idiosyncratic taste has to spend more. If he makes as much money as someone bereft of individual taste, the individualist must buy fewer things. Or else he must forego indulging his personal taste by buying mass-produced articles. But since these yield less satisfaction to him than they give the person whose widely shared preferences they meet, the individualist would still have a lower *real* income. He cannot benefit from the economies of mass production; on the contrary, he must pay for the factors which mass production has made expensive: worktime and overhead. As mass production techniques improve, the gulf between the real income of consumers with shared taste and consumers with unshared tastes opens wider and wider. The industrial system penalizes individual taste economically, regardless of what goods or services are affected. Either your life is styled in conformity with mass tastes or it becomes a series of deprivations, material if you cling to your taste and forego some purchases to pay for it, psychological if you don't. That much can be said without in the least suggesting that individual taste is necessarily more sensitive to aesthetic values than mass taste, or that the mass taste is necessarily bad. Only it is not individual.

The social repercussions are obvious. Clinging to an individual personality (i.e., a number of individual tastes) is penalized; it is likely to be disapproved and resented by all groups. The individualist must choose between isolation and repression—he cannot, as in former times, live in a personal universe or one shared by a group of kindred spirits. He cannot hope to find a restaurant that caters to his tastes—the owner will soon find it more profitable to cater to more widely shared tastes, possibly by advertising his place as a haunt of individualists—whereupon it becomes a crowded places invaded by great masses for whom individualism has snob appeal almost as great as their fear of it. The same is true for a resort, or an idea. The choice is between isolation and the commonplace, gregariousness and solitude, with no room for mere sociability. (*Sociability* may be defined as a wish to enrich, refine, conserve, and express individuality through relations with others. *Gregariousness* is a wish to lose individuation by merging into a crowd. A sociable person is likely to shun gregariousness and, today, to be isolated and shunned.)

Of course, mass taste can be subdivided. There is a selection of different mass-produced teacups. Still, each can be mass produced only by appealing to a sizable group. Hence the selection cannot fully meet any *individual* taste. Besides, as techniques improve, the number of simultaneously available types dwindles, though the models are changed often in response to changing mass taste, or to stimulate demand. With all this, the actual selection available to a consumer below the middle income groups has broadened, as mentioned before—if he does not develop individual tastes.

If the cultural effects of this state of affairs have not been neglected, they also have not been properly linked to the economics of mass production. For instance, the price of books expected to appeal only to a small group has risen, while the price of books sold on the mass market has fallen. The gap widens as the more popular book profits from the economies of mass production and the book appealing only to a few suffers the diseconomies of being printed in a small edition. (The size of the edition required to profit from economies also has increased.) This situation existed as an effect of book clubs long before paperbacks became respectable in America. Paperbacks may alleviate it a little, as may new printing techniques. (But experience shows such alleviations to be minor and temporary; for instance, distribution remains costly.)

Publishers can count on a mass market for classics or, generally, when authors or works are favorably known; or when the topic or treatment supplies an existing mass demand (for instance, *The Power of Positive Thinking* or *Youngblood Hawke*). Mass production must appeal to an already widely shared taste or one so near formation that the book which is to supply it may be expected to call it into being. Books that appeal only to a few, because they are original in topic or treatment and therefore cannot supply an already widely shared demand, become inordinately expensive (unless the publisher miscalculated and the book is remaindered). These are the books that in the end might *create* new taste. But the process is slow and life is short. As the cost of experimentation rises, so does caution. Publishers will still take a gamble on a possible best seller (rewards have increased, too). But they have no reason to publish a book expected to appeal only to a few people unless they can sell the small edition at a high price (and to an assured market; no reason to gamble here). Periodicals without mass appeal are in a similar situation. Compare the cost of *Kenyon Review* or *Partisan Review* to that of the *Reader's Digest* or *True Stories*. Yet the latter magazines are profitable and pay their contributors well, whereas the former are not and do not.

Still, books that appeal only to a small public are published and sold, though they are comparatively expensive. In this respect, the direct impact of the economics of mass production does not seem very impressive so far. One reason is that publishers tend to be irrational in a business sense. Which is fine. But nothing to count on indefinitely.

THE FORMATION OF MASS TASTE

How is the mass market, on which popular culture is sold, formed and perpetuated? Since individual taste has become uneconomic for the purchaser and for the seller, its growth is stunted through education. Group acceptance, shared taste, takes the place of authority and of individual moral and aesthetic judgments and standards. Any taste that cannot be sloughed off—any *in*-dividual taste, not easily divided from the person in whom it dwells—becomes an obstacle to adaptation also because people often move from group to group.

Numerous precautions are taken, beginning in the nursery school (itself hardly an individualizing institution) to avoid elaboration of personal discernment and to instill fear of separation from the group. Group acceptance is stressed through formal and informal popularity contests, teamwork, and polling. Education altogether stresses group instruction. For instance, the size of his classes and the class average, not the qualities of individual pupils, are often considered the measure of the teacher. (In *Character and Opinion in the United States*, Santayana recounts how he was made aware of this at Harvard University.) The student himself is treated so much as part of a group that, except in higher education (which is only partly immune), he may be automatically promoted with his group regardless of individual achievement or variation. Finally, the surviving individual talent is instructed not to cultivate but to share itself. The writer gives writing courses, the scholar lectures and writes popularizations, the beauty models or appears on TV, and the singer deserts the concert hall for the juke box.

ADVERTISING

The aggregate effect of advertising is to bring about wide sharing of tastes. The actual social function of advertising is not to mold taste in any particular way, nor to debase it. Although the molding of taste to accommodate the product is the short term motivation of each advertiser, in the long run advertisers are equally motivated to mold the products to the prevailing tastes. It is more profitable. The *cumulative* effect of advertising reflects as much, even if particular "campaigns" do not. This goes for manufacturers, publishers, and movie-makers, too. They are quite content to produce and advertise what people want—be it T. S. Eliot or Edgar Guest, Kierkegaard or Norman Vincent Peale, "September Morn" or mobiles. It does not matter what people want to buy, as long as they want to buy enough of the same thing to make mass production possible. Advertising helps to unify taste, to de-individualize it, and thus to make mass production possible.

There is no evidence to support conspiracy theories which

hold that wicked capitalists, through advertising and mass media, deliberately, or stupidly, debauch the originally good, natural taste of the masses. Mass production—capitalist or socialist—demands unified taste; but its efficiency, or profitableness, is independent of the nature of the taste, and dependent only on that taste being common to sizable groups.

In a capitalist system, some men might use their wealth to express their personal taste, even though unprofitable. This is less likely under socialism. Socialist planners would be under moral obligation and political pressure to use public money to satisfy the most widely shared taste. Further, capitalist producers can take risks which they might not be allowed to take with public money under socialism. (If planners have not been subservient to mass desires in Russia, it is because the Soviet Union is not a democracy.) It follows that in a democracy government subsidies to the arts—which, even if successful, would not begin to solve the problem—are likely to make matters worse. (This is particularly so with a Jacksonian tradition which England and France are fortunate in not having.)

Are mass tastes homogenized on the "lowest common denominator"? There seems to be no good reason to assume that the lowest tastes are most widespread. One may say something of the sort about a crowd, united temporarily by crude, common appetites at the expense of reason, restraint, and refinement. But why consider consumers a crowd? Even the fare offered by the entertainment media is usually consumed by people separately or in very small groups. (Except for movies, but movie-goers are isolated from each other though they are together.)

Producers certainly have no interest in lowering taste or in catering to low rather than high taste. They seek to provide for a *modal* average of tastes, which, through advertising, they try to make as congruent with the *mean* average as possible. Neither average can be identical with the lowest common denominator. This average taste is hard to calculate and it is subject to fashion. Popular culture is far more fickle and eager for the new than any other type of culture. Just as frigidity and nymphomania are associated, so are boredom and the eagerness for news and entertainment. There would be no risk for song writers or movie producers if appeal could be calculated mechanically; but it cannot be. Indeed, it takes a special talent to sense what might appeal, the talent the editor of a popular magazine, the advertising man and the "stylist" must possess—and an equally special talent to produce it, the talent of the writer of best sellers and of the popular entertainer.

DE-INDIVIDUALIZATION

The mass-produced article need not aim low but it must aim at an average of tastes. In this sense, consumers are treated as a crowd: their individual tastes are not catered to. In satisfying all (or at least many) individual tastes in some respects, mass production violates each in other respects. For there are—so far —no average persons having average tastes; averages are statistical composites. A mass-produced article, reflecting nearly everybody's taste to some extent, is unlikely to embody anybody's taste fully. This is one source of the sense of violation which is rationalized vaguely in theories about deliberate debasement of taste.

The sense of violation springs from the same thwarting of individuality that makes prostitution (or promiscuity) psychologically offensive. The precondition of cheap and easy availability, of mass production, is wide appeal; and the cost of wide appeal is de-individualization of the relationship between those who cater and those who are catered to; and of the relationship of both to the object of the transaction. By using each other indiscriminately as impersonal instruments (the seller for profit, the buyer for sensation—or in promiscuity, both parties for sensation and relief of anxiety), the prostitute and her client sacrifice to seemingly more urgent material demands the self which, in order to grow, needs continuity, discrimination, and completeness in relationships. (Prostitution is not always the greater evil, of course, and it may spring from many motives, as do objections to it. There is no doubt, though, that it becomes psychologically injurious, or reflects a psychological injury suffered, when it is the only and permanent form of sexual activity.) Though profit and sensation can be obtained by depersonalization, the satisfaction ultimately sought cannot be, for the very part of the personality in which it would be felt—the individual self—is stunted and atrophied, at least if de-individualization continues long enough and is comprehensive. Ultimately, the sense of violation, too, is numbed.

Now, the depersonalizing effects of the mass production of some things—say electric clocks—may be minor as far as consumers are concerned, and more than offset by the advantages of cheapness. The same cannot be said for mass entertainment or education. And though some individuals may, society cannot have one without the other. The effects of mass production on people as producers and consumers are likely to be cumulative. Besides, even goods that seem purely utilitarian include elements of nonutilitarian, of aesthetic and psychic (for example, prestige) appeal. Indeed, less than half of consumer expenditure goes for the satisfaction of simple biological needs. (Much less in the higher income group.) Distinctions of this kind are necessarily hazy, but if cigarettes, newspapers, television, drinks, shaving lotion or lipstick, the prestige location of one's apartment, the fashionableness of one's clothing, and so forth are taken to satisfy nonbiological needs—and we can do without them biologically—then we are motivated by psychic needs in spending most of our money. This is not in itself objectionable, except that the processes by which many of these needs now arise and are stilled bring to mind the processes by which bread is now mass produced.

In milling and baking, bread is deprived of any taste whatever and of all vitamins. Some of the vitamins are then added again (taste presumably being provided by advertising). Quite so with mass-produced articles. They no more express the individual taste of producers than that of consumers. They become impersonal objects—however pseudo-personalized. Producers and consumers themselves go through the mass production mill to come out homogenized and de-characterized—only it does not seem possible to reinject the individualities which have been ground out the way vitamins are added to enriched bread. The "Human Relations" industry tries to do just that, and it doubtlessly supplies a demand and can be helpful, just as chemical sedatives or stimulants can be. But it seems unlikely that any assembly line—including one manned by human relations counselors—can give more than the illusion of individuality. Nor can books on "How to Become an Individual," "How to Acquire a Personality"—books, in short, that insist that by following a general recipe you will bake an individual cake—or restaurants advertising "home-cooked" meals, provide more than self-deception.

To produce more, people work under de-individualizing conditions and are rewarded by high income and leisure. Thus they can and do consume more. But as consumers they must once more rid themselves of individual tastes. The benefits of mass production are reaped only by matching de-individualizing work with equally de-individualizing consumption. The more discontinuous earning and spending become physically, the more continuous they seem to become psychologically. Failure to repress individual peronality in or after working hours is costly—in the end the production of standardized things demands also the production of standardized persons.

In a material sense, this assembly line shaping, packaging, and distributing of persons, or life, already occurs. Most people perch unsteadily in mass-produced, impermanent dwellings throughout their lives. They are born in hospitals, fed in cafeterias, married in hotels. After terminal care, they die in hospitals, are shelved briefly in funeral homes, and are finally incinerated. On each of these occasions—and how many others?—efficiency and economy are obtained at the expense of individuality and continuity. If one lives and dies discontinuously and promiscuously in anonymous surroundings, it becomes hard to identify with anything, even the self, and uneconomic to be attached to anything, even one's own individuality. The rhythm of individual life loses autonomy, spontaneity, and distinction when it is tied into a stream of traffic and carried along, according to the speed of the road, as we are in going to work or play, or in doing anything. Traffic lights signal when to stop and go and, much as we seem to be driving, we are driven. To stop spontaneously, to exclaim, *Verweile doch Du bist so schön* ("Stay, for you are so beautiful") may not lose the modern Faust his soul but it will cause a traffic jam—unless he stops together with all the other Fausts. (Besides, would the devil still be interested in individual souls?)

One motive for delinquency—a way of getting out of line—

is, possibly, a preference for occasional prison terms to imprison-
ment by routine. Crime, by its ultimate irrationality, may protest
against the subordination of individual spontaneity to social
efficiency. Three further reactions to anonymity may be noted:

1. The prestige of histrionics has risen. We long to imper-
    sonate, to get a name—better a pseudonym than to remain
    nameless; better a borrowed character than none; better
    to impersonate than never to feel a person. The wish to
    be oneself is felt but dimly and inchoately— for the only
    self known is empty and expects naïvely to be filled from
    the outside.
2. There are attempts to become "interesting" (unconsciously
    to become interested) by buying a ready-made individual-
    ity through "sending for," "enrolling in," or "reading up
    on" something, or "going places."
3. Impersonal and abstract things and instrumental relation-
    ships are cozily "personalized" as though to offset the
    depersonalization of individual life.

De-individualization, however, should not be viewed as a grim,
deliberate, or coercive process. It is induced gradually by economic rewards and not experienced as de-individualization at
all—though the symptoms are demonstrable. Most of the people
nourished by homogenized pap never had solid food on which to
cut their teeth. They feel vaguely restless and dissatisfied, but do
not know what they are pining for, and could not masticate or
digest it if they had it. The cooks are kept busy ransacking all
the recipes the world has ever known to prepare new dishes.
Nothing could be as various as the elements of our popular
culture. Yet the texture is always the same, always mushy, for the
materials are strained, blended, beaten, heated, and cooled until
it is.

MASS MEDIA: THE EXCLUSION OF ART

Let us briefly tour the institutional kitchens where "recreation" is cooked up—movies, radio, television.

Mass media cannot afford to step on anyone's toes—and
this implies a number of restrictions which, though less significant

than the positive prescriptions, are not negligible. We can forebear rehearsing tiresome minutiae—forbidden words, topics, situations, actions; but the countless dangerous associations mass media must avoid deserve some scrutiny.

No religious, racial, occupational, national, economic, political, or other group can be offended. Hence: can an evil man be Jewish? left-handed? pipe-smoking? Can a good man man be an atheist or bigamist? Can he perish in an airplane accident? Can a villain have any qualities shared with nonvillains and a hero have disapproved traits? In short, can either be human? The playwright or script writer may not mean to say that Jews are evil, or evil men left-handed or pipe smokers; he may not intend to advocate bigamy or to suggest that airplanes are dangerous or that we ought to be atheists. Joseph Conrad did not intend *The Nigger of the Narcissus* as an anti-Negro tract any more than Shakespeare intended *Othello* as a tract against handkerchiefs (in favor of Kleenex?). No matter. There is a danger that the play will be so understood. In Shylock and Fagin, Shakespeare and Dickens created individuals, experiences, and ideas and, unlike copy writers or propagandists, did not intend them as instructions on how to act and think. Yet the groups that press restrictions on the mass media are not wrong, for the audience tends to react as though such instruction had been received.

The audience of mass media always expects to be sold goods, stereotypes, and recipes for living—a new vitamin for that tired, listless feeling, or a new *line* for romance. And the audience is usually right: the same actress, who just implored her soap opera husband not to leave her and the kids, turns and implores one and all, in identically sincere and personal tones, to buy insurance or perfume. The small boy's heroes admonish him to get mommy to buy this or that. In many breakfast and news shows, advertising recommendations are deliberately mixed in with "actual" expressions of opinion. Even nonprofessionals— society leaders, well-known novelists, successful and "average" common men—ringingly declare their profound "personal" convictions on brands of soap, or beer, or God: "This I believe." The line dividing views and characters presented as fiction or "real" becomes hazy and the audience is necessarily muddled about separating advertisements, pleas, and recipes from art.

In such a context, the audience cannot receive art as individual experience and perspective on experience. Art becomes irrelevant. It is not perceived in its own terms, but first reduced to, then accepted or rejected as a series of rules and opinions on what to expect or do.

The idea that something must be sold is held by the media managers as fervently as it is held by the audience. It transcends the commercial motives which begot it. Thus public or educational stations, which do not accept commercial advertising, spend nearly as much time on (noncommercial) attempts to sell something as do commercial ones. They sell themselves or their program, or next week's offering—anything at all, as long as something is sold: "please listen again tomorrow," "please send for our booklet," "please do this," or "don't do that"—the listener must always be hectored about, sold on, or wheedled into something. Within institutionally set limits, noncommercial stations try to enlarge more than to instruct or delight their audiences. They play classical music—but whenever possible, the popular classics in popular versions. All the advertising techniques are used, including the "theme" (trademark) stripped from some symphony to introduce "symphony hours," and many outrageous multilations of works of art. How then can the audience see that a character like Shylock simply *is*? A character in the audience's experience is always used to sell something—a point of view, or himself; he is never an end in himself. Hence the audience always asks, should we buy his line?

Art, like love, can be experienced only as a personal, continuous, cumulative relationship. Or else art becomes entertainment—dull entertainment often—just as love is reduced to sex or prestige. Not that art should not be entertaining; but it is no more deliberately aimed at entertainment than love is. Art (and love) must be felt—they cannot be manufactured by someone to suit the taste of someone else. Yet mass media fare is prepared for consumers devoted to amusement, not to art. The circumstances which permit the experience of art are rare in our society anyway, and absent in the reception of mass media offerings. The audience is dispersed and heterogeneous and, though it listens often, it does so incidentally and intermittently, poised to leave if not immediately enthralled and kept amused. Such an audience is captured by loud, broad, and easy charms, by advertising posters, by copy writer's prose. And the conditions and conditioning of the audience demand a mad mixture of important and trivial matters, atom bombs, hit tunes, symphonies, B.O., sob stories, hotcha girls, round tables, and jokes. It jells into one thing: diversion. (Noncommercial stations do the same thing, though more insipidly, by mixing dentistry and Dante.) Hence what art is presented is received as entertainment or propaganda. Shylock would be understood as an anti-Semitic stereotype. The mass media may as well fit their offerings to the audience which they address; they cannot disregard the kind of understanding and misunderstanding their offerings will meet. They must, therefore, omit all human experience likely to be misunderstood—all experience and expression the meaning of which is not obvious and approved. Which is to say that the mass media cannot touch the experiences art, philosophy, and literature deal with: relevant and significant human experience presented in relevant and significant form. For if it is such, it is new, doubtful, difficult, perhaps offensive, at any rate easily misunderstood. Art is not concerned with making the obvious and approved more obvious and approved—it is precisely after this point that art begins and the mass media stop.

When attempting to be serious, the mass media rig up pseudo-problems and solve them by cliché. They cannot touch real problems or real solutions. Plots are packed with action—which obscures the vagueness and irrelevance of meanings and solutions. Similarly, to replace actual individuality, each character and situation is tricked up with numerous identifying details and mannerisms. The more realistic the characteristics, the less real the character usually, or the situation, and the less revealing. Literal realism cannot replace relevance. Mass media inveigh against sin and against all evils accepted as such. But they cannot question things not acknowledged as evil or appear to support things felt as evil. Even *Rigoletto*, were it a modern work, could not be broadcast, since crime and immorality pay and the ending is unhappy for everybody but the villain.

Past audiences were fairly homogeneous and accustomed to the artistic traditions being developed, whereas the mass audience comes from many traditions, or none. Therefore, some segments of it would be shocked by a presentation which, though not actually offering anything new, offered what is new and shocking to them. Hence, the mass media often present even classics in mutilated form, sometimes to the point of disemboweling them or reversing the moral. (For instance, Tolstoi's *Anna Karenina* once was recalled to the studio to make it more palatable by a happy ending. And Nabokov's novel *Lolita*, describing the relationship between a man and a pre-adolescent girl, was transformed into a movie depicting an affair between a man and a sexy teenager.) The original censor objected to the possibly subversive *political* implications of *Rigoletto*. Victor Hugo's play was suspected of casting aspersions on monarchy or monarchs. It did not occur to the Austrian censor to object to the essential content of the play, to its view of the human predicament, of love, crime, violence. The situation has been reversed. We could not wish for a better illustration of the argument.

Fighting legal censorship, organized group pressures, and advertising agencies is gallantly romantic—and as quixotic as a man's rage against his own mirrored image. These agencies are interested only in presenting what is wanted and in preventing what might offend people. They are not always right in their estimates. But who would be? They have an interest in gauging correctly—apart from fairly small side interests favoring *organized opinion*. (On these I invoke *de minimis non curat scriptor*.) Perhaps they are nuisances. But things would not be very different without them. Policemen do not create the law, though they become the target of the few who would defy it.

The very nature of mass media excludes art and requires surrogation by popular culture. Though the Hays production code applies only to movies, its basic rule states a principle which all mass media must follow: "Correct standards of life, subject only to the requirements of drama and entertainment" must be upheld. Doubtless, "correct standards" are those standards most of the audience is likely to believe correct (though they do not necessarily observe these standards in practice). They authorize whatever does not upset or offend the audience—and nothing else. (Classics are presented occasionally since they are sterilized by remoteness; tolerance is the tribute ignorance pays to reputation.) "Correct standards of life" must exclude art. For art is bound to differ from the accepted, the customary moral and aesthetic view, at least as it takes shape in the audience's mind. Art is always a fresh vision of the world, a new experience or creation of life. If it does not break, or develop, or renew in significant aspects the traditional, customary, accepted aesthetic and moral standards, if it merely repeats without creating, it is not art. If it does, it is incompatible with the "correct standards of life" which must control mass media.

Mass media thus can never question man's fate where it is questionable—they cannot sow doubt about an accepted style of life or an approved major principle. To be sure, mass media often feature challenges to this or that, and clashes of opinion. These are part of our accepted style of life—as long as challenges do not defy anything but sin and evil in the accepted place and manner. The mass media must hold up "correct standards of life," whereas art must create, not uphold, views. When filmed or broadcast, the visions of the playwright or novelist cannot deviate from the accepted "correct standards," and they must be entertaining. They must conform to the taste of the audience; they cannot form it. Virtue must triumph entertainingly—virtue as the audience sees it.

THE POWER OF CONSUMERS

The poets, Shelley thought, are "the unacknowledged legislators of the world." Shelley's poets wrote for a few who would take the trouble to understand them. They addressed an audience that knew, respected, and shared the common traditions they were developing. High culture was cultivated in special institutions—courts, monasteries, churches, universities—by people who devoted their lives to the development of its traditions, and who were neither isolated nor surrounded by masses wishing to be entertained. (Besides, there were no means of addressing a mass.) There was no need and no temptation for the artist to do anything but to create in his own terms. There was censorship at times, and desires of specific patrons had to be considered. But though they restricted expression, they seldom prescribed it. And, in particular, they did not insist on things being made easy.

Poets, painters, and philosophers lived in, and were of the group
for whom they produced, as did most people, whether they were
peasants, artisans, or artists. The relations between producers
of culture and consumers were so personal—as were the relations
between producers and consumers generally—that one can hardly
speak of an impersonal market in which one sold, the other
bought.

In both high and folk culture, each bounded and autonomous
universe—court or village—relied on the particular cultivators
and inventors of its arts and sciences no less than the latter relied
on their patrons. Each region or court depended on its musicians
as it depended on its craftsmen and vice versa. The mutual personal dependence had disadvantages and advantages, as has any
close relationship. Michelangelo or Beethoven depended on irksome individual patrons more than they would today. On the
other hand, whatever the patrons' tastes or demands, they were
individual and not "average" tastes or demands. Folk culture
grew without professional help. High culture was cultivated like
an orchard or garden. But both folk and high cultures grew from
within the groups they distinguished, and remained within them.

High culture was entirely dominated by people with more
than average prestige, power, and income—by the elite as a
group, who also dominated politics and society in general. (The
distance between the elite and other groups was greater and
mobility lower than today.) This group determined what was
to be produced, culturally and otherwise; and they took their
toll often by oppression and spoliation of the mass of people
whom they ruled.

With the development of industry, the elite as a group lost its
power. The great mass of consumers now determines what is to
be produced. Elite status, leadership in any form, is achieved,
and kept today by *catering* to the masses—not by plundering
or oppressing them. The nobleman may have become rich by
robbing (taking from) his peasants, as well as by protecting them
from other robbers and from each other. But the industrialist becomes a millionaire by selling to (exchanging with) farmers. And
his business is helped by giving his customers, via television, the
entertainers they want. These, in turn, reach elite status by
appealing to the masses. So do politicians. (Ortega y Gasset

described but did not explain this change in his prescient *Revolt of the Masses.*)

The elite, then, no longer determines what is produced, any more than it dominates society in other respects. Rather, the elite becomes the elite by supplying the goods that sell—the goods that cater to an average of tastes. The elite neither imposes any taste nor cultivates one of its own. It markets and helps homogenize and distribute popular culture—that which appeals to an average of tastes—through the mass media. The changes in income distribution, mobility, and communication, the economics of mass production already discussed, have caused the power of individual consumers to wane. But the power of consumers as a group has risen and that of producers as a group has dwindled.

With the invention of mass media, a mass market for culture became possible. The economies yielded by the mass production of automobiles became available in the mass production of entertainment. Producers of popular culture supply this new mass market. Popular cultures does not *grow* within a group. It is manufactured by one group for sale to another, or rather to an anonymous mass market. The product must meet an average of tastes, and it loses in spontaneity and individuality what it gains in accessibility and cheapness.

The creators of popular culture are not a sovereign group of "unacknowledged legislators." They work to give people what they want. Above all, they are salesmen—they sell entertainment and produce it with sales in mind. The creators of high culture are no longer insulated from the demands of the mass market by an educated elite—as they still were during the nineteenth century (and there are no stable, isolated communities in which folk culture could grow). They do not create for, or have personal relationships with, patrons whom they can lead as a man may lead in a conversation. A personal tutor is much more dependent on a few persons than a television lecturer. But his influence on his pupil is also much greater than the influence of any one television lecturer on any one pupil.

Today's movie producer, singer, or writer is less dependent on the taste of an individual customer, or village, or court, than was the artist of yore. But he does depend far more on the average of tastes, and he can influence it far less. He need not

cater to any individual taste—not even his own—because he
caters to an impersonal market. He is not involved in a conversation. He is like a speaker addressing a mass meeting and attempting to curry favor with it.

THE CORRUPTION OF NEWLY PRODUCED HIGH CULTURE

Why is Brooklyn, so much richer and bigger, so much more
literate and educated—and with more leisure—so much less productive culturally than was Florence? Though the absence of demand from the mass media has a bearing, it does not fully explain
why so little high culture is produced. After all, high culture
existed before mass media were invented. To account for the
blight of high and folk culture, we must consider the *positive* pull
of the mass market on artists and intellectuals. This pull, which
was absent in former times, explains why artists are more "market
oriented" and less "taste oriented," why they create for the sake
of anonymous consumers rather than for the sake of creation,
why the mass market tends to be internalized and to draw the
talent that otherwise might have been devoted to high culture.

Similar reasoning helps explain why even in the natural sciences,
American success has so largely consisted of ingenious application
and mass production of major discoveries made elsewhere. This
can surely be said up to and including radar, penicillin, and
atomic fission. Not that Americans have less talent for pure
research; but American talent was more drawn to application.
The difference in profitability was greater. Now that the pragmatic importance of pure theory has been more fully understood,
a change may be expected—but it will come because of basically
utilitarian considerations. There is no evidence to indicate that
Americans are less talented with regard to art (or science) than
other nations or that less talent is born in our times. In the
absence of such evidence, a non-biological explanation for the
dearth of creation is required. One reason that fewer artists seem
to appear in the population than, say, in the Middle Ages, is
that talent is directed elsewhere by our culture.

By cheapening his product or making it easier, Dante could

not have gained success and prestige as today's writer might. Had he renamed the *Divine Comedy, Florence Confidential,* the number of copies sold would not have risen much—the market was restricted. There was no mass market for anything, good or bad. And the techniques that give mass production advantages had not been invented yet. Had Dante written a best seller more in demand than his work actually was, it still could not have been sold at a cheaper price. (On the contrary, the price might have risen.) Today, however the more something appeals, the cheaper it becomes for the consumer and the greater the reward for the producer. The temptation to meet the average of tastes rather than one's own (or not to develop one's own) grows accordingly.

Past inducements which might have tempted producers to defile or deflect their talents were small. Dante was not tempted to write for *Sports Illustrated,* to condense his work for *Reader's Digest,* or to adapt it for the movies. He had no chance to write television scripts or commercial jingles, *Saturday Evening Post* stories or newspaper columns. If he was impelled to write, there were no alternatives to being as good a writer as his talent permitted. It is unlikely that the possibility of doing hackwork ever was totally absent. "Grubstreet" came into existence in the seventeenth century. Some sort of hackwork probably existed even in Dante's time. But the difference between then and now remains immense though, like the difference between being tempted by one dollar and one million dollars, it is quantitative. And there were, of course, political and religious pressures concerning the philosophical ideas one might express. But there was no mass market to entice the author into streamlining the esthetic vehicle of these ideas, to make it a common carrier, so that the average man could ride along without effort or understanding. Today the alternatives and temptations are very real. The rewards of the mass market are immense—and so are the deprivations of the creator of, one is tempted to say, custom-made literature. The real income of producers who do not cater to mass tastes has fallen even more than that of individualistic consumers. Cole Porter has described the situation and for him popular appeal was not a matter of sour grapes,[1]

Why be a great composer with your rent in arrears?
Why be a major poet and you'll owe it for years!
When crowds will pay to giggle
If you wiggle
Your ears. . . .

1. "Be a Clown," copyright © (unpub.) 1946 by Loew's Incorporated. Copyright © 1948 by Chappel & Co., Inc.

Our society may not treat the creator of great works of art much worse than he was treated in the past. But we treat the creator of popular art so much better that the inducement becomes almost irrestible. There was no such temptation in the past. And it was, of course, easier to decide to please yourself when pleasing others instead was not overwhelmingly rewarded anyway. Most talent is plastic to some extent.

There are some who doggedly insist on being themselves—but the temptations are infinite, and infinitely disguised, and insinuating. The psychological burden of isolation is crushing. Finally, isolation, too, has drawbacks affecting creation. The ability and the will to communicate are impaired if there is no public; and the defense against the temptations of popular culture uses much of the energy needed for creating. The artist who, by refusing to work for the mass market, becomes marginal cannot create what he might have created had there been no mass market. One may prefer a monologue to addressing a mass meeting. But it is not a conversation. And a marginal clique is not an elite, whatever its claims. Perhaps it should be. But it is not, as a social fact, unless society gives it that status. We are dealing with the recognition, not with the presence, of value.

We need not maintain that the taste of the masses has become worse than it was, only that it has become more important to the potential producers of high culture—important enough to isolate them or draw them to the mass market. However good or bad, mass taste could not interfere much with the production of high culture until the pull of the mass market became as mighty as it is now.

Probably the mass taste itself was debased by the de-individualizing and tradition-destroying developments already discussed. Folk culture developed a set of potentialities which requires the personal and communal relations that industrialism destroyed.

But another set of potentialities now fully developed by mass media always existed and has been complained about since Plato's time. The mass media suffice to bring out these potentialities and overwhelm folk (and high) culture. Full-fledged industrialism is not needed, though it might be required to create (rather than spread) popular culture. When movies are imported into a nonindustrial society, into remote parts of Pakistan, Spain, Burma, or the Congo, they easily take the place of native plays and rituals for the upper as well as the lower classes: an industrial product aimed at an average of tastes draws better than the best of folk or high culture in nearly any setting.

Industrialization is a prerequisite of popular culture; and it erodes high and folk culture. Not that without industrialism there can be no widespread bad taste. No one who has seen the frescoes at Pompeii or studied Rome in its decadence can fail to be impressed—as were Arnold Toynbee, Guglielmo Ferrero, and M. T. Rostovtzeff—with some parallels to our popular culture. Indeed, there were parallel developments with regard to mobility, urbanization, and commerce. But lacking machinery to spread it, Rome's "popular culture" was a fairly local affair, though it may have sufficed to dry up the flow of Roman high culture, which had never been copious. Our own popular culture is related to its ancestors as a jet-propelled airplane is to the pony express: without the marvels of modern technology, there could be crowds and traditions could decay. But thoroughgoing, pervasive, and (at least potentially) permanent de-individualization was impossible. Once more, elements of popular culture have existed throughout history. What is new is that industrialism has caused the *prevalence* of popular culture.

Apart from the degree of industrialization, invasion by popular culture is facilitated by two conditions: (1) The absence of strong, native-grown, preindustrial high and folk culture traditions. In the United States, for instance, these traditions, where they existed, were swamped by the influx of great masses with heterogeneous traditions finally homogenized through popular culture. Native traditions were not entrenched within these masses: they included few high culture bearers; and the folk cultures were not adaptable to an urbanized industrial civilization. (2) The suddenness of industrialization, its fragmentariness, and particularly the

316 PART THREE: POPULAR CULTURE

entrance of mass media before the industrialization of production generally. These two hypotheses—and they are necessarily quite speculative—may help explain why popular culture is so pervasive in the United States and so penetrating in the underdeveloped countries, while at the same time, in England, the oldest industrial country, sizable islands of folk and high culture, though embattled, have so far survived.

THE ROLE OF UNIVERSITIES AND FOUNDATIONS

No doubt universities and foundations provide some shelter for high culture, however leaky. They can't quite resist infiltration by popular culture, and they imprison high culture as much as they shelter it. Nevertheless they often fight a remarkable rear guard battle.

There is, however, an unfortunate difference between the largesse of a foundation and that of a Maecenas or of a Medici court. The administrators of foundations are keenly aware of spending trust funds. They feel that they must account for their activities. They try, therefore, to spend money in accordance with some publicly approved standard, or a least in a manner they feel is of demonstrable social usefulness. Thus they spend funds on empirical research and on tangible welfare projects so as to produce measurable results, data, or activities. If foundations attempt to aid literature and the arts, they help artists sufficiently established to exonerate administrators from any suspicion of following personal predilecions or individual tastes. (When an award to Ezra Pound was opposed by much public opinion, the Library of Congress refused to be involved further in these awards. Never mind the merits of Ezra Pound. The point is that public opinion, right or wrong, can veto and, in the end, determine who is to be helped by public money and ultimately by foundations, too.) Foundations help those who cater to already formed (genteel) tastes, not those who might form them. The chances of foundation grants for a budding Proust, Kafka, or Dostoevski before he has formed his public are slim—the chances of followers and imitators afterward are reasonable. Foundations even tempt artists and often seduce scholars to write or do what will find support in foundations—which, though it is not what might appeal to the mass market, is also not what the writer or scholar might have done had he been unseduced.

The situation in universities is a little better partly by reason of tradition, partly because universities pay their personnel mostly for teaching, though they insist on publications. Since they do not scrutinize closely the quality of publications, the instructor can maintain some independence—unless he is very ambitious for promotion and success. If he is, he would be ill advised to spend ten years on a major work which he could spend on minor or less thought-out publications. (This is less true for the exact sciences—with established criteria of value—and more for those endeavors for which standards are difficult to formulate.) And he would be well advised to engage in "teamwork" or other foundation fashions.

Foundations and universities are more useful in cultivating high culture created in the past than in helping new developments. But even their attempts to transmit the heritage of the past are severely marred by the prevalent conception of their educational function. To be educationally effective, that is, to attract an audience in an age of popular culture, universities and foundations tend to compete with the alternatives open to that audience. They end up not by bringing the audience to art, or any form of high culture, but by bringing art to the audience—by sufficiently adulterating high culture to make it palatable to the mass market.

Sometimes foundations and universities have simply followed the mass media at a dignified distance. The work of art is jazzed up a little or simplified to "make the unskillful laugh [though it] cannot but make the judicious grieve," even though "the censure of the which one must in your allowance overweigh a whole theatre of others." Hamlet's admonition is not easily heeded by an administrator who does not know who the "which one" would be—whereas he can identify "the whole theatre of others." Matters would not be helped much if the wealthy spent their money personally. The American rich would not be less sensitive to public opinion than their foundations. Even a hundred years ago, when direct "conspicuous consumption" was still fashionable, money was used to display certified culture—antiques or imitations—rather than to support creation. A wealthy class who became wealthy fairly suddenly and temporarily by catering to mass tastes seems less likely to create or support an autonomous culture of its own than an entrenched upper class with traditions of independence from the masses. (However, the situation a hundred years ago had a few advantages: some wealthy people— for example, the James family—cultivated themselves. Today, they would be more likely to run a newspaper or something else along popular lines.)

THE ADULTERATION OF PAST CULTURE

Corruption of past high culture by popular culture takes numerous forms, starting with direct adulteration. Bach candied by Stokowski, Bizet coarsened by Rodgers and Hammerstein, the Bible discolored and smoothed down into academic prose, Shakespeare spiced and made into a treacly musical comedy, Freud vulgarized into columns of newspaper correspondence advice (how to be happy, though well-adjusted)—the listing could be infinitely prolonged.

Corruption also takes the form of mutilation and condensation. Mozart meanders, Tolstoi was tedious, Dostoevski dawdled. To spare us trouble, to save our time for more important things (such as commercials), their works are cut, condensed, simplified, and rewritten until all possibilities of unfamiliar or aesthetic experience are strained out and plot and action become meaningless thrills with an obligato of maudlin simperings and grandiose defiances. Music is reduced to clatter and tinkle or cloying sentimentalities. Of course, these authors have their vices—necessary to their virtues (or so they felt). In a composition, one part may well be better or more important than another. Shall we then cut the great canvases to pieces accordingly? What of the composition as such? At any rate, the condenser cuts out the virtues with the vices. He is interesting in making it easier, shorter, or simpler, not better.

Editors who do not simply pretend that they know better than Tolstoi how to write his novels, or better than Beethoven how to compose his symphonies, say that half a loaf is better than none. Or, they argue that their mutilated versions will stimulate appetite for the work of art they ravished. This argument is without merit. Why should a reader, listener, or viewer accustomed to having all difficulties, complexities, and originalities streamlined out develop an appetite for the undigested work? Will it not be indigestible to him? How could its more subtle, and perhaps slow and cumulative appeal rival the succession of action-packed climaxes he is accustomed to? Mothers who give in to a child's whining and feed him candy, unlike popularizers, at least do not pretend that they are arousing the child's appetite for nourishment to follow.

Even if a predigested version were to lead to the original work, the public would be confronted with ideas and tropes which in their adulterated form have become commonplace. The garish image from "Classic Comics," the gaudy phrase from *Carmen Jones*, the gloss of the condensation overlay and spotlight the actual work, altering perception of colors and proportions and reducing it to the familiar clichés. No pin-up girl can surfeit appetite for a real one (though it may influence what satisfies it), just as no picture of a steak dulls our hunger. But the pin-up can spoil the appetite for other *images* of girls, particularly for more subtle, less reductive ones. And, if the calendar girl is a streamlined Goya, it certainly obstructs later experience of the actual painting by an untutored eye. Some people may be able to slough off the tawdriness. But even for them, the surprise and delight of freshness are blunted. Besides, how many people are drawn to actual mountaineering by riding a comfortable funicular? In making mountains more accessible, don't funiculars reduce elevation for the passengers?

DO-IT-YOURSELF CULTURE

The "Hundred Great Books" which Drs. Hutchins and Adler want everybody to read are unadulterated and mostly undigested. And according to the advertisements, anyone who reads them will be educated, entertained, and helped in "getting along in business . . . with associates and family." He will also learn

to meet whatever problem bothers him "squarely and conquer it."
(Does the end justify *these* means? May false claims for great
works not weaken their real claims to greatness and foster expectations sure to be disappointed?) The praiseworthy motive of
the plan nonetheless was revolt against corruption and neglect
of our cultural heritage. But on closer inspection, the nostrum
turns out to be a more ambitious and pretentious form of
digesting, the more dangerous because disguised.

By rewriting and paring, the condensers insist they get rid of
dross and compress the essentials for us. The contrivers of the
"Hundred Great Books" program instead brightly discovered
that culture is already concentrated in one hundred specific books
which, as it were, naturally contain the essentials of all ages.
No rewriting needed. Both the condensers and Hutchins' followers believe that there are essentials in the cultural heritage
which they know and have isolated—by distillation, the condensers
say; by simply picking them, Dr. Hutchins says. They insist that
everybody can understand, enjoy, and use these essentials: by
reading the same selection of works, Aristotle to Einstein, but no
systematic expositions of physics or philosophy and no com-
mentaries (Hutchins) or the same selection within works (di-
gesters). They have done the "research" for us, we need not
bother. Culture is reduced to capsules all can take to become
healthy, wealthy, and wise.

In condensation, the elements indigestible to popular culture
are omitted and the whole thing is reduced to pap. In the Hutchins approach, the reader jumps from landmark to landmark without regard, without a view even of the land they are marking.
(When there are no outstanding landmarks, when ideas and views
are not found in particular great books, they are ignored, however influential or important.) The works burst on the reader
as though grown on the same timeless soil. The connecting tissue
of history, which makes them intelligible, is omitted. There is no
history of, say, economic ideas or of the economy, nor is there a
systematic exposition of economics: the reader is simply given
some famous but unrelated works concerned with the subject
matter. But there is no way of understanding a classic except
through the tradition of which it is a part, and no way of understanding a subject except through systematic study. Finally, there
is no way of becoming educated except by absorbing and critically

working through a tradition *and* a subject matter. After all, even a baseball game is meaningless to a spectator who does not know the rules and the background of the contest. The understanding of ideas requires even more knowledge.

THE POPULARITY OF CLASSICS

What about the many excellent uncut and inexpensive editions of the classics, the fine recordings of musical masterpieces which are not hawked as shortcuts to culture? Many are sold under incongruous titles and with ludicrous covers which make promises sure to disappoint the readers enticed by them. But others are decently dressed. Both, it goes without saying, are a boon to individuals still clinging to high culture. And the symphony orchestras springing up in small towns? And the museums and clubs devoted to culture? Though Americans spend untold time reading newspapers and watching television, they also spend more money on attending concerts than on attending baseball games. Twelve million people listen to the New York Philharmonic each month. And the paperbound classics sell well—though, of course, there is no comparison with *Reader's Digest* (c. ten million copies sold per issue in the United States), or *Life*, not to speak of comic books, pulps, slicks, or Norman Vincent Peale. The data suggest that at least a few previously indifferent people buy some classics and go to some concerts. Is popular culture receding then, or being transformed?

The range of widely shared tastes has become broader. In particular, "middle-brow" tastes are more eclectic and now include material that was formerly "high-brow" as well as material formerly reserved to "low-brows." The borderlines are more blurred than ever. The size of the "middle-brow" group itself has grown and its attitudes are less aggressively crude and ignorant than in Sinclair Lewis's and H. L. Mencken's heyday. In short, a wider range of taste is more widely shared and, as was pointed out, this does not imply reduction to "the lowest common denominator." Yet middle-brow culture remains popular culture, even if the Book-of-the-Month Club sends its subscribers Proust, even if more and more people go to college and the *New Yorker* magazine penetrates to Kansas City. The effect is not less but more homogenization. The high and folk culture works, even when they are not *physically* altered, change their function when they are absorbed into the stream of popular culture. They cannot change the function or the basic character of popular culture.

Years ago a naked African chief wearing a top hat was among the stock figures of humorous magazines. The incongruous setting for the hat, worn in obvious ignorance of its ceremonial function in our society and without the complements its requires, struck us as funny. When other fragments of our civilization are put to uses quite alien to them—outside the patterns that give them their meaning in our society—we are similarly amused. Slowly accruing new meanings which become part of a new integrated pattern do not strike us as funny or tasteless. But when, in changed circumstances, the physical object does not become part of a new pattern or retain its old meaning, when it is simply used for its exotic charm, as the chief uses the top hat, we rightly ridicule the pretentious ignorance displayed. Evelyn Waugh, in condemning the protagonist of his *Handful of Dust* to spend the rest of his life reading Dickens to an illiterate, entertainment-hungry native in the Brazilian wilds, makes the point sharply. The situation must seem familiar to many a college professor.

American homes are now decorated with African masks and statues of Mexican gods, with Gothic crucifixions and Japanese prints as incongruous in them as the top hat on the tribal chief. Whether they come from past civilizations—including Western high and folk cultures—or from contemporary Africa, whether they are tacked to the wall, worn, read, listened to, viewed, or danced, such fragments, however entertaining or even instructive do not change popular culture but intensify its syncretistic stylessness. The very kaleidoscopic variety of chips from nearly all cultures the world has known helps to devalue and denature each, just as the colors of the spectrum fuse into a monochrome white when they are rotated rapidly before our eyes. Oddly enough, we pride ourselves on mixing a variety of culture patterns. We take to jamborees featuring "folk dances (or songs) of all nations"—as though the occasion would not deprive the folk dances of each nation of what meaning they might retain singly, and reduce them all to quaint imports. But isn't our life already such a jamboree?

Why do the classics clutter rather than enrich the minds of so many readers? Why do we find the glamorous items assembled indiscriminately like "celebrities" in a nightclub? Why do they not make a whole that organizes minds and sharpens sensibilities? Besides innate capacity, at least some of the following are needed to tutor intellects and sensibilities so that the aesthetic and intellectual values of high culture are apprehended as meaningful: time (and patience), inclination, discipline, focus, guidance, and environment in which style can be experienced.

These conditions have become rare even in our better institutions of higher learning. Were they more available in the past? The evidence is anecdotal, though sweeping assertions are not missing. But the relevant thing is not that possibly more people were devoted to high culture in proportion to the total population, nor even that they were better supported (which is likely), but that practically none were devoted to popular culture. The high culture of the past, however limited, formed a style. The near absence of popular culture and of industrialism meant that high culture functioned under conditions favorable to its continued influence and development, at least in one social stratum. Today, however widely spread, high culture in every stratum of society is a minor ripple in a great flood.

What eagerness for high culture there is in popular culture has abetted the invasion of high culture with unfortunate effect on the invaded territory. Often the effect on the invaders has been unhappy, too. In biting into strange fruits they are not equipped to digest, they are in danger of spoiling their appetite for what might actually nourish them. It is not new or disastrous that few people read classics. It is new that so many people misread them. Doubtless they are eager for intellectual and aesthetic experience. Yet their quest is not likely to succeed. A partial response may sometimes be achieved. But it takes far more than training (and even that is often lacking) and formal preparation fully to experience a work of art as meaningful. It takes an environment and a life experience which do not easily grow on the soil of our society.

CHAPTER XIX

Of Happiness and of
Despair We Have No Measure

MORAL ISOLATION AND GREGARIOUSNESS

What is the impact of the stream of popular culture on persons? Much research on short-run effects of mass media and their specific "campaigns" has been done (and a great deal of nonsense is talked about the effects of specific program contents). But there is hardly anything on the long-run cumulative effects of the total setting. Such research is difficult and unprofitable in more senses than one. But important. The following general observations may help stimulate it.

All mass media in the end alienate people from personal experience and, though appearing to offset it, intensify their moral isolation from each other, from reality, and from themselves. One may turn to the mass media when lonely or bored. But mass media, once they become a habit, impair the capacity for meaningful experience. Though more diffuse and not as gripping, the habit feeds on itself, establishing a vicious circle as addictions do.

The mass media do not physically replace individual activities and contacts—excursions, travel, parties, and so forth. But they impinge on all. The portable radio is taken everywhere—from seashore to mountaintop—and everywhere it isolates the bearer from his surroundings, from other people, and from himself.

324

Most people escape being by themselves at any time by voluntarily tuning in on something or somebody. Anyway, it is nearly beyond the power of individuals to escape broadcasts. Music and public announcements are piped into elevators, restaurants, bars, shops, cafés, and lobbies, into public means of transportation and even taxis. You can turn off your radio but not your neighbor's— nor can you silence his portable or the set at the restaurant. Fortunately, most persons do not seem to miss privacy, the cost of which is even more beyond the average income than the cost of individuality.

People are never quite in one place or group without at the same time, singly or collectively, gravitating somewhere else, abstracted, if not transported by the mass media. The incessant announcements, arpeggios, croonings, sobs, bellows, brayings, and jingles draw everybody to some faraway world at large and, by weakening community with immediate surroundings, make people lonely even when in a crowd, and crowded even when alone.

We have already stressed that mass media must offer homogenized fare to meet an average of tastes. Further, whatever the quality of the offerings, the very fact that one after the other is absorbed continuously, indiscriminately, and casually trivializes all. Even the most profound of experiences, articulated too often on the same level, is reduced to a cliché. The impact of each of the offerings of the mass media is thus weakened by the next one. But the impact of the stream of all mass media offerings is cumulative and strong. It lessens people's capacity to experience life itself.

Sometimes it is argued that the audience reacts to soap opera and comic strip characters and situations as though they were real. (Wedding presents are sent to fictional couples.) People may attempt to live the fiction because they prefer it to their own lives. However, the significant effect is not the (quite limited) investment of fiction with reality, but the de-realization of life lived in largely fictitious terms. Art can deepen the perception of reality. But popular culture veils it, diverts from it, and becomes an obstacle to experiencing it. It is not so much an escape from life as an invasion of life first, and ultimately evasion altogether.

CHILDREN AND VIOLENCE

Parents, well knowing that mass media can absorb energy, often lighten the strain that the attempts of their children to reach for activity and direct experience would impose: they allow some energy to be absorbed by the vicarious experience of the television screen. Before television, the cradle was rocked or poppy juice given to inhibit the initiative and motility of small children. Television, unlike these physical sedatives, tranquilizes by means of substitute gratifications. Manufactured activities and plots are offered to still the child's hunger for experiencing life. They effectively neutralize initiative and channel imagination. But the early introduction of de-individualized characters and situations and the early homogenization of taste on a diet of meaningless activity hardly foster development of individual imagination.

The fact that comic books or television neither express nor appeal to individuality seems far more injurious to the child's mind and character than the violence they feature, though it is the latter that is often blamed for juvenile delinquency. The blame is misplaced. Violence is not new to life or fiction. It waxed large in ancient fables, in fairy tales, and in tragedies from Sophocles to Shakespeare.

Mom always knew that "her boy could not have thought of it," that the other boys must have seduced him. Dr. Frederic Wertham's belief that viewing or reading about violence persuades children to engage in it is Mom's ancient conviction disguised as psychiatry. (See his *Seduction of the Innocent*.) Of course, the impact of a comic strip or movie on a particularly susceptible child may be bad. But the impact of any otherwise harmless experience may be injurious to especially susceptible persons. Children are quite spontaneously bloodthirsty and need both direct and fantasy outlets for violence. What is wrong with the violence of the mass media is not that it is violence but that it is not art—that it is meaningless violence which thrills but does not gratify. The violence of the desire for life and meaning is displaced and appears as a desire for meaningless violence. But the violence which is ceaselessly supplied cannot ultimately gratify because it does not meet the repressed desire. The same reasoning applies to pornography. It does not seduce and, though it thrills some, it does not gratify. The harm it would do if widespread would lie, as with violence, in the debasement of taste. (If there is a general cause of juvenile deliquency, it is likely to be boredom, which causes addiction to both violent fiction and violent action.)

THE OUTLOOK

Before trying to make more explicit the psychological effects of popular culture, let us summarize the setting.

While immensely augmenting our comforts, our conveniences, and our leisure, and disproportionately raising the real income of the poor, industry has also impoverished life. Mass production and consumption, mobility, the homogenization of taste and finally of society were among the costs of higher productivity. They de-individualized life and drained each of our ends of meaning as we achieved it. Pursuit thus became endless and boundless. The increased leisure time would hang heavy on our hands were it not for the mass media which help us kill it. They inexorably exclude art and anything of significance when it cannot be reduced to mass entertainment, but they divert us from the passage of the time they help kill but not fill. They also tend to draw into the mass market talents and works that might otherwise produce new meanings and visions, and they abstract much of the capacity to experience art or life directly and deeply. What they do, however, is what people demand.

We scrutinized the causes, the effects, and the general characteristics of popular culture and found them unavoidable in a mass production economy. But prophecy is beyond our means. We claim to have stated, with reasonable clarity, a number of connected hypotheses—a theory—which fit one series of facts and help to explain them, that is, to connect them with another series of facts. The latter (industrialism, and so forth) are well established. The former—popular culture—though factual enough, are not easily measured and tested. The conclusions are consistent with what measuring has been done. But most testing so far devised is of little relevance to our actual topic. Many sociologists, therefore, have regarded the topic as irrelevant to sociology. But this merely reduces the relevance of sociology to contemporary culture. Other sociologists have tested where possible, but without venturing on comprehensive hypotheses or concepts. This makes the significance of many factual findings unintelligible. (Some facts tested *ad nauseam* are without relevance to any conceivable theory.) We are satisfied then that only the procedure adopted can do justice to the subject matter, though we must rely for verification on the experience and reason of our readers. *Si monumentum quaeris, circumspice.*

Extrapolation of present trends makes a dismal picture. But there is comfort in the fact that no extrapolation has ever predicted the future correctly. Elements can be forecast, but only prophets can do more (and they are unreliable or hard to interpret). History has always had surprises up its sleeve—it would be most surprising if it changed its ways. Our ignorance, then, leaves the rosy as well as the grim possibilities open for the future. But this does not authorize us to avert our gaze from the present and from the outlook it affords. Neither is cheerful.

REPRESSION AND DISCONTENT

The gist of any culture is an ethos which gives meaning to the lives of those who dwell in it. If this be the purport of popular culture, it is foiled. We have suggested how it comes to grief in various aspects. What makes popular culture as a whole so disconcerting is best set forth now by exploring the relationship among diversion, art, and boredom.

Freud thought of art as a diversion, "an illusion in contrast to reality," a "substitute gratification" like a dream. In dreams and in art, ideas and feelings of which the dreamer (or artist) may not be aware are condensed, fused, or split, and expressed, as well as disguised, through symbols. The analogy must not be driven too far, however. The artist needs special gifts to select, shape, control, and organize his materials; and he reveals not himself so much as the world. A dream is not art any more than art is a dream, even if both were only "substitute gratifications." Freud himself did not think that the analogy (or psychoanalysis as a whole) could shed light on artistic gifts or techniques. He realized that the approach, though it may suffice to analyze artistic motivation, does not explain aesthetic quality. Therefore, it cannot define art. Freud was wrong in writing at times as though it did, by sometimes treating the artist as a patient, sometimes as a fellow analyst. Art can be reduced neither to dreams nor to analyses of dreams, though it contains elements of both.

In regarding art as a substitute gratification, an illusion similar to a dream, Freud shared the popular view of art. It is a correct view—of pseudo-art produced to meet the demand for diversion. But it is a mistaken, reductive definition of art. (Freud's actual relation to art was more sophisticated than his theory.) Freud finds the "dreamwork" attempting to hide or disguise the dreamer's true wishes and fears so that they may not alarm his consciousness. The "substitute gratification" produced by the dreamwork, mainly by displacements, helps the dreamer continue sleeping. The dreamwork deals similarly with fears. It displaces and disguises them and attempts to produce illusionary reassurances. However, one major function of art is precisely to undo this dreamwork, to see through disguises, to reveal to our consciousness the true nature of our wishes and fears. The dreamwork covers, to protect sleep. Art discovers and attempts to awaken the sleeper. Whereas the dreamwork tries to aid repression, the work of art intensifies and deepens perception and experience of the world and of the self. It attempts to pluck the heart of the mystery, to show where "the action lies in its true nature."

Though dreams and art both may disregard literal reality, they do so to answer opposite needs. The dream may ignore reality to keep the sleeper's eyes closed. Art transcends immediate reality to encompass wider views, penetrate into deeper experience, and lead to a fuller confrontation of man's predicament. The dreamwork even tries to cover upsetting basic impulses with harmless immediate reality. Art, in contrast, ignores the immediate only to uncover the essential. Artistic revelation need not be concerned with outer or with social reality. It may be purely aesthetic. But it can never be an illusion if it is art. Far from distracting from reality, art is a form of reality which strips life of the fortuitous to lay bare its essentials and permit us to experience them. In psychoanalytic terms, art is not a symptomatic expression of the repressed, but a sublimated and controlled expression—not an escape from, or a limitation or distortion of experience, but an attempt to face it with enhanced awareness, and to deal with its essence. Art differs from science in methods of searching and testing, and because it does reveal rather than predict, and focuses on human reactions and values. Above all, art strives to produce subjective experiences, whereas science produces objective information.

In popular culture, however, "art" is all that Freud said art is, and no more. Like the dreamwork, popular culture distorts human experience to draw "substitute gratifications" or reassurances from it. Like the dreamwork it presents "an illusion in contrast to reality." For this reason, popular "art" falls short. All of popular culture leaves one vaguely discontented because, like popular art, it is only a "substitute gratification"; like a dream, it distracts from life and from real gratification.

Substitute gratifications are uneconomic, as Freud often stressed. They do not, in the end, gratify as much, and they cost more psychologically than the real gratification which they shut out. That is why sublimation and realistic control are to be preferred to substitution and repression. That is why reality is to be preferred to illusion, full experience to symptomatic displacements and defense mechanisms. Yet substitute gratifications habitually resorted to incapacitate the individual for real ones. In part, they cause or strengthen internalized hindrances to real and gratifying experience; in part they are longed for because internal barriers have already blocked real gratification of the original impulses.

Though the specific role it plays varies with the influence of other formative factors in the life of each individual, popular culture must be counted among the baffling variety of causes and effects of defense mechanisms and repressions. It may do much damage, or none at all, or be the only relief possible, however deficient. But when popular culture plays a major role in life, significant repressions have taken (or are taking) place. Popular culture supplants those gratifications which are no longer sought because of the repression of the original impulses. But it is a substitute and spurious. It founders and cannot succeed because neither desire nor gratification are true. "Nought's had, all's spent/Where desire is got without content."

It may seem paradoxical to describe popular culture in terms of repression. Far from appearing repressed, it strikes one as uninhibited. Yet the seeming paradox disappears if we assume that the uproarious din, the raucous noise, and the shouting are attempts to drown the shriek of unused capacities, of individuality repressed and bent into futility.

BOREDOM AND DIVERSION

Repression bars impulses from awareness without satisfying them. This damming up always generates a feeling of futility and apathy or, in defense against it, an agitated need for action. The former may be called listless, the latter restless boredom. They may alternate and they may enter consciousness only through anxiety and a sense of meaninglessness, fatigue, and nonfulfillment. Sometimes there is such a general numbing of the eagerness too often turned aside that only a dull feeling of dreariness and emptiness remains. (In persons suffering from symptom neurosis, the pressure of the repressed impulses may cause so much anxiety that boredom becomes faint. But this is hardly a desirable alternative.) More often there is an insatiable longing for things to happen. The external world is to supply these events to fill the emptiness. Yet the bored person cannot designate what would satisfy a craving as ceaseless as it is vague. It is not satisfied by any event supplied.

The yearning for diversion to which popular culture caters cannot be sated by diversion "whereof a little more than a little is by much too much," because no displaced craving can be satisfied by catering to it in its displaced form. Only when it becomes possible to experience the desire in its true form and to dispense with the internalized processes that balked and displaced it does actual gratification become possible. Diversion at most, through weariness and fatigue, can numb and distract.

For instance, in many popular movies the tear ducts are massaged and thrills are produced by mechanized assaults on the centers of sensation. We are diverted temporarily and in the end perhaps drained—but not gratified. Direct manipulation of sensations can produce increases and discharges of tension, as does masturbation, but it is a substitute. It does not involve the individual as an individual, it does not involve reality but counterfeits it. Sensations directly stimulated and discharged without being intensified and completed through feelings sifted and acknowledged by the intellect are debasing because reductive, because they do not involve the whole individual in his relation to reality. When one becomes inured to bypassing reality and individuality in favor of meaningless excitement, ultimate gratification becomes impossible.

WHO IS SLAIN WHEN TIME IS KILLED?

Once fundamental impulses are thwarted beyond retrieving, once they are so deeply repressed that no awareness is left of their aims, once the desire for a meaningful life has been lost as well as the capacity to create it, only a void remains. Life fades into tedium when the barrier between impulses and aims is so high that neither penetrates into consciousness and no sublimation whatever takes place. Diversion, however frantic, can overwhelm temporarily but not ultimately relieve the boredom which oozes from nonfulfillment.

Though the bored person hungers for things to happen to him, the disheartening fact is that when they do, he empties them of the very meaning he unconsciously yearns for by using them as distractions. In popular culture, even the Second Coming would become just another barren thrill to be watched on television till the next newscast comes on. No distraction can cure boredom—just as the company so unceasingly pursued cannot stave off loneliness. The bored person is lonely for himself, not, as he thinks, for others. He misses the individuality he lost, the capacity for experience from which he is barred. No distraction can restore it. Hence he goes unrelieved and insatiable.

The popular demand for "inside" stories, for vicarious sharing of the private lives of "personalities" rests on the craving for a private life—even someone else's—by those who are dimly aware of having none whatever, or at least no life that holds their interest. The attempts to allay boredom are as assiduous as they are unavailing. Countless books pretend to teach by general rules and devices what cannot be learned by devices and rules. Individual personalities cannot be mass-produced (with happiness thrown in or your money back). Nevertheless, the message of much popular culture is "you, too, can be happy" if you only buy this car or that hair tonic; you will be thrilled, you will have adventure, romance, popularity—you will no longer be lonely and left out if you follow this formula. And success, happiness, or at least freedom from anxiety, is also the burden of popular religion, as unchristian in these, its aims, as it is in its means. "Make People Like You—Increase Your Earnings," advertises Dr. Peale. These aims are not found in the Gospels, in Luther, or in Calvin, and not even in Pelagius and Coelestius. From Dale Carnegie to Norman Vincent Peale to Harry and Bonaro Overstreet only the vocabulary changes. The principle remains the same. The formula is well illustrated in the following (taken from the *Indianapolis News*):

Warm Smile Is an Attribute of Charm
For this, train the upper lip by this method:
1. Stretch the upper lip down over the teeth. Say "Mo-o-o-o."
2. Hold the lip between the teeth and smile.
3. Purse the lips, pull them downward and grin.
4. Let the lower jaw fall and try to touch your nose with your upper lip.
Months of daily practice are necessary to eliminate strain from the new way of smiling, but it, too, can become as natural as all beguiling smiles must be.

One doubts somehow that it will be possible "to eliminate strain," for, whatever the formula, nothing can be more tiresome than the tireless, cheerless pursuit of pleasure. Days go slowly when they are empty; one cannot tell one from the other. And yet the years go fast. When time is endlessly killed, one lives in an endless present until time ends without ever having passed, leaving a person who never lived to exclaim: "I wasted time and now doth time waste me."

OF HAPPINESS AND OF DESPAIR

To the Christian, despair is a sin, not because there is anything
to be hoped for in this life, but because to despair is to lack faith
in redemption from it—in the life everlasting. As for the pleasures
of this life, Lancelot Andrewes described them: ". . . though
they fade not of themselves yet to us they fade. We are hungry
and we eat. Eat we not till that fades and we are as weary of
our fulness as we were of our fasting? We are weary and we rest.
Rest we not till that fades and we are as weary of our rest as
ever we were of our weariness?" Our bodies and minds themselves fade as do their pleasures. The insults of time are spared to
none of us. Such is the human predicament.

A little more than a hundred years ago, Henry David Thoreau
wrote in *Walden*: "The mass of men lead lives of quiet desperation. . . . A stereotyped but unconscious despair is concealed
even under what are called the games and amusements of mankind." Despair, we find, is no longer quiet. Popular culture
tries to exorcise it with much clanging and banging. Perhaps
it takes more noise to drone it out. Perhaps we are less willing
to face it.

But whether, wrapped in popular culture, we are less happy
than our quieter ancestors, or the natives of Bali, must remain
an open question. There have been periods happier and others
more desperate than ours. But we don't know which. And
even an assertion as reasonable as this is a conjecture, like any
comparison of today's bliss with yesterday's. The happiness felt
in disparate groups, in disparate periods and places cannot be
measured and compared. Even in examining a single life it seems
absurd to throw onto the same scale the separate raptures generated by hearing chamber music, eating a peach, loving, or
winning a fight; harder still to measure the depth of despair into
which one sinks if he fails or suffers positive sorrows. Yet to
sum, we must set sorrow off against delight and add the net to
that of other persons. (Perhaps desire can be measured. But does
desire fulfilled bring happiness?) The whole idea does violence to
our actual experience and creates problems which cannot be

solved by any observation. What about intensity versus duration or depth? Or suppose the net "amount" of happiness drawn from a life replete with great joys and sorrows equals the "sum" drawn from a life lacking both? Did the two lives lead to equal happiness?

Perhaps we can order the relish elicited by homogeneous segments of life in terms of "none," "some," "much"; thus we might speak of "more" or "less." But even such ordering can only be undertaken from a given standpoint in time and from a given viewpoint. It would differ from person to person.

Our contention is simply that by distracting from the human predicament and blocking individuation and experience, popular culture impoverishes life without leading to contentment. But whether "the mass of men" felt better or worse without the mass production techniques of which popular culture is an ineluctable part we shall never know. Of happiness and of despair we have no measure.

PART FOUR

The Proper Study
of Mankind

CHAPTER XX   *Man as an Object of Science*

Over the last few centuries, the influence of science has mounted at a steadily accelerating rate. Scientists have annexed more and more realms to their domain, and scientific methods are applied to almost all human activity. As it grew, science became self-conscious. An elaborate philosophy of science, a metascience, now analyzes the methods science uses, as well as its scope, the meaning of its theories, and the kind and degree of certainty it can yield.

This self-consciousness was intensified as scientific study was extended to human behavior itself. The social sciences (including psychology) posed anew questions about the range and the effects of science which had lingered since its beginnings. Can science deal with human beings as with the rest of nature? Is the behavior of people as predictable by scientific methods as the behavior of other bodies and organisms? Are the social sciences, then, as scientific as, say, physics? (This, of course, implies some answer to the question: what makes science scientific?) Further, can the social sciences solve the problems besetting humanity in the same way in which chemistry solves a chemical problem? What precisely is the potential role of the social sciences in the direction of human behavior, particularly in controlling the social changes which the progress of the natural sciences brings about? (By "control" we mean what is meant in

339

the physical sicences: the attempt to bring about an intended effect—e.g., war, peace, prosperity, freedom—any kind of desired behavior.)

OBJECTIVITY

The purpose and method of the natural sciences were thought at first to be impious and immoral, as Galileo can testify; this objection is still with us with regard to the social sciences though usually in disguised form.

As soon as political science was refounded in the Renaissance, moralists asked whether it is permissible to do what Machiavelli did—in Bacon's words, "to describe frankly and without dissimilation what men do, and not what they ought to do." (*Quod homines facere soleant non quod debeant.*) Actually, Machiavelli generalized too much from his particular surroundings; yet many of his observations remain applicable. *The Prince* describes how power is or can be achieved, held, and lost. This is what politics *qua* politics is about—whatever the ends for which power is desired or used—and, therefore, what political science must be concerned with. Yet the thought is still repugnant to many, as witness Machiavelli's reputation through the ages, and such redundancies as "power politics," which are as sensible, Jacques Barzun rightly remarks, as "food nutrition" would be.

Machiavelli was particularly vulnerable to moral objections because his description of political behavior was cast into the prescriptive form of advice to a ruler. His critics thought he must approve of the prince's goal—power at any price—and of all the means for the achievement of this goal which he recommended as effective. (The word "good," which sometimes means "effective" and sometimes "morally right," helps to confuse matters here.) Whether or not he did and, if so, for what ulterior reason, should be irrelevant to the political scientist. What matters is whether the means recommended are as effective as Machiavelli thought—whether he correctly observed the relation between cause and effect in politics.

Somewhat later, when economists studied how a man exclusively concerned with maximizing his income and wealth would have to act, the same question was raised: *should* men act thus?

The misunderstanding of the nature of science on which such questions are based, far from being confined to outsiders, is shared by many social scientists. Yet approval or disapproval of the behavior he studies is as irrelevant to the task of the economist as it is to the task of the political scientist. In this respect, social scientists do not differ from meteorologists, though people are usually more resigned about the weather than they are about themselves. Perhaps we can do more about human behavior (and certainly we feel more responsible for it) than about the weather. But we will succeed only if we first study it, without ignoring undesirable aspects and possibilities. Whether abortions should be undertaken or permitted is a moral question. But it can be decided only if we know what the means and material effects are (both of permitting and prohibiting). Scientific knowledge is never alone sufficient to answer a moral question; but it is necessary most of the time.

There is, however, one consideration—to which not enough attention has been paid—which lends some force to the view that the study of social behavior cannot be morally quite neutral: such a study may have *automatic* effects, desirable or undesirable, apart from increasing our knowledge. Something analogous to the Heisenberg effect in physics may occur in the social sciences; the observation, the attendant requirements, and the publication of results may unavoidably influence that which is being observed (for better or for worse). So far this effect has been minor, but to the extent to which it does occur, it modifies the assumption of neutrality. The information the Kinsey report purveyed about the sexual behavior of some Americans is likely to influence imitative readers, whereas rats, unlike Americans, are not influenced by reading scientific reports about the behavior of other rats. (The scientific validity of Professor Kinsey's entomological enterprise—particularly the statistical techniques— seems doubtful. At any rate it makes me feel waspish.) Social scientists have accorded but fitful recognition to the fact that observation, to the extent to which it is likely automatically to influence what is being observed, is not neutral in its effects, and possibly does not record what would have occurred had there been no observation.

MODELS

Uneasiness about the moral aspects of behavioral studies probably also prompts those questions about "economic man" which appear to be based on modern psychology: *do* men really act to maximize their income? and do they do so as rationally as economists assume? Actually, in building a model of man as income maximizer, economists need not assume anything about the psychology or the nature of man, or even about his ordinary behavior; they need to explore only how a man would have to act, if (all other things being equal) he wanted to maximize his income. Nor does such a model assume anything about the rationality with which we *actually* pursue the fulfillment of our desires.

The economic model depicts the behavior that would be rational if a given end—income maximization—is postulated. But, in essence, economic calculation is simply rational calculation: how to achieve *any* goal with the least expenditure of whatever is valued, i.e., to be economized. Hence, if we replace the goal of income with some other goal, or, better, add some other goals, economic analysis still can and must be applied. In this respect, economics may serve as a paradigm for all social sciences, as was pointed out by the political sociologist Gaetano Mosca.

The importance of the economic model in predicting actual behavior (as distinguished from indicating the implications of conceivable behavior) depends on the actual presence and importance of the included variables (e.g., the income-maximizing tendency) in human activities and the influence of the excluded variables. This is so with *any* theoretical model: its relevance to reality depends on the importance of the included variables in reality; and models become models by excluding some variables to concentrate on others.

This exclusion is not a defect but a virtue—a model is a simplification, not a reproduction of reality. The virtue of simplification becomes a vice only if the model builder is unaware of his exclusions, or forgets about them, and attempts to apply conclu-

Man as an Object of Science

sions drawn from the model directly to human behavior. This, of course, has happened often, but is no more reason for throwing out models in the social sciences than anywhere else. On the contrary, it is a good reason for constructing models which include the variables excluded before, whether separately or together. Sociology, anthropology, and other sciences are attempting, however haltingly, to do so.

METHODOLOGICAL ALTERNATIVES

It is possible to abandon the assumption of rational behavior altogether. We need retain only the assumption that we can find regularities of behavior—for without that no study could bear fruit. Scientific study is nothing if not an attempt to find regularities—recurrent relationships—which permit us to predict and which are tested by predictions. However, the provisional assumption of rationality is useful in some social sciences. It guides our search for regularities and helps make these regularities intelligible. Finally, if we wish to *apply* the social sciences to the control of human behavior, we have to postulate ends and calculate the most rational ways of attaining them. To assume rational behavior is simply to assume ends and to prescribe effective and economic means to attain them. The means then are justified by the ends (nothing else can ever justify *any* means *qua* means, though no end can justify all means).

To say that people act rationally, then, is to make a judgment about how suitable the means are to the ends they pursue. Such a judgment requires us to know not only what people do, but also what they want to achieve. We will be misled if the true objective of the behavior studied is not what it is assumed to be. True or apparent irrationality may occur because people are vague, ambivalent, or misleading about their objectives. Yet not much would be gained if we were to drop the teleological (rational) model altogether in the social sciences. The real difficulties lie in empirically establishing regularities of human behavior, regardless of the form—purposive or not—in which they are described. The heuristic value of the teleological model is considerable. Besides, if we are to apply our knowledge to the control of human behavior, we will have to investigate actual human ends anyway, and decide among possible ones.

Some problems of attaining knowledge about human behavior, though not peculiar to the social sciences, characterize them more than other disciplines. Individuals, groups, and societies are streams of historical events which, unlike the models abstracted from them, take place in nonrecurrent situations. The events have enough in common to fall into classes signified by such words as "war," "depression," and "family." But each war, depression, or family differs immensely from another, if only because each develops in unique historical circumstances. Strictly speaking, this is true as well for the events studied by the natural sciences. But in the natural sciences the most relevant features appear to be repetitive, whereas in the social sciences repetitiveness can be postulated only by abstracting from relevant and often decisive features which, though not themselves unique, combine into unique situations. What is worse for the social sciences is that it is nearly impossible to *reproduce* any of the situations they are concerned with. Because of this, we cannot *actually* isolate variables from one another so as to ascertain which are necessary and sufficient to produce the effects of which we suspect them to be the cause; we can do so only in our analytical models.

We must rely on observation, without the basic advantage, offered by experiment, of keeping constant the actual environment of the phenomena under observation, and thus testing our hypotheses. The evidence for the theories of the social sciences is therefore unlikely ever to be as conclusive as the evidence for propositions in physics can be. The propositions of the social sciences are unlikely ever to be definitively tested. If a prediction which follows from a theory does not come true, it may be that the theory is wrong. It may be as well that it would have come true were it not that some of the circumstances presumed to remain unchanged—*ceteris paribus*—did not remain unchanged. And we cannot ascertain *empirically* whether this would have been the case.

Moreover, for the sake of simplicity, we often must presume circumstances to remain constant which we know will actually change (though we do not know which way). Further, these circumstances are known to be relevant to what we study—for example, political developments are relevant to economic ones. Yet, the major attempts to create a unified social science—from Comte, to Marx, to Spengler or Toynbee—have proved to be without scientific value themselves, though they have served as sources for manifold inspirations, and are sometimes admirable as works of art or metaphysics.

VALUE JUDGMENTS

Even if the social sciences could predict with the degree of probability which characterizes the natural sciences, there are peculiar difficulties in applying such knowledge. In physics, for instance, controlling energy means to utilize our knowledge so as to arrange matters in such a way as to produce or channel the energy wanted. But in the social sciences we would have to arrange not matters, but ourselves so as to produce the desired result; we are not only the manipulators but also the manipulated. To some extent the natural sciences, when applied, also involve the manipulation of human beings, for instance, in medicine. Usually, however, the individual is free to take the physician's prescription or pour it down the drain. The decision is seldom collective and compulsory, and when it is (e.g., vaccination and other public health measures) people tend to accept it because they are fairly agreed on what they wish to achieve. In contrast, in the social sciences we are not agreed on what we want. To be sure, if aims are stated vaguely enough, agreement is easily reached. But each goal is achievable only at the expense of other valued aims. And when the all-important question of alternative goals, of costs, is faced, there is no agreement. Yet the attainment of social goals requires social action and acquiescence. This last point is, perhaps, most serious. For, unfortunately, disagreements on what changes are worthwhile—on what ends we *should* strive for, individually and collectively—are not amenable to resolution by scientific means. Hence, to the extent to which social problems are rooted in divergent values (goals), they are not likely to be solved by the social sciences, which at most clarify the alternatives and their costs. Yet collective decisions have to be taken.

Clarification by the social sciences can be of great assistance, however. Divergent ends may be attained by different persons without conflict, and it is for scientific analysis to establish whether this is possible. Further, ends may be pursued in ignorance of the means actually required to achieve them and of their cost, or in ignorance of their unattainability, or of their incompatibility with other ends simultaneously pursued. Knowledge of means and of effects may influence the ends people wish to pursue; and the social sciences yield such knowledge.

Some American philosophers even feel that most conflicts which appear to be about ultimate ends can be eliminated by increased knowledge. And some social scientists believe that a philosophical anthropology (or psychology) could establish the needs of human nature, and therewith the ends we should strive for. These views have the merit of calling attention to the fact that agreement on ultimate values is often greater than it appears to be, that many apparent conflicts about ends are due to ignorance of the precise implications of each end—the means needed and the effects achieved by it. Nonetheless, I think that the views are false if they are interpreted to assert that perfect knowledge would eliminate conflicts about values—about what is good or right, about what should be done, about the ultimate ends that people should pursue in preference to others. ("Instrumental ends"—things that are "good for" the attainment of other ends in any given situation—are here referred to as "means.")

James Madison went too far when he wrote "if men were angels, no government would be necessary," if he meant that perfect knowledge, goodness, and wisdom, such as may be attributed to angels, would lead to agreement on ends and means and thus make a government superfluous. Not so. If the angels do not all come from the same mold (and to assume that they do is to define away the problem and not to solve it), they may have different preferences. Some, for instance, may wish to leave nature unspoiled; others, in concrete circumstances, might want to give up some natural beauty in favor of, say, electric power or housing developments. Government is not needed only, as Madison implied, because human nature is corrupt and requires restraint; the conflict is not only between good and evil; collective decisions about alternative goods are required when these are indivisible; and science, or knowledge, or wisdom, or absence of evil are not sufficient to make them. No social science, indeed no knowledge at all, however angelic, can decide what should be done, what is better, or even by what means the decision should be made. For the process by which the decision is to be made requires criteria for decision making which ultimately must be based on values. Yet decisions must be made all the time, and we are not even angels.

"HAPPINESS" NO HELP

Bentham's famous formula (actually it was current before him), which is still popularly accepted—the greatest happiness of the greatest number—is of little help; the greatest happiness (if measurable at all) is not necessarily the happiness of the greatest number; the greatest total happiness may be achieved by enslavement of some to others. Total happiness might be increased by rape, murder, and theft, if the victim's happiness is decreased less than the perpetrators' is increased. The Marquis de Sade (who fantasied just that), was a malevolent utilitarian. Bentham was a benevolent one. The premises are really the same; the ultimate values differ, but though one may prefer one set to the other, one cannot prove it right on the basis of the "felicific calculus" (or any other). Note how this kind of problem crops up in many decisions. Is the "happiness" of Southern Negroes or that of Southern whites, of Algerian *colons* or Arabs, to be preferred? Should local majorities or over-all majorities decide, or the interpretation of the will of a generation long dead?

On the other hand, the happiness of the greatest number if each counts equally, as Bentham intended, might be the least possible happiness in sum, and surely less than the maximum one. All this on the assumption that there is a homogeneous and measurable quantity called happiness. But then Bentham's assumption seems wrong for each person, and of course, interpersonally. "Happiness" is the name of a number of heterogeneous qualities which have only some aspects or symptoms in common. The positive feelings generated by different actions—solving a problem; making an advantageous deal; marrying; being honored; slaking one's thirst; contemplating a work of art; creating it—

are not commensurable. Nor are negative feelings. Certainly positive feelings cannot be quantified and added up so that after
negative feelings are subtracted a net amount of happiness remains. A life replete with joys and sorrows does not yield the
same net happiness as one that has little of either, even if the
arithmetic net could be calculated. The quantities are not homogeneous enough to make even ordinal measurement meaningful.

Preferences can be observed; happiness is hard to observe,
impossible to calculate. Anyone who thinks otherwise ought to
read some of the great novels which describe man's career on
earth. Yet we act—and must act—as though we knew what
action will lead to a net increase of happiness. From the building
of a highway to the imposition of a tax, such an assumption,
though perhaps not causing the action, is used to justify it.

Moreover, that happiness is desirable at the expense, possibly,
of other things, is to be shown, not to be assumed, and it cannot
be shown by showing that it is desired. (For "desirable" means
that which ought to be desired, not that which is.) And, unless
we deprive "happiness" of specific meaning and assert, by definition, that everything people do they do because they desire to,
and everything that is desired is desired because it is believed to
lead to happiness, we can observe that people do many things
even though aware that they will not lead to happiness—e.g., we
make sacrifices and observe duties and obligations. The
morally right is certainly not always the individually happy-
making. And if we were to accept a definition that makes "striving for happiness" synonymous with "striving for whatever
people strive for" we would not be helped much in choosing
among goals, for we would be saying that we ought to strive
for whatever we want to strive for.

Finally, one decisive contribution of the social sciences to the
problem has not been fully recognized—least of all by those
who made it. It is somewhat paradoxical at that: the social
sciences have demonstrated that happiness as a goal for society
is meaningless for the simple reason that its contents are largely
determined by society. In other words, what makes a group or
individual happy is not, apparently, altogether dependent on
biological or other inherent needs; it is decided largely by social
conditioning. Inherent factors at most set a limit to the range

of possibilities. Cultural conditioning influences individual personalities sufficiently to influence greatly, if not to decide, what will make them happy or unhappy. A native of New Guinea may be made happy by hunting heads successfully; an American, by making money; a medieval person, by becoming a martyr for his faith. Martial glory may make for happiness among some tribes; and peaceful, non-competitive living, among others. If this be so, clearly it does not help at all to say that society shoud do or permit those things that make for the greatest happiness of its members. For society in the first place appears to determine what the things (values) are that will make its members happy. In this decision—what social values shall we foster?—the rule "those conducive to happiness" (apart from all the other objections) is meaningless, for it is the choice of social values which determines what will be conducive to happiness.

LIMITS OF SCIENCE

The social sciences can nonetheless assist in making social decisions. They can ascertain who wants what, what makes people want what they do want, and how their desires may be fulfilled, or changed. Such desires may arise from wrong beliefs —prejudices. If this is so, knowledge provided by science can influence the (pseudo) radional aspect of the desires. Unfortunately, they are usually not decisive: the desire leads to the prejudice more often than conversely. And if this is so, the desire will not change with increased knowledge. On the contrary, though available, such knowledge is unlikely to be absorbed. Further, the desire itself—apart from its rationalization (prejudice)—cannot be proved to be right or wrong by any science. The one thing the social sciences cannot do, the one thing, indeed, no science can decide is whether desires ought to be fulfilled or changed or frustrated.

If we could believe that people can pursue their aims independently, fewer social decisions would have to be made. But this is seldom so; worse, it is not at all certain that individual and group satisfaction do not require dissatisfaction of other individuals and groups. St. Thomas Aquinas might have been a good psychologist when he wrote that those who are in heaven will see the punishment inflicted on the damned "so that their ecstasy will be greatly heightened." Perhaps we ought to do without that ecstasy (though this "ought" cannot be proved to be "right"). But it might well be that such things as the enjoyment of riches, and certainly of prestige and power, are all predicated not on having some—which it might be possible to grant everyone—but on having more than others have, which obviously is something that cannot be granted to everybody. Surely prestige and power exist only inasmuch as they are unequally distributed—inasmuch as some are, relatively, deprived.

Even in simpler matters, valuation based on aesthetic or moral decisions, and not on observation, is unavoidable, though the questions to be decided on are largely framed by observation. Thus, economists may come to the conclusion that a certain degree of social mobility is required to achieve maximum social income. Sociologists, however, may conclude that the required degree of social mobility is detrimental to a person's relations with other people (and possibly with himself). In short, the social and the economic *optima* may differ and may require inconsistent conditions. Certainly the Industrial Revolution achieved economic advantages at a fairly high cultural and psychological price. Was it worth our while? No *scientific* answer is possible to such a question about the irreversible past or about the future.

IF NOT SCIENCE, WHAT?

Are we then to despair? Not unless we assume that science is the only method of solving problems. And that assumption seems unwarranted, even though scientists often develop a faith in science which is no more justified by science than religious faith is. (Faith—belief in "the evidence of things not seen"—is far more justifiable in the religious than in the scientific context. Science is based on the evidence of things perceptible by all who are skilled. Not so religion, which admits divine grace, revelation, and providence not necessarily intelligible to the faithful.) To admit but scientific methods is to assume implicitly that the cosmos is so arranged that its total magnitude and contents cannot exceed the grasp of scientific method—that nothing can exist that cannot also be known intersubjectively and proved scientifically. Values, then, can be proved to be "right"—or the universe becomes valueless.

Yet, this seems an unnecessary dilemma, explainable by the psychological impact of science, but in no way inherent in its methods or results. Only science can make *testable* predictions, and thus prove scientific theories. But, if it is correct to say that only what is true can be proved to be so, it does not follow that only what is proved, or provable, can be true. Demonstrability and truth are not the same. And there are many matters which pose problems that will not yield to scientific methods. To ignore such problems surely is not to solve them; to pretend that science can solve them is to create pseudoscientific morals and to discredit science by pretending that it can prove what it cannot prove. Philosophical reasoning is needed here. Such reasoning takes account of what science tells us about the facts of the situation, and about the probable effects of any move we might make. But philosophical reasoning goes beyond that, by offering an analysis of moral premises, and of whether the various solutions are compatible with them. Such analysis will not prove the premises, and, therefore, will not prove the solutions to be correct or incorrect. But it can clarify precisely what is implied, and thus help choose in full awareness of both the factual and the moral implication of our choice. This has been our task ever since Adam's fall. And science, though it cannot reconduct us into the Garden of Eden, can help us to get our bearings in this limited world.

As for the "truth" of such moral implications, of values, of ends and purposes of life, though science cannot establish it, one may well allow that there is such a truth—even though people disagree on where and how to find it. A difference of beliefs does not imply that there is no truth or that it cannot be found. It implies only that it has not been found. The situation is not very different from the situation in art: it is probably impossible to prove that one composer is a great musician and another is not, that one novelist is a great writer, and another is not. Yet I shall continue to hold very strong convictions on the value of their respective works; and I shall not regard them as matters of taste but of esthetic truth. Analogously, I hold moral values to be matters of moral truth. Science will help somewhat —it will clear the underbrush—but reason and faith cannot be dispensed with, if we wish to map a transcendent road; and without it we will be lost in this world, if not in the next.

Bibliography

The purpose of this list is to assist the reader to pursue further the subjects here discussed. Only works broadly concerned with the main topics have been included. The list is selective, not exhaustive; and the selection is unavoidably arbitrary. However, most of the works contain bibliographies of their own. Books of interest mainly to specialists are omitted. The most recent and least expensive American edition is given wherever possible. (All authors mentioned here in the text will be found also in the Index.)

CHAPTERS I-VI

Sigmund Freud, *A General Introduction to Psychoanalysis* (paperback).
   New Introductory Lectures on Psychoanalysis (paperback).
   Group-Psychology and the Analysis of the Ego, Hogarth, London, 1949.
   Civilization and Its Discontents, Hogarth, London, 1953.

This constitutes a basic though by no means complete introduction to psychoanalysis. The history of psychoanalysis and some newer developments are found in

Ernest Jones, *The Life and Work of Sigmund Freud*, Vol. I, Vol.
        II, Vol. III, Basic Books; or abridgement thereof, also
        Basic Books.

A succinct general view is found in

Charles Brenner, *An Elementary Textbook of Psychoanalysis*,
        Doubleday Anchor Book, 1957.
Ruth L. Munroe, *Schools of Psychoanalytic Thought*, Dryden
        Press, 1955.
Sylvia Brody, *Patterns of Mothering*, International Universities
        Press, 1956.

Therapeutic applications are thoroughly surveyed in

Otto Fenichel, *The Psychoanalytic Theory of Neuroses*, Norton,
        1945.

Among general introductory texts the following should be mentioned.

Ernest R. Hilgard, *Introduction to Psychology*, Second Edition,
        Harcourt, Brace & World, 1957.
Clifford T. Morgan, *Introduction to Psychology*, McGraw-Hill,
        1956.
Norman Cameron, *The Psychology of Behavior Disorders*,
        Houghton Mifflin, 1947.
Charles E. Osgood, *Method and Theory in Experimental Psychology*, Oxford University Press, 1953.
Clyde Kluckhohn, Henry A. Murray and David M. M. Schneider,
        eds., *Personality in Nature, Society and Culture*, Alfred
        A. Knopf, 1953.

Theodore M. Newcomb and Eugene L. Hartley, eds., *Readings in Social Psychology*, Henry Holt, 1947.

CHAPTERS VII-VIII

Among the best general texts of sociology are

Kingsley Davis, *Human Society*, Macmillan, 1954.
Leonard Broom and Philip Selznick, *Sociology*, Row, Peterson, 1955.
Robert Bierstedt, *The Social Order*, McGraw-Hill, 1957.

A good sociological analysis of American society is found in

Robin M. Williams, Jr., *American Society*, Knopf, 1951.
See also under Chapter XI.

Excellent material is found in

Robert K. Merton, Leonard Broom and Leonard S. Cottrell, eds., *Sociology Today*, Basic Books, 1957.
Logan Wilson and William L. Kolb, *Sociological Analysis*, Harcourt, Brace & World, 1949.

CHAPTER IX

Interesting material is found in

George Simmel, *Conflict* and *The Web of Group Affiliations*, Free Press, 1955, and in
Margaret Mead, ed., *Cooperation and Competition among Primitive Peoples*, McGraw-Hill, 1937.

CHAPTER X

Robert K. Merton and others, eds., *Reader in Bureaucracy*, Free
    Press, 1952, and
Bertrand de Jouvenel, *Power*, Viking Press, 1952, might be
    consulted.

CHAPTER XI

  Outstanding among the many good texts on anthropology are

A. L. Kroeber, *Anthropology*, Revised Edition, Harcourt, Brace
    & World, 1948.
Ralph Linton, *The Study of Man*, Appleton-Century-Crofts,
    1936.
    The Cultural Background of Personality, Appleton-
    Century-Crofts, 1945, is a concise and brilliant intro-
    duction to that topic.
    The Tree of Culture, Knopf, 1955, is Linton's posthumous
    and most comprehensive popular work.
Melville, J. Herskovitz, *Man and His Works*, Knopf, 1948, is
    equally comprehensive, more systematic, and less
    sparkling.

  On religion, see also

C. J. Ducasse, *A Philosophical Scrutiny of Religion*, Ronald, 1953.
Joachim Wach, *Sociology of Religion*, University of Chicago
    Press, 1944.
G. van de Leeuw, *Religion in Essence and Manifestation*, Allen
    and Unwin, London, 1938.
R. A. Knox, *Enthusiasm*, Oxford University Press, 1950.
Salomon Reinach, *Orpheus*, Liveright, 1942.

CHAPTER XII

The notion of anomie is examined penetratingly in

Robert K. Merton, *Social Theory and Social Structure*, Free
Press, 1949.

The classical analysis of our social system is found in

Alexis de Tocqueville, *Democracy in America*, Knopf Vintage
Books.

It has been brought up to date in

David Riesman, Nathan Glazer and Reuel Denney, *The Lonely
Crowd*, Doubleday Anchor Book, 1953.

An excellent commentary on Riesman and on his subjects is

S. M. Lipset and Leo Lowenthal, *Culture and Social Character*,
Free Press, 1961.

CHAPTERS XIII-XVII

Richard Bendix and Seymour M. Lipset, eds., *Class, Status and
Power*, Free Press, 1953.
Sinclair Lewis' novel, *Babbitt*, read in conjunction with
The Lonely Crowd (see above), helps the reader to
understand changes in our status psychology.

CHAPTERS XVIII-XIX

Bernard Rosenberg and David White, eds., reader in *Mass Culture*, Free Press, 1957.
William H. Whyte, Jr., *The Organization Man*, Simon and Schuster, 1956.
George Santayana, *Character and Opinion in the United States*, Doubleday Anchor Book, 1956.
Leo Lowenthal, *Literature, Popular Culture and Society*, Spectrum Books, Prentice-Hall, 1961.
See also the works listed under Chapter XII.

CHAPTER XX

Karl R. Popper, *The Logic of Scientific Discovery*, Science Editions, 1961.
Hans Reichenbach, *The Rise of Scientific Philosophy*, University of California Press, 1961.
J. W. N. Sullivan, *The Limits of Science*, Mentor Books, 1956.
Ernest Nagel, *The Structure of Science*, Harcourt, Brace & World, 1961.

Index

Blake, William ("Infant Sorrow"), 7, 83
Bodin, Jean, 116
Boethius, Anicius, 213
Bolling v. *Sharpe*, 279
Book clubs, 297, 321
Book publishing and mass culture, 297-98
Boredom: and Melanesians (Rivers), 175; and repression, 54, 331-32
Breast feeding, 76-77, 79, 80
Brenner, Charles, 33
Brown v. *Board of Education*, 279
Burckhardt, Jacob, 95
Bureaucracy and personal authority, 155
Burgess, Ernest W., 46, 47
Butler, Colin G., on honeybees, 159
Byron, Lord, 126
Byzantine civilization, 105

Calvin, John, 66, 333
Capitalism, (Marx and Marxists on), 190
Capone, Al, 240
Career women and role conflicts, 85-87
Carnegie, Dale, 333
Caste system, 139, 204-05, 223
Castration fears, 31
Categories, social, 235
Causation, joint, in psychoanalysis, 25
Celibacy in priesthood, 226
Censorship of entertainment, 308, 309
Character neuroses, 57, 70-71
Character types, 78
Charisma, 151
Charles VII of France, 155
Charlie's Aunt, 265
Chinooks, 269
Choice, social, 191, 257
Christianity, 35, 160
Churches as groups, 124-25
Circumcision rites, 31
Civil wars, intraparty identification in, 126
Civilization, Freud's theory of, 35. *See also* Culture
Clark, Kenneth B., 283-85

Class system, 204, 205-06; and discrimination, 278; and expansion, 226; and vertical mobility, 223-24. *See also* Marx, Karl; Mobility; Stratification
Classics, literary, 308, 321, 323
Clay, Cassius, 237
Climates, theory of, 116, 117
Coelestius, 333
Cohesion, social, 97, 99, 159-61. *See also* Culture, ethos of
Collective unconscious, 36
Colonial expansion, 219-20
Comic books, 326
Common man, ideal of, 160
Communication. *See* Language
Communism, 245. *See also* Communist Party; Marx
Communist Party and democracy, 143-44. *See also* Communism; Marx
Competition: group, and conflict, 130-38, 140, 144; and Communist parties, 143-44; and cooperation, 140-41; direct, 133-34; indirect, 131-32; and stratification, 204
Comte, Auguste, 345
Compulsive behavior, 53-55, 58
Concepts, 24
Conflicts, group, 130-31, 136-37, 140-44
Conformity, social, 49
Conscience and Superego, 19, 20-21
Consumer power, and popular culture, 310-11
Contacts, and understanding, 122-24
Conversion hysteria, 69
Cooperation, social, and competition, 140-41
Corruption, and power, 158
Countertransference, 72
Creative drives, 41, 42
Crime, 61, 182-87, 304
Crowds as groups, 99-100
Cultural anthropology, 78, 102
Culture: as aggregate of institutions, 104; conditions the individual, 165-68; criteria for comparing different, 169-70; defined, 163; as determinant of groups, 98; do-it-yourself, 319-21; ethos of, 171-